STUDIES ON VOLTAIRE
AND THE
EIGHTEENTH CENTURY

✦

198

General editor

HAYDN MASON

School of European Studies
University of East Anglia
Norwich, England

WILLIAM H. TRAPNELL

VOLTAIRE
AND THE
EUCHARIST

THE VOLTAIRE FOUNDATION

AT THE

TAYLOR INSTITUTION, OXFORD

1981

ISSN 0435-2866
ISBN 0 7294 0264 9

*Printed in England by Cheney & Sons Ltd,
Banbury, Oxfordshire*

Contents

Abbreviations

Best.D   Voltaire, *Correspondence and related documents*, ed. Th. Besterman, Voltaire 85-135 (Genève, Banbury, Oxford 1968-1977)

Denz.   Heinrich Denzinger, *The Sources of Catholic dogma* (St Louis 1957)

Dial.   Voltaire, *Dialogues et anecdotes philosophiques*, ed. R. Naves (Paris 1961)

Dict.   Voltaire, *Dictionnaire philosophique*, ed. R. Naves (Paris 1961)

F.C.   *The Fathers of the Church*

L.W.   Sébastien Longchamp, Jean-Louis Wagnière, *Mémoires sur Voltaire* (Paris 1826)

M.   Voltaire, *Œuvres complètes*, ed. L. Moland (Paris 1877-1883)

Migne   *Patrologiae latinae cursus completus*, ed. J. Migne (Paris 1878-1890)

SLNPF   *A select library of Nicene and post-Nicene Fathers of the Christian Church*

SG   Thomas of Aquinas, *Summa contra Gentiles* (London 1929)

ST   Thomas of Aquinas, *Summa theologiae* (New York 1965-1975)

Voltaire   *The Complete works of Voltaire*, ed. W. H. Barber *et al.* (Genève, Banbury, Oxford 1968-)

W.A.   Martin Luther, *D. Martin Luthers Werke* (Weimar 1901)

Biblical abbreviations:

Ac.	Acts
Co.	Corinthians
Dt.	Deuteronomy
Ex.	Exodus
Gn.	Genesis
Jg.	Judges
Jn.	John
K.	Kings
Lk.	Luke
Lv.	Leviticus
Mk.	Mark
S.	Samuel

Introduction

❧❦❧

CARL Becker's *Heavenly city of the eighteenth-century philosophers* (1932) is one of those irritating reminders of the flowers trampled in a butterfly hunt. Many scholars seem to specialise in the eighteenth century because they are not interested in religion and they believe it to be an age of religious eclipse. They would really rather forget that the Enlightenment sprang from the sincere efforts of Christianity to enlighten itself, that the *philosophes* owed much to their Christian education and that they were fundamentally concerned with the propagation of a new faith which in many insidious ways resembles the old. While every field of study needs an occasional iconoclast, on the other hand no intellectual mutation can escape the kind of debt Becker stresses and the ideas regenerated by the *philosophes* were as fresh as ideas can be, so fresh in fact that most of them still apply. Their most dynamic and yet inexplicit rediscovery, the liberty of conscience, remains the essential issue, even though the predominant object of belief has shifted, as any honest preacher will admit, from God to economics. The elite of earlier ages had already experimented with the liberty of conscience, but rarely with the afterthought of extending it to others, let alone women. The *philosophes* did try to spread the good news, to those at least who could understand it and occasionally to others as well. They inspired a contemporaneous minority, angered a larger minority and left the majority indifferent. Today, they enjoy a public they never dreamed of, not even in their wildest fantasies. If Becker, like Isaiah, should return, perhaps he would remind us of that, for prophecy really consists in remembrance of things past.

Everybody knows that the *philosophes* were a small band of heroes outnumbered and encircled by evil forces bent on annihilating them. Had Voltaire never entered the fray – as if he could have refrained! – he would be just another eighteenth-century poet, admired in his day and forgotten in ours. Not even his stories, especially not his stories, lack the inspiration of battle. But some of his tactics were less conventional than others and tend to escape the epidemic army of scholars in the field. He waged one of his most subtle campaigns against the eucharist and

this one has been neglected, if not ignored, because his personal behaviour appears to contradict the polemic in his publications.[1] No more
evident to his contemporaries than ours, his intention nonetheless
remained, in this area as in others, to substitute faith in reason for faith in
Christianity. He was not so naive as to think that one could simply
obliterate religion, the dream of rival *philosophes* like d'Holbach.
Yet his reasons are museum pieces: persistent determinism inspired by
the watchwork universe of Newton and scepticism about the morality of
atheists, despite the apology of Bayle and the erroneous, but fully
credited, example of Spinoza. What remains entirely valid is his faith
in the reason received by all men from the source of life. We know it
exists, it has to come from somewhere and he plausibly attributed it to
his deist or theist God.[2] He wanted, in some measure, to replace external
authority by internal authority, in other words, replace authority
claimed on one pretext or another, exercised and transmitted by other
men, usually selfish and ambitious men as history demonstrated, by an
authority guaranteed in its integrity by its divine origin which even
Christians, and especially after Malebranche, could hardly dispute.
The attempt to substitute a superior faith for an inferior one does not
deserve the customary accusations of negative or destructive intent
consistently levelled at him. This purpose also governed his campaign
against the eucharist, and, although he used a novel manœuvre, the
publicity stunt, along with his habitual ones, criticism and satire, he
never lost sight of it. The failure to perceive the usual design behind
the unusual tactic has obscured this aspect of his antichristian polemic.

An effective study of his campaign against the eucharist requires
preliminary knowledge of the development from which the dogma

---

[1] in *La Religion de Voltaire* (Paris 1956), René Pomeau treats of Voltaire's Easter
communions in Colmar in 1754 and at Ferney in 1768-1769. Eugène Kieffer considers the
first of these communions in 'De la vie et de la "mort" de m. de Voltaire à Colmar',
Annuaire de la Société historique et littéraire de Colmar 3 (1953), pp.85-115, and Fernand
Caussy, the last two in 'Les Pâques de m. de Voltaire', *Le Figaro littéraire* (13 April 1912).
Neither do they take Voltaire's behaviour seriously, nor do they suspect anything more
than a superficial motive on his part, to say nothing of investigating this motive in its
relation to his polemic against the Eucharist.

[2] Besterman finds that Voltaire makes no real distinction between *deist* and *theist*: 'At
first he tended to use the first word, and later the second, but this was simply [because]
churchmen [. . .] sought to discredit [. . .] *deist* by using it synonymously with *atheist*
[. . .] In the *Dictionnaire philosophique* [. . .] "Théisme" ostensibly dates from 1756, but
[. . .] in fact was first published in 1742 under the title "Déisme"' (*Voltaire* (New York
1969), pp.212-13).

emerged, a field remote from the usual interests of Enlightenment scholarship. A critical historian himself, Voltaire investigated this necessary background and used his research to advantage in his polemic. The present study therefore begins with a chapter on the history of the eucharist. The subject is vast, however, and a comprehensive account of it would dwarf the second chapter, which presents Voltaire's reactions to it. His own historiography nonetheless indicates a solution to this problem. From classical dramaturgy, he borrowed the technique of concentrating on the moments of power or crisis that generate the waves of history. The first chapter of the present study reviews such moments, which have been determined especially by Voltaire's interest in them. The technique seems to allow concision without the sacrifice of essential information. Also predominantly chronological, the second chapter progresses from one phase of his career to another, whether the phase centres on a particular activity or work. In each case, however, all significant revisions of such a work are generally treated in the section devoted to it and not reserved for later sections. The conclusion, which appears as usual in a final section, is not meant to revolutionise Voltaire studies, but rather to supplement them by the addition of a practically untreated subject.

Practically, because Pomeau does not omit the subject in *La Religion de Voltaire* (1956), but gives it little attention in a comprehensive examination of the writer's preoccupation with religion. He describes Voltaire's communions as an 'hommage ironique, mais hommage tout de même, à l'utilité de l'Eglise' (p.432). The second chapter of the present study is intended to demonstrate, among other points, that the writer went considerably further than mere homage to this utility. It is also intended to go beyond existing commentary, in Pomeau and elsewhere, on Voltaire's polemic against the eucharist, which should not be treated as – the usual tendency – a minor aspect of his war on Christianity. Critics often remind us, moreover, that the writer was a polemicist and not a scholar, so one must not expect scholarly rigour of him. Yet his polemic against the eucharist depends on his knowledge of the sacrament and its development, which one can scarcely evaluate without a review of the subject according to modern standards. Hence the first chapter in the present study.

I

The eucharist

⚜

THE Christian rite designated by the word *eucharist* derived from the
Jewish cult practised by Jesus, but exactly which Jewish rite served as a
prototype and how this derivation took place are controversial questions. The Christian rite could have deviated from the Jewish prototype
only after his death, because the evidence of the New Testament proves
conclusively that he was a devout Jew. His immediate followers must
have initiated this deviation and most of them came, as he did, from rural
Galilee, where an archaic form of Judaism predominated. The sacrificial
tradition reaching back to the ancient Hebrews enjoyed tremendous
prestige among such Jews. The probable influence of this tradition on
the earliest stage of Christian sacrifice necessitates study of the most
ancient record of the Hebraic cult, Exodus.

Although Voltaire accuses the ancient Hebrews of human sacrifice,[1]
the evidence of the Old Testament suggests that it played no more than
an occasional part in their cult.[2] Animal sacrifice, on the other hand,
flourished from the earliest period in their history. Two kinds predominated, communion meals sharing the victim with Yahweh and
burnt offerings or holocausts consuming it entirely on the altar. The
Hebrews apparently borrowed both types from the Canaanites, who
were in Palestine when they invaded it. In communion sacrifice, certain
parts of the victim's body belonged to Yahweh, such as the fat, the
intestines and the kidneys, while the rest, which we consider choice,
remained to the worshippers. The smoke which rose from the burning

[1] he implies that such sacrifice was customary: 'Les Juifs immolaient des hommes à la
divinité, témoin le sacrifice de Jephté [Jg.xi.30-31, 34-39], témoin le roi Agag coupé en
morceaux par le prêtre Samuel' (1 S.xv.32-33) (*Traité sur la tolérance*, M.xxv.72-73).
[M. designates Louis Moland, ed., *Œuvres complètes de Voltaire* (Paris 1877-1883).]
Note that Samuel's murder of Agag is not an example of human sacrifice, strictly speaking.

[2] Abraham is about to sacrifice his son Isaac to Yahweh, when an angel tells him that it
will not be necessary (Gn.xxii). In return for victory, Jephthah vows to sacrifice the
first person he meets upon entering his house. He thus incurs the obligation to sacrifice his
own daughter (Jg.xi).

flesh in both cases returned the life substance of the victim to the author of life. A blood rite, inherited no doubt from the Hebrews' nomad ancestors, usually accompanied both kinds of sacrifice. Blood being the essence of life, they sprinkled it over the altar where Yahweh was always present.

For several centuries, burnt offering commemorated the legendary ratification of the Covenant in the Sinai Desert,[3] but the Hebrews eventually came to look upon it rather as atonement for sin. They continued to practise local sacrifice in the form of thanksgiving meals, which they no longer shared with Yahweh as in communion sacrifice. They had inherited Passover, in which they dined on a spring lamb, from their nomad ancestors and Matzoth, the feast of unleavened bread, from the Canaanites. They used both of these rites concurrently to celebrate Yahweh's legendary deliverance of his chosen people from Egypt. According to the Synoptic Gospels, Jesus's Last Supper coincides with the Passover feast, but the Fourth Gospel sets this event on the evening before Passover began. Jaubert[4] resolves this conflict by referring to two different calendars, one followed by conservative and the other by progressive elements of the population, but some specialists do not accept her solution. Nor do scholars agree on whether the Last Supper was a Passover feast. The scanty information in the New Testament does not exclude the possibility that it was merely the kind of meal that Jesus habitually ate with his followers or even a farewell dinner in anticipation of his forthcoming death.

Whatever the occasion, Jesus almost certainly did not intend what later became the eucharist, but rather a sacrificial meal conforming to Jewish custom.[5] Among the four detailed accounts of this event in the New Testament, Paul, Mark and possibly Luke offer distinct versions of a presumably common Aramaic source which may have existed before 40 AD. Matthew as usual elaborates on Mark, while John omits the institution of the eucharist.[6] Specialists in Aramaic have always noted

---

[3] see Ex.xxiv.1-11.   [4] Annie Jaubert, *La Date de la Cène* (Paris 1957).

[5] 'There is one point on which many influential scholars are agreed, though at first glance they may appear to have almost nothing in common – that is, a willingness to admit that in apostolic times the Eucharist was understood as a sacrificial meal' (Edward Kilmartin, *The Eucharist in the primitive Church* (Englewood Cliffs, N.J. 1965), p.23).

[6] here are the three passages in question (*The Jerusalem Bible* (New York 1966)): The Lord Jesus took some bread, and thanked God for it and broke it, and said, 'This is my body, which is for you; do this as a memorial of me.' In the same way he took the cup after supper, and said, 'This cup is the new covenant in my blood. Whenever you drink it, do this as a memorial of me' (1 Co.xi.23-25).

that the originals of *This is my body* in all three passages and *This is my blood* in Mark (and Matthew) could not have expressed the idea of *is*. At best they could only have implied it, for Aramaic has no explicit equivalent for the verb *to be*. Literally, the probable Aramaic originals translate as *This my body* and *This my blood*, phrases whose semantics embrace everything from identity to symbolic association. If Jesus actually said these phrases, did he mean that he was holding his body in his hands and his blood in his cup as Voltaire facetiously (see p.197) and others seriously claim? Or that the bread in his hands represented his body and that the wine in his cup represented his blood? Either solution raises difficulties, not only over what an unsophisticated Galilean Jew might have meant, but also over how he could have said such a thing to begin with. The idea of drinking blood or eating human flesh would ordinarily have disgusted his fellow Jews, ever fearful of defilement.[7] Traditionally materialistic, his unhellenised Judaism could probably not accommodate the distinction between material and spiritual existence, but hellenised Judaism is a different matter. Paul and John speak of the eucharistic bread and wine as if they were really, but spiritually and not materially, the body and blood of Christ. Eating a spiritual equivalent of human flesh and drinking a spiritual equivalent of blood would be far less offensive to them than the material substance. It seems likely therefore that, in the process of oral transmission, hellenised Christians altered Jesus's language so that it would conform to their independently evolving conception of the eucharist.

The passages ascribing the institution of this sacrament to him reveal other inappropriate ambitions as well. 'This cup is the new covenant in my blood' in Paul and Luke confirms 'This is my blood, the blood of the covenant' in Mark. But did Jesus himself want to replace the Mosaic

He took some bread, and when he had given thanks, broke it and gave it to them, saying, 'This is my body, which will be given for you; do this as a memorial of me.' He did the same with the cup after supper, and said, 'This cup is the new covenant in my blood which will be poured out for you' (Lk.xxii.19-20).

He took some bread, and when he had said the blessing he broke it and gave it to them. 'Take it,' he said, 'this is my body.' Then he took a cup, and when he had returned thanks he gave it to them, and all drank from it, and he said to them, 'This is my blood, the blood of the covenant, which is to be poured out for many' (Mk.xiv.22-24).

7 'In the Aramaic tradition transmitted through Syriac, the "eater of flesh" is the title of the devil, the slanderer and adversary par excellence. The drinking of blood was looked on as an horrendous thing forbidden by God's law (Gn.ix.4; Lv.iii.17; Dt.xii.23; Ac.xv.20). Its transferred symbolical meaning was that of brutal slaughter.' (John translated by Raymond Brown, *The Anchor Bible*, xxix (New York 1966), p.284).

Covenant by a new one of his own invention? His profound respect for traditional Judaism practically ruins this hypothesis. Such an ambition more appropriately characterises the early Christian rivals of Judaism, who were separating the new religion from the old, but not from their prestigious common heritage. Despite radical mutation, all the important ingredients of the ancient Hebraic cult remain in the eucharist. No longer does the lifeblood of livestock seal an alliance with God, the source of all life, but rather does that of Christ, the incarnate Son of God soon to be sacrificed on the cross. Instead of smoke from a burning carcass, his body will ascend to heaven intact. How earthly communicants could partake of a body in heaven, moreover, would occasion much debate. In his version of the Last Supper, Matthew quotes Jesus as having said that whoever communes on his body and blood will obtain remission of sins and hence eternal life. He likewise reproduces the command in Paul and Luke to 'do this as a memorial of me', which resembles liturgical discipline rather than the mind of Jesus. Such promises, conditions and requirements tend to found a new cult and by no means foresee an impending kingdom of God, Jesus's all-absorbing preoccupation. Behind them, one detects the desire to establish a permanent priesthood, an ambition apparently foreign to Jesus himself. Did he himself drink of the wine he allegedly designated as his own blood? Since several different ceremonial cups were passed in Jewish ritual meals like the Last Supper, Mark and Luke do not clarify this point: 'Take this and share it among you, because from now on I shall not drink wine until the kingdom of God comes' (Lk.xxii.18); 'I will not drink any more wine until the day I drink the new wine in the kingdom of God' (Mk.xiv.25). Assuming he did drink this wine, how could he possibly have pretended to drink his own blood? This seems possible only in satire and horror stories. Yet custom required Jesus to share the cup with his fellows and none of the sacred writers saw fit to inform us that he did otherwise. The greatest probability therefore lies in his drinking of the cup and his utterance of no words intended to suggest what we call the eucharist. If the passage in Mark is authentic, however, Jesus may have had a very different idea in mind. His prediction that he would not drink wine again before the kingdom of God may well have referred to the eschatological banquet which many Jews, and especially those of rural Galilee, expected at the end of time.

In the early Church, on the other hand, the eucharist served to heighten the tension in the minds of the faithful between the redemptive martyrdom of Christ and his imminent return (constantly postponed) to judge the world. In 1 Corinthians x.17, Paul described the faithful as many sharing in the same loaf. The rewards promised by him and other missionaries for communion with Christ and fellow Christians obviously appealed to the multitudes embracing Christianity in the early centuries. No doubt the idea of sharing in the very substance of the divinity by the most natural of bodily functions, eating bread and drinking wine, had a powerful impact on the psychology of the Roman world. One can readily understand why the term communion soon began to designate the sacrament itself.

What may once have been John's version of the institution[8] follows Jesus's feeding of five thousand people with five loaves of bread and two fish. If it is indeed, he has converted his institution narrative into the second of two discourses by Jesus on this miracle. Since the miracle occurs 'shortly before [the] Passover' (Jn.vi.4) of Jesus's arrest, eucharistic material does not seem out of place. Perhaps John's passion for rhetoric and metaphor moved him to transform the institution narrative into a rhetorical commentary on the miraculous feeding of the multitude.

Continuing a series of *I am* statements, Jesus cries: 'I am the living bread which has come down from heaven. Anyone who eats this bread will live for ever; and the bread that I shall give is my flesh' (Jn.vi.51). The God of the Old Testament continues to give life, but Jesus's own body replaces manna as the bread of divine sustenance. Not only does it assure longevity in this life, the only one conceivable to the ancient Hebrews, but also an eternal afterlife. As usual in John, the Jewish (Judean) listeners argue with each other over the significance of Jesus's words, and well they might, for cannibalism was repulsive to them.[9] But Jesus adds insult to injury by exhorting them to drink his blood too. Whoever drinks of his blood, the Son of Man 'will raise him up on the last day' (Jn.vi.54) when he comes to judge the world. The cup of the eucharist therefore promises resurrection, but resurrection just before Last Judgement as in the Jewish tradition. Jesus further antagonises his audience by insisting, 'My flesh is real food and my blood is real drink'

---

[8] 'The backbone of [Jn.vi.] 51-58 is made up of material from the Johannine narrative of the institution of the Eucharist which originally was located in the Last Supper scene and [. . .] this material has been recast into a duplicate of the Bread of Life Discourse' (*Anchor Bible* xxix, p.287).

[9] this incident occurs in Capernaum, hence *Capernaism*, the heretical belief in communion on Christ's physical body and blood.

17

(Jn.vi.55). Opposition to Docetism, which denied that Christ had ever assumed bodily form, probably motivated this gruesome insistence. It is unlikely, however, that Jesus ever exhorted his fellow Jews to eat his body or drink his blood to begin with. This interpretation must have evolved from efforts to justify his ignominious death to the Hellenistic world.

John's interpretation of the eucharist differs from that of the extra-canonical Didache, written about the same time, towards the end of the first century. This manual offers Christians worshipping without the guidance of a priest a liturgy and brief recommendations by the author. His text indicates that in his community the eucharist typically accompanied the agape, or sacrificial Christian meal. One of the blessings prescribed for the end of the meal gives thanks for the holy name of God 'enshrined in our hearts' (x.2);[10] another explains this enshrinement by comparing spiritual to physical food and drink. The physical ingestion of bread and wine results in a spiritual indwelling of the divinity. But none of these prayers acknowledges the presence of Christ's body and blood; none calls upon Christians to remember his propitiatory martyrdom. The author addresses them all to God and speaks of Christ only in the third person. Unless his allusion to the vine of David proves otherwise, nowhere does he even recognise the eucharist as a commemoration of the Last Supper. Instead, he dwells on the admiration and awe that Christians owe God for the gift of life transmitted by Christ. He therefore demonstrates that some early Christians were not in agreement with Paul and the evangelists on the significance of the eucharist.

Fathers like Ignatius of Antioch, who died a martyr in Rome *ca.*110, better represent what has come to be regarded as the mainstream of early tradition. A pagan convert, he became one of the earliest bishops of Antioch and left seven epistles written during his voyage to Rome. Although none of them concentrates on the eucharist, they contain rudimentary elements of future dogma. In describing Christ's presence in the sacrament, Ignatius mingles spiritual and realistic terms in the manner of John. He probably believed in a presence both spiritual and real after the consecration of the bread and wine by the bishop or his delegate. The body and blood of Christ, who had risen from the dead, brought eternal life to those who communed on them in Christian sacrifice. This opportunity was available only from 'the catholic church',

[10] *The Didache, the Epistle of Barnabas*, translated by James Kleist (Westminster Md. 1961).

by which Ignatius did not mean a universal organisation, but rather a union of all who receive divine inspiration. In denying the physical reality of Christ's body, the Docetists, he believed, excluded themselves from the church, communion and eternal life.

Justin Martyr (died *ca*.165), a Platonic philosopher who found spiritual fulfilment in Christianity, had a more comprehensive doctrine of the sacrament. Addressing his *First apology* to the emperor Pius Augustus, he twice describes the eucharist known to him, first as the final step in the baptism of pagan converts and then as the climax of the regular Sunday service, the earliest known version of the mass. In both cases, bread and wine diluted in water are brought to 'the one presiding',[11] probably an explanatory periphrasis for *bishop*. The bishop says a prayer of thanksgiving and the congregation replies 'Amen!' Hebrew (Aramaic) for 'So be it!' as Justin explains. Finally, deacons distribute the bread and diluted wine to the congregation and take them to absentees. Justin's testimony implies that the congregation remained standing during the eucharist and that the bishop improvised at least some of the prayers. The agape, unmentioned here, had apparently disappeared from the service, but the celebrant had obviously become a dominant figure, while the congregation had assumed a subordinate role. Had the emergence of a hierarchy brought changes in the ritual or vice versa? This the evidence does not tell us.

'We call this food the eucharist', Justin informs Pius (66). Only baptised Christians who believe in the Christian doctrine and who lead Christian lives may receive it. They fortify themselves with eternal life by eating and drinking of the flesh and blood assumed by the Saviour in the Incarnation. Just as the word of God incarnated him, it converts the food and drink of the eucharist into his body and blood. This passage[12] demonstrates a working knowledge of the theory in Plato's *Timaeus* according to which the blood circulating in the body nourishes it by the distribution of food particles.[13] Ordinary bread and

---

[11] *Writings of Justin Martyr*, translated by Thomas Falls, *F.C.* xiii (New York 1948), 65, 67. *F.C.* designates *The Fathers of the Church*.

[12] 'Not as ordinary bread or as ordinary drink do we partake of them, but just as, through the word of God, our Saviour Jesus Christ became incarnate and took upon himself flesh and blood for our salvation, so [. . .] the food which has been made the Eucharist by the prayer of his word, and which nourishes our flesh and blood by assimilation, is both the flesh and blood of that Jesus who was made flesh' (66).

[13] 'When the breath passes inwardly and outwardly, an interior fire attends it in its course; and being diffused through the belly, when it meets with solid and liquid aliments, it reduces them to a state of fluidity; and, distributing them into the smallest parts, educes

wine become a part of the body and the blood by digestion. But bread
and wine consecrated by the words Jesus pronounced at the Last Supper
are already identical with his body and blood before being consumed by
the communicant. While spirit became flesh in the Incarnation, flesh
becomes spirit (without losing its physical qualities) in the eucharist.
As a Platonist, Justin could accept the coexistence of material bread and
wine with spiritual body and blood in the same substances. The distinction between the material and spiritual content of the eucharist
answered accusations, already current in his day, that Christians were
indulging in Capernaism or pretending to eat the physical flesh of
Christ. In the quotation above, moreover, he implies that communion
holds the promise of salvation ('for our salvation'). He makes no
allusions to a return by Jesus, for disappointment had long since dashed
the eschatological hopes associated with the eucharist earlier.

In his *Dialogue with Trypho*, he also amplified Jesus's order to celebrate the eucharist in remembrance of him: 'Christ commanded us
to offer [the Eucharistic bread] in remembrance of the passion he en-
dured for all those souls who are cleansed from sin' (41). Thus Justin
reminds us that communion removes sin and provides access to redemption through Jesus's self-sacrifice. None of these points appears
in the *Didache*, but its author has at least one thing in common with
Justin. Both consider the eucharist a sacrifice offered to God, though in
the name of the Son according to Justin. He assures the Jew Trypho:
'God has [. . .] announced in advance that all the sacrifices offered in his
name, which Jesus Christ commanded [. . .] that is, in the Eucharist of
the bread and of the chalice [. . .] are pleasing to him' (117). Christians
in fact constitute 'the true priestly family of God' (116.3), for sacrifices
offered by Jewish priests no longer please God. One can well imagine
the impression this remark made on Trypho. But Justin bases his claim
on an Old Testament passage, Malachi i.10-11,[14] which the prophet
probably intended to shame his fellow Jews into reform of their cult by
this reference to a widespread and superior form of sacrifice. Since the

them as from a fountain through the avenues of its progression: pouring these small
particles into the channels of the veins, and deducing rivers through the body as through
a valley of veins' (*The Timaeus and the Critias or Atlanticus*, translated by Thomas Taylor,
(Washington 1944), p.206).

[14] 'Is there no one among you who [. . .] will stop you from lighting useless fires on
my altar? [. . .] From your hands I find no offerings acceptable. But from farthest east to
farthest west my name is honoured among the nations and everywhere a sacrifice of incense
is offered to my name.'

book was composed before 445 BC, he may have been thinking of the Persians who had a vast empire and worshipped a supreme God. Ancient Christians insisted, however, that 'Malachi' was prophesying the transfer of God's favour from the material sacrifice of Judaism to the spiritual sacrifice of the eucharist. In the *First apology*, Justin objects to the useless slaughter and immolation of animals, typical not only of the Judaic Temple cult, but also of his own pagan background: 'The only worship worthy of [the Creator] is not to consume by fire those things that he created for our sustenance' (13). Evidently the idealistic sensibility of a Gentile Platonist like Justin required a spiritual form of sacrifice. The appeal of the eucharist must have contributed to the conversion of many such Platonists to Christianity.

After Justin, eucharistic theology continued to broaden and deepen its interpretation of eucharistic liturgy which itself, like all liturgies, evolved slowly if at all. According to Irenaeus, who became bishop of Lyons towards 160, spiritual fortification of the body preserves it from decay in preparation for resurrection, just as it had in the resurrection of Christ. What is to prevent an unworthy communicant from obtaining salvation, however? 'He who [. . .] cherishes secret sin does not deceive God by that sacrifice which is offered correctly as to outward appearance,' he warns. On the contrary, 'that sin may the more, by means of the hypocritical action, render him the destroyer of himself' (4.18.3).[15] He does not offer any example of death from this cause, but perhaps that would be asking too much.

For nearly ten centuries no serious controversy arose over the eucharist, because theologians generally agreed on the proper doctrine. They did not even see fit to devote a work to this subject in particular until Cyprian's Letter 63, in the middle of the third century, and Cyprian himself merely recapitulates traditional practice and doctrine.[16] Over a century later, Theodore of Mopsuestia and Cyril of Alexandria did not clash over the eucharist, but rather its christological consequences. Historians anxious to trace medieval controversy back to the

[15] *Irenaeus against heresies*, translated by Alexander Roberts and James Donaldson, *The Ante-Nicene Fathers*, i (Buffalo 1887).

[16] 'If Christ Jesus, our Lord and God, is himself the high priest of God and Father and first offered himself as a sacrifice to his Father and commanded this to be done in commemoration of himself, certainly the priest who imitates that which Christ did and then offers the true and full sacrifice in the Church of God the Father, if he thus begins to offer according to what he sees Christ himself offered, performs truly in the place of Christ' (14) – St Cyprian, *Letters 1-81*, translated by Rose Donna, *F.C.*, li (Washington 1964).

Fathers detect a realistic tendency among some of them and a symbolic one among others. But the ancient conviction that a symbol contains at least some of the reality it represents blurs this distinction. Kelly is more convincing when he divides the Fathers into those who believe that consecration of the bread and wine by Jesus's words actually converts them into his body and blood, and those who do not try to explain how they come to be present, a curious oversight. Cyril of Jerusalem, Gregory of Nyssa and Ambrose, according to Kelly, advocate such a theory, while Tertullian, Cyprian and Augustine ignore the problem.[17] In fact, Ambrose and Augustine unknowingly laid the foundations of mutually antagonistic tendencies that would emerge only later.

Since Cyril of Jerusalem pioneered the theory developed by Ambrose, a preliminary assessment of his contribution to the theology of the eucharist would be useful here. Though bishop of Jerusalem from 348 until 387, Cyril was exiled three times for his fidelity to the Council of Nicaea (325). His *Catecheses*, a series of lectures delivered to catechumens, include several on the eucharist which are more explicit than any previous text. Since Jesus converted water into wine for the marriage feast in Cana, Cyril reasons, he can also convert wine into his blood. In response to our prayers, God sends the Holy Spirit to operate this conversion. Before the consecration, bread and wine are on the altar but, afterwards, only the body and blood of Christ remain under the appearances of bread and wine. Did not Jesus himself say, 'This is my body; this is my blood?' Faith tells us what the senses cannot perceive and he who communes without believing in the real presence of Christ's body and blood eats and drinks his own condemnation. Yet Cyril scoffs at the Jews in John vi.52, who assume that Jesus is inciting them to cannibalism. Like the other Fathers, he does not look upon the consumption of human flesh imperceptible to the senses as cannibalism. In view of the real presence, he draws two conclusions. When we commune, we offer the body and blood of Christ as a propitiatory victim in a spiritual sacrifice, which bears no resemblance to the gory spectacles of pagan and Hebrew rites. But when we commune, we likewise partake of Christ's body and blood which, diffused throughout our bodies, integrate us into the body of Christ. While Augustine would clarify this strange idea, the other elements of Cyril's doctrine would reappear in Ambrose's writings.

[17] John Kelly, *Early Christian doctrines* (London 1958), p.440.

Ambrose, bishop of Milan, who died in 397, shared Cyprian's respect for tradition, but his clarification of the eucharist harboured potentially radical ramifications. In a study of the bishop's eucharistic doctrine, Johanny recommends his semantic exploitation of the *divine word* as a point of departure.[18] Ambrose effectively welcomes the flexibility of a term whose meaning ranges from sacred language to the Son of God. He reminds us that the Word, who served as God's agent in the creation, is the same being as the pre-existent Christ. He further reminds us that it was Christ who first pronounced the words of consecration in the eucharist. These words therefore have creative power: 'Cannot the words of Christ, which were able to make what was not out of nothing, change those things that are into the things that were not?'[19] Changing what already exists into something else or metabolism seems easier to Ambrose than making something out of nothing. The recitation of Jesus's words, 'This is my body [...] This is my blood', actually reproduces his body and blood. This consecration, according to *On the Christian faith*, transforms the bread and wine into the body and blood[20] and, according to *The Sacrament of the Incarnation*, the body and blood, into the bread and wine.[21] Although, as Johanny indicates,[22] the two explanations appear to contradict each other, they are actually complementary. Despite the loss of their appearances, the body and blood become the reality of the eucharist, while the bread and wine keep their appearances, despite the loss of their reality. Ambrose's distinction between the spiritual reality of Christ's body and blood and the physical appearances of bread and wine foreshadows the scholastic distinction

[18] he in fact quotes the passage which I quote below (*The Mysteries*, 52). Raymond Johanny, *L'Eucharistie centre de l'histoire du salut* (Paris 1968), p.13.

[19] *The Mysteries*, 52; *St Ambrose: theological and dogmatic works*, translated by Roy Deferrari, F.C., xliv (Washington 1963). Quotations of Ambrose come from this text unless otherwise indicated.

[20] 'We receive the sacramental elements, which by the mysterious efficacy of holy prayer are transformed into the flesh and blood [of Christ]' (10.125) – St Ambrose, *Select works and letters*, translated by H. de Romestin, *SLNPF*, 2d Series, x (Grand Rapids 1955). *SLNPF* designates *A select library of Nicene and post-Nicene Fathers of the Christian Church*.

[21] 'You believe that true flesh was assumed by Christ, and you offer his body to be transfigured on the altar' (4.23).

[22] 'Le verbe *transfigurare* sert à traduire une double relation, d'une part la relation pain-corps du Christ et d'autre part la relation corps du Christ-pain [...] Les oblats sont convertis au corps du Christ, le pain d'avant la consécration devenant la vraie chair du Christ, mais cette chair du Christ [...] ne pouvant pas nous être donnée sous une forme sanglante doit revêtir la figure du pain' (p.104).

between substance and accidents. 'There was no body of Christ before the consecration,' he further explains, 'but after the consecration [. . .] there is the body of Christ' (*The Sacraments* 4.4.6). Having applied the same before-and-after description to the blood of Christ, he insists that both the body and the blood are really present in the eucharist. He believed the body to be the same as the one born of Mary and crucified by Pilate,[23] the one which rose from the dead and ascended to heaven where it now resides, but, as he learned from the Greek Fathers, it is a spiritualised body[24] no longer susceptible to decay. In communing on this body, one actually partakes of Christ's divinity, the source of eternal life. We might object that the eucharist neither looks nor tastes like flesh: so much the better! Ambrose applauds, for if the eucharist disgusted the communicant, there would be no candidates for redemption. The communicant, he teaches, eats a symbol of Christ's body and drinks a symbol of his blood, yet both of these symbols contain the spiritual reality of the thing represented. Augustine would amplify this doctrine and his name would especially come to be associated with it, though it was already traditional when Ambrose adopted it.

Ambrose follows the other Fathers in describing the eucharist as both a continuation and improvement of Hebrew and Jewish sacrifice: 'In old times a lamb, a calf was offered; now Christ is offered. But he is offered as man and as enduring suffering. And he offers himself as a priest to take away our sins.'[25] Not only does Christ replace the animal victims of Jewish sacrifice, but also he assumes the sacrificial function of the priest by offering his own life, an idea borrowed from Hebrews.[26] After expiating our sins by his martyrdom, the resurrected victim intercedes on our behalf, something no animal could do. Ambrose naturally believes that the expiatory value of his suffering on the cross far exceeds that of a burning animal carcass. As many Fathers, therefore, he considers the eucharist a sacrifice as well as a sacrament, for it re-actualises a sacrifice, even though the latter has already taken place

[23] 'This body which we make is from the Virgin [. . .] Surely it is the true flesh of Christ, which was crucified, which was buried; therefore it is truly the sacrament of that flesh' (*The Mysteries*, 53). We will be seeing part of this passage again (see pp.28, 33, and 35).

[24] 'Ambroise [. . .] rappelait fortement l'état spirituel qui est celui du Sauveur depuis le matin de Pâques' (Henri de Lubac, *Corpus mysticum: l'eucharistie et l'Eglise au moyen âge* (Paris 1949), p.150).

[25] *On the duties of the clergy* (1.48.248), translated by H. de Romestin.

[26] 'The ideal high priest [. . .] would not need to offer sacrifices every day [. . .] because he had done this once and for all by offering himself' (He.vii.26-27).

once and for all: 'For the sins of the people, Christ died once and for all, but in order to redeem the sins of the people.'[27]

Thinking no doubt of those for whose souls he was responsible, Ambrose frequently urges his readers to take advantage of the opportunity offered by communion. He even recommends a pious form of inebriation which he identifies with the gift of the Spirit in Acts: 'As often as you drink, you receive the remission of sins and you are inebriated in spirit' (*The Sacraments*, 5.3.17). He nevertheless distinguishes between sacred ecstasy and vulgar drunkenness, which of course he condemns. Eucharistic inebriation has an effect unknown to common drink: 'The body does not stagger because of this inebriation, but it is reinvigorated; the soul is not confounded, but immortalised.'[28] This spiritual exaltation is a symptom of the communicant's liberation from sin. The eucharist replenishes his soul with life, potentially eternal life. By the time of Ambrose, the sacramental means to this end had long since become the exclusive monopoly of the priesthood. However generous they may sound, the bishop's exhortations to partake heartily of the eucharist tended to consolidate his power over his diocesans. Nothing reinforced the claim of the Church to control access to salvation like frequent and massive participation in the eucharist. To be sure, Ambrose and his fellow Christians saw this privilege in a different light: 'Christ [. . .] feeds his Church on these mysteries' (*The Mysteries*, 55). Challenging such assumptions seems to have tempted few dissidents (other than the Albigensians) before the Reformation. Nor is there any reason to suspect Ambrose, or Augustine for that matter, of worse than a saintly paternalism.

A student of Ambrose, Augustine spent much of his long career as a theologian and as bishop of Hippo[29] fighting heresies. His war on Manichaeanism, from which he himself had converted to Christianity, inspired a statement of principle: 'There can be no religious society, whether the religion be true or false, without some sacrament or visible symbol to serve as a bond of union' (19.11).[30] True religion nonetheless differs from false, he thought, in that its sacraments designate a mysterious reality and Christianity enjoys this exclusive privilege. The

[27] *Commentary on the Gospel according to Luke* (10.8), my translation from *Patrologiae Latinae cursus completus*, ed. J. Migne (Paris 1845), xv.

[28] *Commentary on Psalms* (118.15.28), my translation from Migne, xv.

[29] the modern seaport of Bône in northeastern Algeria.

[30] *Reply to Faustus the Manichaean*, translated by R. Stothert, *SLNPF*, 1st Series, iv (Grand Rapids 1956).

bread and wine of the eucharist are perceptible signs indicating the spiritual presence of Christ's body and blood, but only to faith. This convenient restriction preserves the alleged truth of Christianity from verification by anyone who does not already believe in it. However suspect, this theory is not the work of a cynical schemer, but rather a zealous proselyte, who passionately believed in the unique truth of Christianity. Less than the appetite for power in numbers, the common-sense conviction that a belief shared by many people must be true and the Neoplatonic faith in the excellence of unity seem to have motivated his crusades against the Manichaeans, the Donatists, the Pelagians and the Arians.

He valued the unity of the Church so highly that he built it right into his theory of the eucharist. According to this theory, the head of Christ's body on the altar, which differs from the one in heaven, is Christ himself and the members of this body are the true Church, the predestinate elite of Christendom.[31] Augustine derived this theological monster from 1 Corinthians x.17, where Paul is discussing 'communion with the body of Christ [. . .] Though there are many of us, we form a single body because we share in [. . .] one loaf.' Paul's ambivalent use of the Greek word for body (*soma*) does not literally exclude Augustine's interpretation, which nonetheless probably exceeds the Apostle's intentions. The bishop of Hippo took him literally, pushed his reasoning to the limit and added Christ the head to the body of the faithful, although the whole likewise remained the body of Christ. One Easter, he taught newly baptised Christians, who had taken their first communion the night before, 'You are the body and members of Christ [. . .] The mystery of what you are is placed on the Lord's table: you receive this mystery' (Sermon 272).[32] Communion simultaneously introduces the communicants into the Church and the Church into the communicants.

While the sacrament accomplishes this reciprocal integration, the accompanying sacrifice commemorates the redemptive martydom of

[31] 'He would have this meat and drink to be understood as meaning the fellowship of his own body and members, which is the holy Church in his predestinated, and called, and justified, and glorified saints and believers' (*Homelies on the Gospel according to st John* (26.15), translated by John Gibb and James Innes, *SLNPF*, 1st Series, vii (Grand Rapids 1956)).

[32] my translation from *Textos eucharisticos primitivos*, ed. Jesus Solana (Madrid 1952-1954), ii.210.

Christ and presents the figure of the self-sacrificing priest. But Augustine's conception of the eucharistic body results in a modification of the latter principle: 'He is both the priest who offers and the sacrifice offered. And he designed that there should be a daily[33] sign of this in the sacrifice of the Church, which, being his body, learns to offer herself through him.'[34] As members of the eucharistic body, communicants therefore offer themselves in sacrifice, and yet Augustine's insatiable pursuit of unity does not stop there. In the sentence preceding the quotation, he reminds us that the persons in his trinity function concurrently, thus the divinity is sacrificing its body to itself. Since this body without the head consists of the faithful, they are daily re-enacting the original sacrifice by the crucifixion of the body to which they now belong. In this way, Augustine's eucharistic body allows him to achieve a Christian solution for the Neoplatonic problem of reconciling transcendent unity with immanent multiplicity.

The contradictions implied by this theory would persuade Protestants who denied the real presence that Augustine justified them. His habit of distinguishing between the perceptible sacrament and its mysterious effect (*virtus*), as if he believed in no more than a dynamic presence of Christ's resurrected body, would contribute to earlier disputes. There can be no real doubt, however, that he thought this effect substantive enough to constitute what was later designated as the real presence, a principle defended already by Ignatius. He finds, for instance, that John vi.57[35] 'shows what it is in reality and not [just] sacramentally, to eat his body and drink his blood' (*City of God*, 21.25). Furthermore, the sacrament resembles the mystery sufficiently to allow the naming of the sacrament after the mystery. The bread of the eucharist resembles the body enough to be called the body of Christ and the wine resembles the blood enough to be called the blood of Christ. If there were no such resemblance, Augustine observes, there would be no sacrament. Unwittingly, no doubt, he sowed the seeds of speculation and controversy by writing to his fellow bishop Boniface that the (mystery of the) sacrament *is* the body and blood of Christ *secundum quendam*

[33] Augustine's diocesans practised daily communion.

[34] *City of God*, 10.20, translated by Marcus Dods, *SLNPF*, 1st series, ii (Grand Rapids 1956).

[35] 'As I, who am sent by the living Father, myself draw life from the Father, so whosoever eats me will draw life from me.'

modum,[36] without saying what manner. The expression implies the existence of a manner or manners in which they are not identical, but he may have felt that he had settled this question by his condemnation of Capernaism.

He deplores the attitude of the Jews in Capernaum who (understandably) assumed that when Jesus invited them to eat his body and drink his blood (see p.17), he meant the kind of 'flesh [. . .] sold in the [meat market]'.[37] Given the opportunity, he supposes, Jesus might have commanded, 'Understand spiritually what I have said: you are not to eat this body which you see; nor to drink that blood which they who will crucify me shall pour forth.'[38] Thus Augustine excludes cannibalism in the usual sense and he even finds that Romans viii.6 condemns to death anyone believing in a cannibalistic communion.[39] He probably never wavered in his opposition to Capernaism, but he seems to have yielded occasionally to the temptation of exaggerating his realism for the edification of his public, as in the following statement: 'When [Christ] consumed his own body and blood, he took what the faithful know in his own hands; and he raised himself in a certain manner, saying, "This is my body." '[40] While it harmonises with the reciprocal integration of communicant and Church and does not necessarily negate the real presence, the statement invites a commonsense verdict of autophagia. In his polemic against the Pelagians, Augustine likewise tended to greater realism and to identification of the body on the altar with the one in heaven.

He did not doubt that the body born of Mary and crucified by Pilate was in heaven. Having taught neophytes that they belonged to the body of Christ, he asked them rhetorically, 'Where is your head?' Then he told them that Christ had risen from the dead, ascended to heaven and was seated at the right hand of God: 'therefore, our head is in heaven'.[41] Unlike Ambrose, he believed this body to have remained material and

[36] 'In a certain manner the sacrament of the body of Christ is the body of Christ, and the sacrament of the blood of Christ is the blood of Christ' (98.9) – St Augustine, *Letters 83-130*, translated by Wilfrid Parsons, *F.C.*, viii (New York 1953).

[37] *Homelies on . . . John* (27.5).

[38] *Expositions on the Book of Psalms* (99.8), translated by A. Cleveland, *SLNPF*, 1st Series, viii (Grand Rapids 1956).

[39] 'It is death to limit oneself to what is unspiritual.'

[40] Sermon, 2.2; my translation from Solana, ii.175.

[41] Sermon 227, st Augustine, *Sermon on the liturgical seasons*, translated by Mary Muldowney, *F.C.*, xxxviii (New York 1959).

unilocal in nature,[42] hence his conviction that it stays in heaven.[43] If it does not leave heaven, however, how can it be really present on the altar? While Augustine never answered this question, his Neoplatonism provides an answer which he may have taken for granted. The manner of the identity between the heavenly and the eucharistic bodies seems to be the manner of Platonic ideas which, in contrast with phenomena, are illocal and permanently real.[44] Augustine no doubt assigned a mere perishable reality to the bread and wine in the eucharist and eternal reality to the ideas of Christ's body and blood present after the consecration, even though he believed the physical manifestation of these Ideas to be in heaven.

He agrees with Ambrose on the activation of the real presence by the consecration: 'Until now, as you see, it is bread and wine; after the sanctification this bread will be the body of Christ and this wine, his blood.'[45] This sentence confirms the difference between what is on the altar before and after the consecration, but it does not indicate that one becomes the other. Neither did Augustine adopt Ambrosian metabolism nor did he fashion a conversion theory of his own. Yet he insisted that the body and blood cannot fail to be present after the consecration, provided a Catholic priest, any Catholic priest, repeat the words of Jesus at the Last Supper: 'This is my body [...] This is my blood.' They are present, in his opinion, even when a sinful, corrupt or unworthy priest says them: 'How can God listen to a murderer saying a prayer ... over the eucharist? ... Yet that is done, and validly, by murderers [per homicidas].'[46] Although the bishop of Hippo is following tradition here, this principle assures faith in the sacrament at the expense of clerical discipline. It conveniently eliminates a motive for scrutiny of the celebrant's qualifications, thus shielding the clergy from

[42] 'Un corps, pour Augustin, c'est toujours un organisme individuel, formé de chair et d'os, composé d'organes distincts et strictement localisé [...] Incorruptibles en fait, les membres de ce corps glorieux n'en demeuraient pas moins [...] circonscrits dans l'espace' (de Lubac, *Corpus mysticum*, pp.147-48).

[43] 'For the body of the Lord, in which he rose again from the dead, can be only in one place' (*Homelies*, 30.1).

[44] 'Christ's body is present *ad modum Ideae* [...] When [Augustine] distinguished between the Eucharist and the body born of Mary, he was making a distinction like that which Plato postulated between Idea and phenomenon' (John Fahey, *The Eucharistic teaching of Ratramn* (Mundaleine, Ill. 1951), p.156).

[45] my translation from Sermo Guelferbytana 7, *Tractatus sive sermones inediti ex Codice Guelferbytana* (Zürich 1918).

[46] *On baptism*, 5.20.28; my translation from Migne, xliii.190.

accountability to laymen and leaving discipline to the hierarchy, whose power it enhances.

On the other hand, the eucharist according to his theology does discipline communicants, for sinners and heretics, who do not belong to the body of the predestinate, receive neither the body nor the blood of Christ. On the contrary, they condemn themselves: 'Heretics and schismatics being separate from the unity of this body, are able to receive the same sacrament, but with no profit to themselves, – nay, rather to their own hurt' (*City of God*, 21.25). Augustine does not tell us what punishment this self-condemnation[47] brings or whether it occurs in this life or the next. But his sacramental trap and the implied threat of such punishment militate in favour of a laity subservient to the wishes of the bishop. Thus his disinterest suffers when he restricts the effect of the eucharist or divine grace to members of Christ's mystic body: 'He [...] who is in the unity of Christ's body, that is to say, in the membership [of his Church] that man is truly said to eat the body and drink the blood of Christ' (*City of God*, 21.25).

He also concerns himself with the manner in which one eats the body and drinks the blood of Christ. He distinguishes in fact between the spiritual ingestion of the mystery and the physical consumption of the sacrament, the same as that of ordinary food and drink. In spiritual ingestion, 'He who eats in his heart does not chew with his teeth' (*Treatises*, 26.12). Wary of Stercoranism, Augustine warns against confusing the routine digestion of the sacrament with the spiritual assimilation of the mystery, a delicate distinction. 'What you see passes,' he taught the neophytes, 'but [...] that which is not seen, does not pass; it remains' (Sermon 227). Under no circumstances must we imagine that the body and blood of Christ suffer the destruction and indignity inflicted on the bread and wine of the eucharist. Augustine therefore typically approves of the rule requiring Christians to fast before communion on the doubtful grounds of respect for Christ. What need, one might ask, do immaterial body and blood have of such respect?

Despite his typical claim merely to clarify the traditional theology of the eucharist, he obviously supplemented it with major innovations, including his conception of the eucharistic body, on which he refounded the whole doctrine. Then why was he not condemned for heresy? Condemnation for heresy usually results from the triumph of enemies

---

[47] 'Accipere ergo incipitis quod et esse coepistis, si non indigne accipiatis, ne judicium vobis manducetis et bibatis' ('Easter day sermon on the sacraments', Solana, ii.216).

and, with his intelligence, authority and aggressiveness, he was a dangerous adversary. He probably avoided the posthumous fate of Origen, a comparable figure, because his innovations strengthened the privileges and power of the clergy, the only class who could make such a condemnation. They especially benefited from the relatively idealistic commitment of an original genius to the unity of the Church. How far would he have gone in this direction, moreover, if uninhibited by the Christian horror of theological originality?

By the ninth century, Augustine and Ambrose were almost unquestionable authorities in Western Europe. The eucharistic realism of the Gallican church, which had evolved from Ambrose, conditioned the popular theology of the Benedictine Paschase Radbert. In his concern for monastic discipline, Paschase sought to edify ordinary monks rather than inform his fellow theologians. His *Body and blood of the Lord*[48] reproduces the text of a parallel between the crucified and sacramental bodies of Christ in Ambrose with only trivial inaccuracy: 'Vera utique caro Christi quae crucifixa est [. . .] vere ergo carnis illius sacramentum est' (Ambrose, *On mystery*, 53; Solana, i.384); 'Vera utique caro Christi quae crucifixa est [. . .] vere illius carnis sacramentum' (Paschase, *On the body*, iv.1; Migne, cxx). He derived his eucharistic doctrine from Ambrose in particular, but he reconciled it with Augustine as much as he could. Along with others, he adopted a definition of sacrament which Isidore of Seville had compiled from the works of Augustine available to him. While transmitting the Augustinian doctrine faithfully, Isidore stressed the idea of mystery, which he defined as divine power concealed beneath a corporeal veil. Paschase accordingly emphasises the mystery of the eucharist and describes it as the spiritual body and blood of Christ hidden beneath the corporeal veil of bread and wine, which are the figure of the mystery. He supplements the mysterious power by the objective presence of the body and blood, and reduces the corporeal veil to a sensory illusion sustained by God. In this way, he shifts the Augustinian dynamics of Isidore towards Ambrosian realism, with consequences that would embroil him in the first significant controversy over the eucharist in history.

Seeking nonetheless merely to recapitulate tradition, he retains as many of Augustine's ideas as possible. He accepts the mystic body of the predestinate and agrees that communion integrates the faithful into

[48] written in 831. Later, Paschase published extracts under Augustine's name. Having rewritten the work, he published it in 844.

this body. He locates the resurrected body in heaven, but identifies it with the mystic body. He shares the early medieval phobia against Capernaism and Stercoranism, which had emerged from Augustine's vigilance against the possibility of these heresies. Although they prevailed only among the ignorant majority in the form of superstition, the theologians of the period, who lacked confidence in their philosophical background, accused each other of committing them. Paschase himself condemns Capernaism, 'quia Christum vorari fas dentibus non est' (iv.1). Suspecting Stercoranism, on the other hand, he rebukes Christians who refrain from food and drink after communion, as if to avoid digestion of the eucharist. Though really present, the body and blood are immaterial and can only be assimilated spiritually. Paschase follows Augustine in declaring that a corrupt priest can consecrate the eucharist, 'quia non in merito consecrantis, sed in verbo efficitur Creatoris et virtute Spiritus sancti' (xii.1). While the idea of the power behind the word of God comes from Ambrose, Augustine contributes the thesis of a rite unaffected by priestly corruption. In keeping with Augustinian theology, Paschase considers the celebrant a mere representative behind whom Christ, the invisible priest, stands separating the unworthy communicants from the worthy. Augustine persuades him that the merit of communicants determines whether they receive the body and blood rather than mere bread and wine. Only through faith, which Paschase regards as a faculty of the mind,[49] can they commune on this spiritual food and drink. In passages inspired by Ambrose, however, he commits himself to their necessary presence after the consecration and, by implication, whether communicants deserve them or not. Nor does he provide for their removal before they reach unworthy communicants. Such conflicts between elements borrowed from Augustine's subjective realism and Ambrose's objective realism detract from his doctrine.

The Augustinian problem of the relationship between the bodies on the altar and in heaven had not occurred to Ambrose, because the latter believed the heavenly body to be in a spiritual state and therefore illocal. Did Paschase realise that? He seems rather to have assumed that Ambrose had already solved the problem without seeking to learn his solution. He in any case identifies the eucharistic body with one passing through all the stages of Christ's earthly and heavenly existence

[49] he added this supernatural faculty to four natural faculties: the senses, the imagination, reason and intelligence.

from the Virgin birth onwards. The body in the sacrament, he says is
the same as 'illud corpus quod natum est de Maria virgine [. . .] quod
pependit in cruce, sepultum est in sepulcro, resurrexit a mortuis, pene-
travit coelos, et nunc pontifex in aeternum, quotidie interpellat pro
nobis' (vii.2). No more than Augustine, therefore, does he acknowledge
any change in the body between its earthly and heavenly sojourns. The
identity of this unchanging body with the one on the altar does not
exclude Capernaism, despite his condemnation of this heresy. He might
have avoided opposition from fellow Benedictines, if he had qualified
such statements by what he wrote elsewhere in the same book, and other
statements might have benefited from this precaution too. He submits,
for instance, that the eucharist contains both the body and the blood of
Christ because the communicants' human nature consists of both.[50]
In isolation, this remark suggests that the eucharistic body and blood
nourish the human body and blood of the communicant. Elsewhere in
the *Body*, Paschase dissipates this impression: 'Bibimus quoque et nos
spiritaliter ac comedimus spiritalem Christi carnem' (v.3). Another
remark echoes the ancient belief in the life-giving power of blood.
The soul of Christ, residing in the blood of the eucharist, mediates
between the soul of the communicant and God, thus renewing and
sanctifying the entire man.[51] The location of Christ's evidently immaterial soul in the blood of the eucharist suggests that this blood is in a
physical state, yet Paschase obviously considers it spiritual. Such
statements invited attacks on the *Body* from the start, but he made
further trouble for himself by inserting a number of miracle stories
drawn from popular superstition to edify monks recently converted to
Christianity.[52] Accounts of bleeding communion wafers and the like
did little to reassure his critics on the spirituality of his realism.

While overstating Ambrose's realism, he also imitates his metabolism and finds precedents for eucharistic conversion in the Incarnation
and the creation. If God can create a world from nothing, if he can
engender a human body for his Son, then he can convert bread and wine
into the body and blood of this Son: 'voluit in mysterio hunc panem et

[50] 'Et ideo quam recte caro sanguini sociatur quia nec caro sine sanguine utique, nec
sanguis sine carne jure communicatur. Totus enim homo, qui ex duabus constant sub-
stantiis, redimitur, et ideo carne simul Christi et sanguine saginatur' (xix.1).
[51] 'Ut caro habeat relationem ad animam, quae in sanguine christi est, et anima vivi-
ficatrix carnis per sanguinem relationem habeat ad Deum, atque ita totus homo sanetur'
(xix.2).
[52] those in the Benedictine monastery of Corvey in Saxony, a satellite of Corbey.

33

vinum vere carnem suam et sanguinem consecratione Spiritus sancti potentialiter creari [. . .] ut sicut de Virgine per Spiritum vera caro sine coitu creatur' (iv.1). Whenever a celebrant recites the words of consecration, God re-creates a small portion of his creation,[53] thus converting material bread and wine into the spiritual body and blood of Christ. While the senses continue to perceive bread and wine, a figure of the underlying mystery, the body and blood of Christ manifest themselves to faith alone. The prospect of countless and unceasing miracles performed by God does not deter Paschase. His unscholastic reliance on the divinity for the solution of difficult problems precludes the elaboration of anything so complicated as impanation or transubstantiation. He shares Ambrose's convenient enthusiasm for the versatile power of the divine word, 'qui verbo cuncta creavit, haec verbo una cum Spiritu sancto cooperatur, et ideo nihil dubitandum, ubi Deus Trinitas jure opifex creditur' (xiii.1). Once the trinitarian God has uttered such a word, whether to empower the creation or the eucharist, the effect continues forever. After the multiplication of animals in creation and of bread in the feeding of the five thousand, the production of the eucharistic body and blood seems a matter of course to Paschase. But each celebration of the sacrament also miraculously reactualises the sacrifice of the cross, even though Christ suffered only once.[54] Thus Paschase records tradition, as he intended throughout the *Body*. His combination of Ambrose and Augustine nonetheless went further than either, and even he himself, intended. His introduction of ingredients from Augustine's dynamic symbolism into the metabolic realism of Ambrose, with which they clash, did not particularly upset his fellow theologians. The identification of the sacramental and heavenly bodies, on the other hand, did shock some of them and especially in passages where he neglected to confine this identification to immaterial existence. Nor did his attacks on Capernaism convince them that he understood the real presence in a truly spiritual sense.

Several fellow Benedictines criticised the *Body* when he published it in 844, the year he became abbot of Corbey (near Amiens). Among them were Raban Moor, Gottshalk of Orbais and particularly Ratramn, a

---

[53] the re-creation of Christ implies that he is a creature to begin with, hence Arianism, which Paschase did not intend.

[54] 'Et ideo in cruce nos cum illo simul crucifixi sumus,' he wrote in his *Letter to Frudegard*, a consequence of the identity between the historical body and the body of all believers (the Church) (Migne, cxx.1364C).

monk in his abbey and a former pupil of his. In contrast with Ratramn, Paschase did not enjoy imperial favour, but he gave his book to Charles the Bald, who dabbled in theology, for Christmas. Hearing of the controversy, however, Charles must have anticipated a political opportunity, for he submitted two treacherous questions to Paschase's opponent Ratramn: 1. Are the body and blood of Christ in the eucharist perceptible to the senses (truth) or can they be known only to faith (mystery)? 2. Is this body the same as the one born of Mary, crucified, resurrected and seated at the right hand of the Father? The first alternative in the first question implies Capernaism, of which Paschase was apparently being accused, and the second question raises the very point under dispute in his doctrine. Perhaps Charles was inviting Ratramn to implicate an unwanted abbot in heresy, although nothing of the sort actually happened, but an abbot agreeable to the emperor did replace Paschase in 849.

In answering Charles's first question, Ratramn gives a definition of figure closer to Isidore and Augustine than Paschase's. Ratramn agrees that a figure is a corporeal veil covering a spiritual mystery, but the Paschasian veil conceals the mystery, while the Ratramnian veil reveals it, though indistinctly. Ratramn cites the example of the Johannine Jesus describing himself as living bread which has come down from heaven. Such figures, he explains, say one thing and indicate another, which is similar yet different. Thus the image of the object seen through the veil resembles the object as it would appear without the veil. Perceived by the senses, the bread and wine of the eucharist resemble the underlying body and blood of Christ known only to faith. Ratramn accordingly interprets Augustine's enigmatic 'secundum quendam modum' as 'the manner of figure' (lxxxiv).[55] Instead of relegating this figure to the status of sensory illusion like Paschase, however, he recognises its objective existence. He even emphasises the validity of sensory perception after the consecration: 'Taste it, there is the savour of wine; smell it, there is the scent of wine; behold it, there is the colour of wine' (x). Such commonsense observations would mislead Calvinists and Voltaire into assuming that he confined the reality of the eucharist to material existence. On the contrary, the inability of the senses to detect any alteration, persuades him that they change spiritually and not materially. To deny that they are the body and blood of Christ,

[55] *The Book of Ratramn*, translated by H. W. and W. C. C. (Oxford 1838).

he warns, would be impious. 'Under the corporeal veil of bread and wine, the spiritual body and blood of Christ do exist' (xvi): clearly he believes in the real presence, but what kind of real presence? The mystery behind the figure contains spiritual power to nourish the soul with eternal life and this secret power contrasts with the perceptible manifestation of the sacrament. Ratramn does not conceive of power in the modern sense as either potential or kinetic energy devoid of any substantial existence. A dynamic concept of this sort would indeed eliminate the real presence of the body and blood, a conclusion to which interpreters have often leaped.[56] Ratramn evidently believes power to be something substantial, for he defines the eucharistic mystery as both power and 'spiritual structure'.[57] As if to discourage an exclusively dynamic interpretation, in fact, he refers to the 'food of the Lord's body and [. . .] drink of his blood' (lxxxiii) as well as 'spiritual meat and spiritual drink' (ci). Needless to say, he castigates Capernaism, on the other hand, as 'a horrible crime' (xix)!

In answering Charles's second question, he quotes the same parallel between the heavenly and the eucharistic bodies from Ambrose and even more accurately than Paschase: 'Vera utique caro Christi, quae crucifixa est [. . .] vere ergo carnis illius sacramentum est' (Ambrose, *On Mystery*, 53); 'Vera utique caro Christi, quae crucifixa est [. . .] verae ergo carnis illius sacramentum est' (Ratramn, *On the body*, lvi). He agrees with Ambrose on this parallel, but not with Paschase on the identity of the two bodies, despite his belief in the real presence. Augustine's conviction that the same body could not be in heaven and on the altar at the same time strikes him as decisive. He likewise joins Augustine in reasoning that, while the disciples could see and touch Christ after his resurrection, communicants cannot perceive the body in the eucharist by any of their senses. He therefore distinguishes between the two bodies as follows: 'The body in which Christ was crucified and buried is no mystery, but true and natural; while the body which now in a mystery contains the similitude of the former is not a perceptible, but rather a

---

[56] among them, two Catholic theologians: H. Peletier, 'Ratramne', *Dictionnaire de théologie* (Paris 1930-1950) and Josef Geiselmann, *Die Eucharistielehre der Vorscholastik* (Paderborn 1926).

[57] 'Secundum potentiam vero quod spiritaliter factae sunt, mysteria sunt corporis et sanguis christi' (xvi) – *Ratramnus: De corpore et sanguine domini*, ed. Bakhuizen van den Brink (Amsterdam 1974).

sacramental manifestation.'[58] Like Charles, he conceives of truth as an antonym of mystery and as evidence unobscured by figure. Since the body in the eucharist does not qualify as truth in this sense, it cannot be identical with the historical body which does. Then how can Christ's body be really present in the eucharist? Ratramn takes no steps to solve this dilemma and, in fact, does not even seem aware of it. Nor, as Fahey demonstrates, is it necessarily a dilemma for the Neoplatonic mind (see p.29). If reality exists only in the world of ideas, then the reality of Christ's body escapes the limitations of space and time. From a Neoplatonic viewpoint, therefore, this reality can be in heaven and on every altar at the same time, even though its perceptible manifestation remains at the right hand of God. The perceptible figure of the sacrament in Ratramn's thinking replaces this manifestation in its function of revealing the spiritual reality behind it. According to him, moreover, this figure designates and resembles another mystery, the body of people who believe in Christ. He supports this claim by Paul's comparison of the grain concentrated in the bread with Christians united by the Church. His language implies, as one might expect, that the mystic and heavenly bodies differ from each other too: '[This] mystery [. . .] bears the figure of either [utrius] body, that is, the body of Christ which suffered and rose again, and the body of the people who are born again and quickened from the dead' (xcviii). Does the body of believers then relate to the heavenly body in the same way as the sacramental body? Ratramn does not say. Nor does he examine eucharistic sacrifice in terms of figure and mystery, but these terms seem to apply. In commemoration of Christ's redemptive martyrdom, celebration of the eucharist renews what he once accomplished on the cross.[59] Apparently, the act of celebration itself is a figure of the sacrificial mystery conferring the redemption already obtained by Christ. Another passage suggests that the eucharist offers a pledge of salvation, the fruit of redemption: 'This body and blood are the pledge of some future thing [. . .] which [. . .] will hereafter be openly revealed' (lxxxvi). Here figure assumes the role of a pledge in a prophetic mystery promising the revelation of what must be salvation, although Ratramn does not specify. Despite such examples, reason weighed more heavily in his

---

[58] 'Haec vero caro quae nunc similitudinem illius in misterio continet, non sit specie caro sed sacramento' (lxvii).

[59] 'Quod dominus iesus christus semel se offerens ademplevit, hoc in eius passionis memoriam cotidie geritur per misteriorum celebrationem' (xxxix).

mind than Paschase's, and faith, though still essential, proportionately less. Yet one cannot take his wish to conform 'to the authority of the ancients' (xii) any less seriously.

The opposition from fellow Benedictines did not incline Paschase to conciliation. When he came to the institution of the eucharist in writing his *Commentary on st Matthew* (after 851), he sharpened the elements of his doctrine offensive to his opponents. As if to browbeat them, in fact, he belabours the apparent meaning of Jesus's words: 'Necque itaque dixit cum fregit et dedit eis panem, hoc est, vel in hoc mysterio est virtus vel figura corporis mei, sed ait non ficte, "Hoc est corpus meum" ' (Migne, cxx.890C). The denial that Jesus said anything about mystery or power, essential components in Ratramn's doctrine, may well be a reply to him. This naive argument, in any case, reveals the chasm between the kind of docile piety that Voltaire would call fanaticism and intellectual curiosity in the ninth-century controversy. Paschase further rebukes the objections to his theory by amplifying the human inability to comprehend the effects of God's activity. Having accepted Ambrose's belief in the spirituality of the risen body, he does not concern himself with how the body and blood can be in more than one place at the same time, not even at the Last Supper: 'Erat autem integer Christus et corpus Christi coram oculis omnium positum; necnon et sanguis in corpore, sicut et adhuc hodie integerrimum est et manet, qui vere dabatur eis ad comedendum, et ad bibendum' (Migne, cxx.891A). The disciples not only partook of a body living among them without wounding or diminishing it in any way, but also, ever since, communicants everywhere unceasingly consume the same body, which nonetheless remains intact at the right hand of God. Paschase now affirms that the heavenly, the sacramental and the mystic bodies are all one and the same. He also repairs the defect in the solution he advances for the problem of keeping the body and blood away from unworthy recipients. No longer does their impiety prevent them from receiving the body and blood already in the eucharist, but rather the body and blood do them harm. Against insinuations of Capernaism, he continually repeats that communion takes place *spiritaliter* and not *corporaliter*. Since his opponents agreed, this point might have served as a point of departure for negotiation, but the dispute never attained the proportions necessary to activate pressure for conciliation or precipitate arbitration by higher authority.

Adopted by the Benedictines of Cluny, Paschase's doctrine prospered in a climate of exaggerated realism over the next two centuries, while Ratramn's subsisted obscurely. The latter's *Body* nonetheless found an enthusiastic reader in Berengar of Tours, who attributed it to John the Scot Erigena, the author's name having been lost. Before 1059, the master of St Martin's School in Tours based his eucharistic theology on his interpretation of Ratramn, whom he vigorously defended from the Paschasian majority. 'Si tu tiens [Jean Scot] pour hérétique,' he warned Lanfranc, 'tu dois également regarder comme hérétiques saint Ambroise [...] et saint Augustin.'[60] The letter in which this challenge appears was forwarded to Rheims where the addressee was attending a council against Berengar. Intercepted there, it eventually resulted in the condemnation of Berengar by a Roman council in 1050. Also disciplined by councils at Vercelli and Brionne in 1050, Paris in 1051, Tours in 1051-1052 and 1054, Florence in 1055, Rouen in 1055 and 1063, Rome again and decisively in 1059 and 1079, Angers in 1062, Lisieux in 1064, Poitiers in 1076 and Bordeaux in 1080, he obviously had a reputation for heresy. Yet he himself was convinced of his orthodoxy. As usual, the attempt to obliterate his opinion resulted in the destruction of so many of his writings, that one cannot easily reconstitute it. To what extent have his enemies tampered with the surviving quotations, letters and manuscript of his *On the Holy Communion*? To what extent have they misrepresented his character in an age of ecclesiastical truculence and cynicism? Whether he was stubborn or steadfast depends on the point of view, but his enemies complain of his ability to twist the meaning of the texts they forced him to accept. The master dialectician changed his mind significantly only once, after the Council of Rome in 1059, and even then only to defend a less conciliatory position. For he abandoned the dynamic symbolism of the earlier period for a pure symbolism attenuating the logic of his persistent belief in the real presence.

He had in fact outgrown the legacy of Ratramn, whose commonsense criticism seems puny in comparison with his empirical dialectic. In the *Communion*, he finds reason imcomparably superior to sacred authority itself as a guide in the search for truth. He tells Lanfranc: 'Maximi plane cordis est, per omnia ad dialecticam confugere, quia confugere ad eam ad rationem est confugere, quo qui non confugit, cum secundum

[60] Charles-Joseph Hefele and Henri Leclercq, *Histoire des conciles* (Paris 1916), iv, Part 2, p.1047.

rationem sit factus ad imaginem Dei, suum honorem reliquit.'[61] This passage applies the idea of personal honour in chivalry to theological disputation. The more closely one imitates God, the greater the honour and, since human reason is itself an 'image' of God, one must exercise it whenever one can. Berengar naturally considers dialectic the highest form of reason, thus dialecticians, in his opinion, enjoy the greatest honour of all. He is in effect congratulating himself on his arrival at the pinnacle of his feudal aspirations. In the preliminary ritual of single combat, boasting precedes the challenge. Dialectic, by its very nature, tends to provoke polemic, but the passage, which itself demonstrates the art of dialectic, implies a specific challenge to Lanfranc: whoever does not resort to reason dishonours himself. Berengar is challenging his enemy to single combat in the form of dialectical disputation on the customary assumption that God will reward the defender of the truth with victory. His naive enthusiasm for this custom accounts for his role as the much battered scapegoat of Church politics in the eleventh century and of Catholic apology ever since. But Lanfranc may never have read this particular challenge, for Berengar, realising the danger of retaliation, refrained from publishing the *Communion*.[62] Stripped of its medieval baggage, the passage anticipates the Enlightenment by its assurance that 'the natural light' is the most reliable source of truth available to us and even more reliable than authority or tradition.

Apparently, the divine source of reason, in Berengar's opinion, guarantees the validity of empirical observation, with which reasoning must begin. He uses Ratramn's commonsense evaluation of consecrated bread and wine as a point of departure in his rational analysis of the eucharist, yet he soon leaves his predecessor far behind. Since the senses cannot detect any change in consecrated bread and wine, he concludes, unlike Ratramn, that none takes place. He does believe, however, that the consecration adds something previously absent, which he calls the sacrament of Christ's body and blood. It corresponds to Augustine's symbol, neglected in the ninth century, and, like Augustine, he distinguishes between the sign and the thing signified. Though separated from the body in heaven, the sacrament resembles it and contains some of its power. Since the body cannot come down, according to Augustine, the hearts of communicants must fly up to it or, in other words, partake of it subjectively. While it is not objectively

[61] Friedrich Vischer, ed., *Berengarii Turonensis De Sacra Coena* (Berlin 1834), p.101.
[62] the work was unknown until Lessing discovered a manuscript copy in 1770.

present in the eucharist, Berengar insists that it is really present. He therefore conformed essentially to Augustine at this stage in his career.

But conformity with the prevailing opinion enjoyed a higher priority with his enemies, who had other axes to grind. They persuaded the Roman council of 1059 to condemn him to a public reading of a profession of faith written by cardinal Humbert. According to this document, he repudiated as heresy their interpretation of his doctrine and embraced a deliberately exaggerated version of theirs. Thus they forced him to disown as erroneous the opinion that 'le pain et le vin placés sur l'autel sont seulement un sacrement (un symbole) et non le véritable corps et le véritable sang de [. . .] Jésus-Christ'.[63] Since in reality he believed as they did in both propositions, the statement implies the admission of an error he never committed. But they also forced him to profess a belief that he had always rejected and particularly in a letter whose language Humbert was imitating in the profession: the body of Christ 'peut d'une manière [sensuelle] et non seulement dans le sacrement, mais en vérité, être traité par les mains du prêtre, être rompu et broyé par les dents des fidèles'.[64] The cardinal included *sensualiter* in the text because Berengar habitually affirmed that communicants receive the body and blood of Christ *intellectualiter* (spiritually) rather than *sensualiter* (materially), *intellectually* being his interpretation of Augustine's *in a certain manner*. Humbert seems to have exaggerated the Paschasian position in order to prevent him from construing the profession in a manner favourable to his own opinion, as he usually did. The cardinal did not himself believe in the Capernaism he was forcing his adversary to profess. These tactics suggest that he never even considered the possibility of reconciliation, but rather concentrated on humiliating his victim. He apparently miscalculated that his tyranny, backed by the authority of the council, would crush what he regarded as impudent dissension. Although Berengar did not have to sign the profession, a curious oversight,[65] his defeat was trumpeted as a great victory over heresy!

In the following years, he bitterly attacked Humbert on the grounds of Capernaism and, when the cardinal died in 1061, Lanfranc felt obliged to defend his memory. Although Berengar and Lanfranc were rival schoolmasters, they may initially have been on good terms.

---

[63] Hefele, iv, Part 2, p.1173 n.   [64] Hefele, iv, Part 2, p.1173 n.

[65] the future Gregory the Great, the legate Hildebrandt, who had befriended Berengar, may have arranged to spare him this humiliation.

Berengar appears to have provoked Lanfranc unintentionally by the letter quoted above, for the addressee had to clear himself of the suspicion that he shared his correspondent's views. He found himself in agreement with the Roman council of 1050 and they approved his development of Paschasian metabolism on the spot. After the same council had condemned his fellow schoolmaster, he soon became his greatest enemy. Not only was he a match for Berengar in disputation, but he also had the political finesse his adversary lacked. Some time between 1066 and 1069, he answered Berengar's assault on Humbert with his own *Body and blood of the Lord*. Though aggressive and poorly written, this work is a milestone in the history of the eucharist. Predictably, the author gives early priority to reversing the Berengarian superiority of reason over sacred authority. Any change in the bread and wine requires a greater reliance on the mysterious power of God than otherwise, but Lanfranc seems rather to accept than welcome this necessity as Paschase and Ambrose do. The redundant series in the following passage, *ineffably, incomprehensibly, and marvellously,* seems for instance to overstate his conviction (Migne, cl.430 BC):

Credimus [. . .] terrenas substantias, quae in mensa Dominica, per sacerdotale mysterium, divinitus sanctificantur, ineffabiliter, incomprehensibiliter, mirabiliter, operante superna potentia, converti in essentiam Dominici corporis, reservatis ipsarum rerum speciebus, et quibusdam aliis qualitatibus.

Despite the semantic confusion and the exploratory imprecision of the text, it undoubtedly anticipates the doctrine eventually known as transubstantiation. The confusion arises in part from a later standardisation of terms, while the imprecision results from the attempt to grasp an unfamiliar concept. The other remaining qualities of the terrestrial substances (bread and wine) blur Lanfranc's distinction between their appearances, on one hand, and the essence of Christ's body, on the other. Furthermore, he accounts neither for the essence of the bread and wine nor the appearances of Christ's body, not to mention the other qualities of the latter. His attempt to clarify the relationship between the bodies in heaven and on the altar also lacks rigour: 'Ipsum corpus quod de Virgine sumptum est nos sumere, et tamen non ipsum. Ipsum quidem, quantum ad essentiam veraeque naturae proprietatem atque virtutem; non ipsum autem, si species panis vinique speciem, caeteraque superius comprehensa' (Migne, cl.430C). Here again, intermediate values blur the promising distinction between essences and appearances. If property and power (as in a dynamic presence!) belong to the true nature of a thing, what remains to be considered appearances? Despite these discrepancies, the two passages indicate definite progress towards a partial solution of the problems that Paschase had left to the miraculous powers of God. Lanfranc, on the other hand, makes a traditional reply to Berengar's charges of Capernaism. The appearances and certain other qualities of bread and wine subsist in the eucharist 'ne percipientes cruda et cruenta, horrerent' (Migne, cl.430C). He thus establishes an argument already advanced by Ambrose on a firmer foundation. Less convincingly, he combines Ambrosian metabolism with Augustinian symbolism; the prestige of both Fathers deterred any open sacrifice of one to the other. This combination nonetheless reinforces his support of the real presence, weakened by the partiality of the identity between the resurrected and the sacramental bodies. In view of his polemical intentions in *The Body and blood of the Lord*, moreover, this partial identity and this accommodation of symbolism served as tactical concessions to Berengar.

Aware of the danger to his own position, the master of St Martin's adjusted his criticism of Paschasian metabolism to meet the new challenge. Although he did not publish *On the Holy Communion*, a reply to Lanfranc's *Body and blood of the Lord* written in 1063, the arguments against transubstantiation in this work are presumably the same as the ones he was using in oral communication and writings since lost. He follows Lanfranc's disordered plan, responds to his insults with insults of his own and, unlike his adversary, indulges in much repetition. Yet he discriminates more successfully between subject and accidents than Lanfranc does between essence and appearances or qualities. By no means, moreover, does this distinction imply that, in his opinion, they can really be separated from each other. On the contrary, accidents necessarily reveal the presence of their subject and a subject cannot exist without its accidents. These considerations clearly reflect his confidence in sense data and the ability of God-given reason to derive the most significant truth from this source. Applied to the substantial conversion of Lanfranc, his analysis wreaks havoc. The consecration does not destroy the subject of bread, because the accidents (colour, taste, etc.) remain. Since the accidents of Christ's body do not appear in the eucharist, their subject is absent. The loss of these accidents, in any case, would necessarily indicate the destruction of an immortal body! The digestion of this subject in communion would produce the same absurd result. It can neither be brought down from heaven nor, since it already exists, be re-created on the altar. Nor can it be chopped into tiny pieces and distributed by the millions at all celebrations of the Lord's Supper. Berengar protests against this Capernaistic atrocity as if he thought his adversary really believed in it, for, according to Berengar's philosophy, he should have. This deliberate caricature of metabolism, a habit with him, illustrates his dialectical technique.

He faced a new enemy after 1070, when Lanfranc, favoured by William the Conqueror, became the archbishop of Canterbury. Guitmund of Aversa, a former pupil of Lanfranc, replaced the latter as the leading proponent of substantial conversion. But Guitmund's *True body and blood of Christ* (1075) reveals a poor knowledge of Berengar's doctrine. Guitmund apparently mistook it for a kind of impanation, the coexistence, after the consecration, of both bread and wine, on one hand, and the body and blood of Christ, on the other. Berengar seems never to have entertained such a compromise with metabolism, but his adhesion to the real presence, which struck most of his enemies as hypocrisy, must have suggested this interpretation. Actually, Berengar may have understood the real presence in terms of Augustine's Neoplatonic belief in the universality of ideas. Guitmund appears to have invented impanation himself and, since his text is obscure on this point, one may wonder whether the invention tempted him. He rejects it in *The True body*, however, and the brunt of his argument commits him to Lanfranc's theory, which he refines and fortifies against Berengar's objections. He liquidates the problem of destruction and re-creation, which the latter had raised, by supposing the direct conversion of one existing substance into another. Despite the originality of this concept, he took a typical precaution: 'Panem et vinum altaris Domini in corpus et sanguinem Christi substantialiter commutari [. . .] universalis Ecclesiae consensione roboratum est.'[66] *Substantialiter commutari* obviously improved upon Lanfranc's *substantialiter mutari* and, together with its context here, offered a practical definition of transubstantiation even before the word was coined. While this doctrine partially rationalises the eucharistic miracle proclaimed by Ambrose, Guitmund by no means reduces the role of mystery in the rite. His repetition of the Capernaistic miracle stories in Paschase's *Body and blood of the Lord* shows that even the metabolistic elite did not entirely

[66] *De corporis et sanguinis Christi veritate in eucharistia*, ed. H. Hurter (London 1879), iii.44.

escape popular superstition. He particularly relies on the mysterious powers of God to repair the weakness in metabolism exposed by Berengar's facetious protest against the division of Christ's body into many pieces: 'Tota hostia est corpus Christi, ut nihilominus unaquaeque particula separata sit totum corpus Christi' (i.16). The body exists in its entirety and remains intact, not only in heaven, but also in every crumb of bread and in every drop of wine consumed by communicants. Known as concomitance, this opinion implies the removal of the necessity for communion on both bread and wine. According to the traditional assumption shared by Lanfranc, the bread becomes flesh and the wine, blood, each exclusive of the other. How could Guitmund have advocated so radical an innovation without being accused of heresy? Perhaps his contribution to the massive and passionate reaction against Berengar brought him unusual privileges.

His influence apparently had a decisive impact on the anti-Berengarian council at Rome in 1079. The publication of *The True body* and further condemnations by provincial councils had contributed to a renewal of the persecution against the master of St Martin's. Anxious to defend himself before an ecumenical council, he appealed to Gregory the Great, who had won his confidence as a legate at the Council of Tours in 1054. Gregory called a council at Rome in 1078 and sought a compromise acceptable to him. Once Berengar had agreed to a profession of faith declaring his belief in the real presence, but leaving substantial conversion unmentioned, the pope actually pronounced him innocent of heresy. Berengar was ready to swear to this oath in public and one of his supporters to grasp a red-hot iron bar to demonstrate God's approval. On the eve of this ceremony, however, Gregory let himself be persuaded to put the final decision off until the next year. Probably he yielded, not to charity for the supporter, but rather to pressure from Berengar's enemies who feared, no doubt, that the bar might not burn his hands. In 1079 they assembled a crushing majority against Berengar, but Gregory had a private conversation with him beforehand and promised him protection in return for flexibility. At the council, his enemies nevertheless, on Guitmund's advice perhaps,[67] obtained amendments in the profession he had accepted, including the insertion of *substantialiter*. It now read as follows (Denz. n.355):

[67] this is A. J. MacDonald's opinion in *Lanfranc: a study of his life, work and writing* (London 1944); see p.185.

The bread and wine [. . .] on the altar are substantially changed into the true[68] and [. . .] living flesh and blood of [. . .] Christ [. . .] and [. . .] after conse-cration it is the true body of Christ which was born of the Virgin and which [. . .] was suspended on the cross, and which [sits] at the right hand of the Father and the true blood of Christ, which was poured out from his side not only through the sign and power of the sacrament, but in its property of nature and in truth of substance.

Known as 'Ego Berengarius', the initial words (omitted here), this text is the earliest endorsement of transubstantiation, as yet unnamed, by the Church. It follows Lanfranc in its use of substance and nature as synonyms; a more rigorous conception of substance evolved only later. It also combines dynamic symbolism with metabolism, thus preserving the heritage of Augustine. But it does not contain any reference to concomitance, a discreet indication that this anti-Beren-garian weapon did not enjoy the confidence of the majority against him. From their viewpoint, the amended profession of faith imprisoned a heretical escape-artist in an orthodox cage likely to put an end to his stubborn subversion of Christianity. The style practically stumbles under the redundant weight of clauses designed to block every possible alternative interpretation. From Berengar's viewpoint, on the other hand, this text threatened to adulterate the faith, frustrate a lifelong struggle and make a monumental scapegoat of him. Having disputed in vain the insertion of *substantialiter*, he resigned himself to the inevitable. His enemies at once suspected, correctly perhaps, that he was as usual secretly interpreting this adverb in a favourable manner. They de-manded that he explain his understanding of the text, but he refused on the grounds that he was not at liberty to divulge a secret agreement he had made with the pope. He may have hoped that this disclosure would force Gregory to keep his promise. But had Gregory not already decided to sacrifice him to the majority? Angered by the disclosure, he ordered him to admit the error of leaving *substantialiter* out of the original oath. Berengar obeyed and the humiliation of signing a pro-fession of faith contradicting his profoundest convictions followed. The only consolation it offered him was the revocation, implied by the very adverb *substantialiter*, of the Capernaism in the profession of 1059.

---

[68] the title of Guitmund's treatise differed from those of Lanfranc, Ratramn and Paschase only by his insertion of the term *veritate*. The reappearance of the term in this oath implies deference to him by his colleagues at the council. The abbreviation Denz. refers to Heinrich Denziger, *The Sources of Catholic dogma*, translated by Roy Deferrari (St Louis 1957).

Thus, typically, Berengar became a heretic by the deviation of orthodoxy, a deviation nonetheless resulting from his opposition to the predominant interpretation of the eucharist and especially the excesses he
saw in it. However cunning and arrogant he may have been in theological disputation, he was a sheep among wolves in the political arena
of the medieval Church. With few exceptions, the councils against him
were particularly intended to relieve pressures and further ambitions
that had little to do with the purification of the faith.[69]

In 1215, the Fourth Lateran Council confirmed the doctrine opposed
by Berengar and designated it as transubstantiation. Called to combat
the Albigensians, it likewise confirmed the real presence, which they
denied. On the disciplinary front, it declared a monopoly over the
distribution of the eucharist, available only from priests ordained by the
Church. According to a 'salutary law' (Denz. n.173), it required of all
Catholics at least one communion every year at Easter, on pain of
excommunication. Anxious to preserve the authority of the Church
and set firm standards of faith, the framers of the conciliar decree gave
little attention to the theological justification of its contents. Scholastic
theology, on the other hand, was already committed to a quest for such
a justification, but the proportions of the grand debate preclude an
exposition of it here.

The eucharistic doctrine of Thomas, whose authority exceeds that of
all other scholastics, nonetheless summarises the results sufficiently
for our purposes. He considers 'this sacrament, which contains Christ
himself [. . .] perfective of all the other sacraments'.[70] Not only does it
bestow grace as they do, but it also unites participants with the very
source of grace, the mysterious body of Christ, the Church in the
Augustinian conception. One need only desire it, said Thomas, in
order to obtain its effect, a remark which he almost certainly did not
intend as a contradiction of Fourth Lateran, for the Church was most
eager to satisfy this desire wherever it occurred. More positively than
any of his predecessors, the Angelic Doctor ascribes an intrinsic and
autonomous power to the words of consecration themselves, so that

[69] 'In the early middle ages, politics, not religion, engaged the attention of the astute
ecclesiastics at Rome, and [in] the case of Berengar [. . .] the natural development of
religious doctrine and the personal rights of an individual were sacrificed to the growing
political program and necessities of the papacy' (MacDonald, p.103).

[70] *Summa theologiae*, lvi-lix, translated by David Bourke, James Cunningham, William
Barden and Thomas Gilby [hereafter *ST*] (New York 1965-1975), 3.85.1.

they actually do what they say.[71] Recited by any priest, 'This is my body' and 'This is my blood' convert bread and wine into the body and blood of Christ. 'In performing this sacrament, [he] has no other act save the pronouncing of the words' (*ST*. 3.77.2). Since Jesus charged these sentences with a self-activating power in his institution of the eucharist, there is no further need for intervention by him. This theory has the advantage of eliminating the necessity for the trivial involvement of the divinity wherever and whenever communion takes place. It has the disadvantage of transforming the consecration into a kind of magic formula and liberating the celebrant from moral responsibility. But these considerations may have influenced Thomas less than the Capernaistic reflex of preserving Christ's body and blood from contamination. A routine instrument of divine power, the celebrant could not degrade the sacrament even if he wanted to. 'The mass of a wicked priest is not of less value than that of a good priest, because the same sacrifice is offered by both' (*ST*. 3.82.5). The tradition behind this statement, one suspects, grew out of fear that a possible invalidation of eucharistic celebrations endangered the authority of the Church. Whoever the celebrant may be, Thomas confidently affirms, his pronunciation of the final syllable in the sentence of the consecration formula triggers the transubstantiation of the bread into Christ's body and of the final syllable in the second sentence, that of the wine into his blood.

How can this body be in heaven and on the altar at the same time? Thomas solves this traditional problem by process of elimination: 'A thing cannot be in any place where it was not previously,' he observes, 'except by change of place, or by the conversion of another thing into itself' (*ST*. 3.75.2). But the body of Christ cannot be in the eucharist by 'local motion' (change of place) for three reasons: 1. If it moved from heaven to earth, it would cease to be in heaven, which is impossible. 2. A moving body occupies successive positions in space, which is not the case here. 3. A moving body cannot occupy different positions in space simultaneously and 'The body of Christ under this sacrament begins at the one time to be in several places' (*ST*. 3.75.2). Having thus eliminated the possibility of local motion. Thomas serenely concludes that Christ's body is in heaven and on the altar 'by the conversion of another thing into itself'. In scholastic terms, the accidents or sensual

71 this opinion is an innovation by Thomas, according to Francis Assisi, *The Eucharist, the end of all the sacraments according to st Thomas and his contemporaries* (Sinsinawa, Wisc. 1972), p.187.

appearances of bread and wine remain after the loss of the substances formerly sustaining them. Thomas rejects impanation on the grounds that 'what is changed into another thing no longer remains after such a change' (*ST.* 3.75.2). Yet he refuses to admit the destruction of the substances underlying the bread and the wine either, because it would be improper for God to destroy a part of his own creation. As Turmel puts it, 'la substance du pain et du vin, qui n'a pas été anéantie par la transubstantiation, a eu un sort équivalent à cela'.[72] After consecration, in any case, the substances of bread and wine become those of Christ's body and blood. While the senses continue to perceive the accidents of bread and wine, faith detects the substances of his body and blood. Then how can these accidents subsist without the support of their own substances? 'They are being kept in existence by God' (*ST.* 3.77.1). This respectful endorsement of the traditional answer, however, could scarcely have satisfied a theologian who devoted his entire career to exposing the details of how God does such things. Accidents could subsist without their substance, he therefore speculated, if a fundamental accident, through which the substance would ordinarily support the others, remained intact. He identifies this fundamental accident as the *dimensive quantity*, by which he means three-dimensional extension or, simply, spatial configuration. In the *Sum of theology*, he explains: 'All the accidents cling to the substance through the medium of the [dimensive) quantity; for [example] the immediate recipient of colour is the extended surface' (*ST.* 3.77.2). Consequently, the spatial configuration of the bread in the eucharist continues to support the other accidents, taste, texture, colour, etc., after they have lost their substance to transubstantiation. The substance of Christ's body produced by this conversion occupies the same spatial configuration. As Thomas wrote in the *Sum against the Gentiles*:

After the change, the dimensive quantity, whereby the bread occupied that place, remains; while the substance of the bread is changed into Christ's body, which thus comes to be under the dimensive quantity of the bread, and consequently occupies the place of the bread; by no means however of the bread's dimensions.[73]

Consequently, transubstantiation in this theology qualifies as a partial conversion, one which includes substance, but stops short of the

[72] Joseph Turmel, *Histoire des dogmes* (1931-1936), v.474.
[73] The English Dominican Fathers, *The Summa contra Gentiles*, iv (London 1929), 4.63.

dimensive quantity, thus leaving all the accidents intact. Presumably, a conversion including both substance and dimensive quantity would be total, since nothing would remain to support the other accidents, but he does not explore this hypothesis. The partiality of substantial conversion spares the communicants the sensual horrors of bloody flesh and deprives the unbeliever of grounds for scorn, or so he believed.

His explanation of what happens to the accidents of Christ's body and blood is perhaps the weakest point in his doctrine. 'The entire Christ is in this sacrament' (*ST*. 3.76.1), he declares, and he supports this claim by the necessary unity of Christ's body, whose substance he has already found to be in the eucharist: 'If any two things be really united, then wherever the one is really, there must the other also be' (*ST*. 3.76.1). According to the *Sum against the Gentiles*, 'both Christ's soul and his divinity are present under the appearance of bread, because both are united to his body' (4.64). The *Sum of theology* concerns itself rather with the means by which the accidents of the body accompany the substance. While transubstantiation cannot produce these accidents, concomitance, in Thomas's opinion, can: 'by [...] concomitance the whole dimensive quantity of Christ's body and all its other accidents are in this sacrament' (*ST*. 3.76.3). He nevertheless admits that this effect of concomitance does not conform to 'the essential demands of the situation [...] The dimensions of Christ's body are [not] in this sacrament [...] in a way that it is normal for dimensions to be' (*ST*. 3.76.4). He thus attempts to preserve the unity of Christ's body in the eucharist by the transubstantiation of bread into its substance, on one hand, and the concomitance of its accidents, on the other. This solution confronted him with two different kinds of presence and this difference detracts from the unity to which he had apparently already committed himself.

His use of concomitance to establish the unity of the body and the blood in the eucharist seems more convincing. 'The whole Christ', he submits, 'is under each of the species [...] This serves to represent Christ's passion, in which the blood was separated from his body' (*ST*. 3.76.2). Like that of the soul from the body, this separation occurred only during the three days between the crucifixion and the resurrection. Thomas therefore accredits the ancient belief that the blood gives life to the body, a belief upon which the institution narrative itself was probably founded. Permanently reunited in the risen Christ, the body and blood must somehow accompany each other in the eucharist. 'In virtue of the consecration', however, 'the body of Christ is under the species of bread, while his blood is under the species of wine' (*ST*. 3.81.4). Thomas apparently believed that transubstantiation necessarily converts a liquid into a liquid and a solid into a solid, further evidence that theological invention ultimately depends on sensory experience. Again, since transubstantiation cannot assure the necessary unity, concomitance must: 'Now that his blood is not really separated from his body; by real concomitance, both his blood is present with the body under the species of the bread, and his body together with the blood under the species of wine' (*ST*. 3.81.4). But this time concomitance, by its complementary effect, achieves a more convincing double unity. As in Guitmund's primitive version of the doctrine, though, it continues to imply the independence of each element and the redundance of either. Thomas informs us, moreover, that some churches were already restricting laymen to the body, while clergymen communed on both body and blood. The excuse for this tardy privilege, suggested no doubt by superstitious exaggeration of the real presence, is the fear of spilling Christ's blood from a cup shared by many communicants. A clergyman himself, Thomas may not have realised that this 'prudent custom' (*ST*. 3.80.12) had apparently developed from the slow, but sure aggrandisement of clerical privilege throughout the history of the Church. Exempted from moral responsibility, yet privileged with access to an additional and more dramatic[74] source of eternal life, the celebrant faced formidable temptations.

Moral and political questions nonetheless aroused the great doctor's curiosity less than the technical problems of theology, such as the traditional dilemma over the simultaneous multilocality of Christ's body. His solution stems from 'the specific nature of [. . .] substance, [which] is prior to its being extended' (*ST*. 3.76.3), that is, prior to spatial configuration. Substance, therefore, does not conform to the laws governing the position and division of matter or, in other words, it escapes common sense. 'If a substantial totality is wholly in the whole of something, it is also wholly in each part of that thing' (*SG*, 4.67). As examples, Thomas cites the total presence of water in water everywhere and the total presence of the soul throughout the body. He does not except the original eucharist, distributed by Jesus himself, from the total consequences of Jesus's participation in the first of all communions: "Christ was the first to fulfill what he required others to observe [. . .]

[74] more dramatic because of the continuing belief that blood contains the essence of life.

When he said [...] 'Take and eat,' and again, 'Take and drink' [...] he himself [...] both ate and drank" (*ST.* 3.81.1). Voltaire would facetiously insinuate that Jesus committed autophagia and his disciples, together with all communicants, cannibalism (see p.197). The material understanding of the real presence in popular superstition, which the Church did little to combat, ran the risk of such an interpretation. But the limitation of the flesh consumed to its substance, an immaterial existence abstracted from the idea of flesh, neutralises the bestial implications of autophagia and cannibalism. Thomas accordingly emphasises the innocence of communing on Christ's substantial body and blood under the appearances of ordinary bread and wine. 'The body of Christ in itself is not broken, but only in its sacramental appearance' (*ST.* 3.77.7). He recommends, in fact, that Humbert's oath of 1059 be interpreted in this wholesome manner. In the twelfth century, however, only an intellectual elite could exercise such sophisticated discrimination.

While the apparent digestion of eucharistic bread and wine would seem to raise a similar problem, Thomas proposes a different solution. Instead of reapplying the theory applied elsewhere he refers to an 'existence [which] is not actually in matter, but of the same kind as the existence of a material thing'. In communion, such an existence is 'taken away by a disintegrating power when the matter is no longer there' (*ST.* 3.77.4). This disintegrating power alludes to the 'natural heat' (*ST.* 3.80.3) of digestion. Why did Thomas settle for this rough approximation of a theory, which involves the destruction of a dimensive quantity unsupported by its substance and the resulting disappearance of its secondary accidents? One cannot say. In any case, he concedes that, like ordinary food and drink, consecrated bread and wine can nourish or even inebriate communicants. The (Augustinian) power of the sacrament, however, can nourish and inebriate the soul itself (an echo of Ambrose: see p.25). While corporal nourishment 'is changed into the substance of the person nourished [...] spiritual food changes a man into itself' (*ST.* 3a.73.3). Communion incorporates the communicant into (Augustine's) mystical body of Christ, which the sacrament does not contain, but rather signifies. Christ's love for sincere believers makes this integration into the Church possible, 'because it is the special feature of friendship to live together with friends' (*ST.* 3.85.1). Should people in mortal sin or animals consume the eucharist, neither would it benefit them, nor could they degrade it. Grace comes only to people who sincerely desire (deserve) it and Jesus exposed his body to worse abuse without loss of dignity. Thomas innocently acknowledges a consequence that Voltaire would find revolting: 'Even though a mouse [. . .] were to eat the consecrated host, the substance of Christ's body would not cease to be under the species.'[75] (*ST*. 3.83.3). On the strength of this conviction, one may appropriately terminate the exposition of the eucharist as sacrament in his teaching.

After so ample a discussion of this panel in the dyptich, his treatment of the eucharist as sacrifice comes as a disappointment. One brief quotation adequately summarises his thought on this subject: 'The celebration of this sacrament is an image representing Christ's passion, which is his true sacrifice [. . .] It is called a sacrifice [. . .] because [. . .] we are made partakers of the fruit of our Lord's passion' (*ST*. 3.83.1). Thomas in effect briefly outlines the relationship between sacrament and sacrifice as well as two themes, the commemoration of the Passion and the access of communicants to salvation. Both of these logically belong to sacrament too and Thomas, along with his predecessors back to Paschase, amply develop them as such. Since, in the *Sum of theology*, he intended to provide students with an exhaustive compendium of theology, his neglect of eucharistic sacrifice is significant. The routine re-actualisation of Jesus's self-sacrifice in the eucharist defies rational analysis even more forbiddingly than the presence of the victim in the sacrament, which is merely a preliminary step. How bread and wine could become the body and blood of Christ is a less formidable mystery than how he could suffer only once as the victim of a sacrifice recurring whenever communicants eat this bread and drink this wine. No major theologian seems to have made any considerable effort to answer this question between Augustine and Trent. Paschase had in fact diverted attention from sacrifice to sacrament by his treatment of the preliminary problem. In the ensuing controversies, sacrifice appears to have been neglected, so that Thomas inherited a highly developed theology of sacrament and a faint tradition of sacrifice. Scholasticism and the nature of his talent oriented him towards the rationalisation of Christian mystery by a systematic revision of existing theology. No incentive inclined him to risk the adventure of reviving a forgotten tradition, risking accusations of heresy and struggling with the primeval difficulties of explaining how the crucifixion could be renewed in every celebration of the eucharist.

[75] *ST*. 3.83.3. Speculation on what would happen in this case is a scholastic commonplace inherited by Meslier and Voltaire. For Voltaire, see p.39.

With the exception of Wyclif, Thomas's fellow scholastics disputed the manner of transubstantiation, but not the fact. They disagreed, for instance, over what sustains the accidents of bread and wine after their loss of substance. Instead of quantity, they proposed quality and weight, while Duns Scotus, the great rival of Thomas, thought they needed no other support than the will of God. Transubstantiating the substances of bread and wine into those of Christ's body and blood, he admitted, amounts to annihilating them. Unwilling to concede a partial destruction of the creation, his admirer William of Ockham, who privately professed impanation, declared that the substances of bread and wine cease to exist, while those of the body and blood *succeed* or replace them on the altar, yet without leaving heaven. William's nominalism may have facilitated this ambiguity. According to this philosophy, phenomena have nothing in common except the general concepts under which we unite them in our minds. If the creation consists of individual substances, each with its own accidents, the conversion of one into another would establish a relation between them, which is impossible in nominalism. In reaction to the philosophy taught by William's disciples at Oxford, John Wyclif went to the opposite extreme of realism.[76] The abstractions by which we designate categories of phenomena, he insists, correspond to underlying realities of universal value. Knowledge of these universals is innate and they form a hierarchy of truth emanating from God himself, the highest of them all. Robson traces this integration of God in the creation to the transmission of Augustine's works by Arab scholars.[77] Wyclif's realism derived in large measure from the Neoplatonism of Augustine, whom he admired as much as Berengar and Ratramn did.

Ockham's version of transubstantiation offended the Oxford realist more acutely than Thomas's, which he also opposed. The most thorough presentation of his arguments appears in *On the eucharist*, a somewhat obscure and incoherent work published (*ca.*1380) towards the end of his life. Two objections to Ockhamist transubstantiation predominate, the impossibility of annihilating a substance and the impossibility of converting a substance no longer in existence into an existing one. The cessation of existence, a periphrasis avoiding the risky implications of substantial destruction, does not fool Wyclif: 'Cessation and de-

[76] philosophical realism, not to be confused with eucharistic realism, as in Paschase, Lanfranc, Guitmund and Thomas.
[77] John Robson, *Wyclif and the Oxford schools* (London 1961), p.146.

struction are exactly the same thing'[78] Having unmasked this hypocrisy, he reinforces the traditional protest against the partial annihilation of the creation by a realist argument. As a general concept, substance qualifies as a universal and, since a particular is an individual manifestation of a universal, annihilation of a particular substance would break the chain of being which descends from God. And that would be impossible. But even if the substances of bread and wine could be destroyed, Wyclif argues, Ockhamist transubstantiation implies a contradiction camouflaged by succession. How could the substance of bread be converted to that of Christ's body when, annihilated, it no longer exists? That would be impossible too. This stricture nonetheless depends on the assumption that destruction and conversion cannot occur simultaneously as the Ockhamists claimed. Actually, Wyclif is exposing the heretical implications of the Ockhamist theory, which does not involve a true conversion and therefore does not deserve to be called transubstantiation. He discovers a further contradiction in his adversaries' criticism of Thomist transubstantiation. In their opinion, the dimensive quantity of bread is destroyed, thus it cannot support the accidents of bread after consecration. Wyclif remarks that they 'deny composition to be continued on the basis of non-existent quantities, yet admit as possible the cessation of the bread at a particular instant and the conversion following immediately thereafter' (3.10). If the dimensive quantity of bread does not subsist and thus cannot sustain the accidents of bread, then certainly the substance of bread, once it is annihilated, cannot be converted into that of Christ's body. Against transubstantiation in general, Ockhamist, Thomist or other, Wyclif joins Berengar in attacking the survival of accidents unsupported by their substance. 'There remaineth nothing but a heap of accidents', he complains in one of his sermons.[79] Although he has less faith in experience than the Ockhamists, he does not disdain the sensualist argument of Berengar and Ratramn. Even if all Catholics should agree on transubstantiation, he contends, 'it does not follow that the bread is identical with the body of Christ, as is clear to anyone who heeds his sensual perception' (7.59). The people, who do not heed theirs, commit idolatry for lack of proper instruction. Here is another allusion to popular superstition, which continued to haunt eucharistic theology. The sensual perception of the accidents, in Wyclif's opinion, proves the

---

[78] *On the eucharist*, translated by Matthew Spinka (London 1953), 3.4.
[79] *The Great sermons of the great preachers* (London 1858), p.116.

substantial presence of bread and wine. But realism provides him with an argument he considers even more potent. Accidents can occur only when God communicates the universal substance to us in a particular manner. The annihilation of the particular substance – as if a universal could be destroyed – would necessarily liquidate its accidents. In Wyclif's language, accidents depend on 'the truth that substance is accidentally of a certain sort [. . .] but no such truth can exist without substance, just as no creature can exist without God' (3.15). The third impossibility, that of accidents unsupported by substance, essentially completes his philosophical refutation of transubstantiation.

He supports this refutation by historical evidence against the authenticity of the dogma, which in his opinion neither scripture nor tradition condone. Like Berengar, whose true opinion he misunderstood, he finds that transubstantiation is a modern perversion of the ancient faith.[80] He misinterprets the oath of 1059 as proof that the Church had preserved the primitive doctrine of the eucharist until the eleventh century. 'The earlier opinion', which he mistook for his own, 'agrees more with sense, reason, the holy doctors and Scripture' (2.6). He consequently pleads for the right to disagree with the Church, when dogma conflicts with the teaching of the Bible: 'No one ought to believe even the pope in matters of faith, except to the extent that his pronouncements are founded in Scripture' (3.13). He may have been the first pre-reformation theologian to demand that all dogma be justified by the text of the Bible. In accordance with his realism, every word in the sacred text enjoyed the status of a truth communicated by God and therefore an absolute priority over any human opinion. 'Neither upon Scripture nor reason', he concludes, 'can the Avignonese[81] Church base the said transubstantiation' (3.13).

In turning from the doctrine he condemns to the doctrine he defends, one encounters obscurity and vacillation, for he was unable to mould his eucharistic theology into a coherent whole before his death in 1384. His exegesis of the institution narrative and the oath of 1059 are nonetheless helpful in the attempt to re-establish his conception of the sacrament.

---

[80] he hardly suspected, however, that the 'notion of transubstantiation appeared for the first time in the Eucharistic theory of a Gnostic sect [the Valentinian Marcosians], and at a period when the Church was still disposed to reject it as a heresy. This is in fact only one of many examples, which show how the Church on capital issues came, in process of time, to make into dogmas ideas which it had originally condemned as heresy' (Martin Werner, *The Formation of Christian dogma* (New York 1957), p.191).

[81] the pope resided in Avignon from 1309 to 1377.

He notes that the text in the gospels differs from the liturgy in an important respect: 'The consecration of the bread preceded the words "This is my body"' (4.13). Thus Jesus's consecration must have referred to the bread and not his body. Nor does Wyclif accept that Jesus took his body in his own hands, broke it and asked his disciples to eat it. 'Since the figurative sense is true,' he reasons, 'it would be false to hold that this is Christ's body in the sense of [identity]' (4.13). If Jesus meant that the bread and wine were his body and blood in the sense of identity, Jesus lied, and that would be unthinkable. On this point, Wyclif agrees, though unknowingly perhaps, with Berengar. Even more flagrantly than Berengar himself, no doubt, he misinterprets the oath of 1059 in a sense favourable to their opinion: 'The same bread and wine which were placed . . . upon the altar remain after the consecration both as sacrament and as the Lord's body' (2.2). Obviously this passage has little in common with Humbert's Capernaistic text, but it does formulate the principle of remanence, according to which the bread and wine remain intact after the consecration. This is Wyclif's opinion. The designation of the bread and wine as both sacrament and body of Christ indicates the dual nature of Christ's bodily presence in his eucharistic theology. While imposing his own doctrine on the oath of 1059, he describes Berengar's heresy as a rejection of the real presence, an error revealing his disapproval of this extreme. In reality, both theologians were more successful in avoiding extremes than in establishing an unambiguous moderate position. They clung to the real presence without being able to formulate exactly what kind of presence they thought appropriate.

According to the moderate position he sought to establish, the consecrated bread and wine not only signify, but also *are* the body and blood of Christ. The question of how they could be as much without substantial identity raised difficulties that he seems never entirely to have overcome. Apparently dissatisfied with dynamic symbolism as such, he tries to use it as a springboard to discovery. The figurative truth of the sacrament, he says, 'has the power to cause the body and blood to exist *de facto* under the sacramental appearances' (4.2). But he fails to ascertain what this power accomplishes or what this *de facto* presence actually consists in. Another attempt to determine the mode of Christ's bodily presence in the prescribed sense involves Paul's concept of 'seeing through a glass darkly':[82] 'We do not see the body of

[82] 1 Co.xiii.12: 'Now we are seeing a dim reflection in a mirror.'

Christ [. . .] with the bodily eye, but rather with the eye of the mind, that is in faith through a mirror darkly' (1.7). The hostia resembles a mirror reflecting a perfect image of Christ, but 'darkly', because faith alone can perceive it. Wyclif concludes this passage with an assurance that we do not chew Christ's body with our teeth, but rather 'receive it in a spiritual manner, perfect and undivided' (1.7). Elsewhere, he evokes the traditional shattered mirror to show how Christ's image can be multiplied in its entirety. Unfortunately, these optical analogies scarcely clarify the ancient mystery of an immaterial existence known only to the believing imagination. His use of *or* instead of *and* in the enumeration of the following passage betrays a groping for conceptualisation: 'The body of Christ in the sacrament of the altar [. . .] is whole, sacramentally, spiritually, or virtually in every part of the consecrated host, even as the soul is in the body' (1.2). And his century boasted no better an explanation of how the soul resides in the body than Voltaire's! Like Berengar, he is wandering along paths already beaten by Augustine, for he in turn acknowledges the one sure landmark established by the great Father, the permanence of Christ's resurrected body in heaven. As with Berengar, his Augustinian philosophy offers the best prospect for approaching the kind of presence he must have had in mind. To divine immanence in Neoplatonism corresponds the hierarchy of universals flowing from God in his realism. Thus the trinity including Christ belongs to the same realist continuum as the universal of material existence, among whose many particular manifestations are the consecrated bread and wine of the eucharist. Perhaps this is what he means when he claims 'that the body of Christ is concealed in [the host]' (1.11). Surely this solution could not have satisfied him, however, for it implies the presence of Christ's body in all other material objects as well. One might infer that he was really thinking of impanation or, in Lutheran terminology, consubstantiation. When properly defined, nevertheless, both terms refer to a substantial co-existence of bread and Christ's body, while Wyclif, as we have seen, adamantly rejects the substantial presence of this body in the eucharist.

An offshoot of metabolism, impanation would not ordinarily harmonise with his inclination to attribute presence or absence to the merit of the communicant. He repeats the Augustinian distinction between carnal and spiritual eating, of which the latter alone feeds the souls of the faithful, thus incorporating them into the mystic body of the Church. He also follows Augustine in denying any benefit to unworthy

58

communicants or animals. 'Beasts can eat the consecrated host,' he concedes, 'but it is the bare sacrament [in this case] and not the body and blood of Christ' (1.2). Yet he likewise speaks of a conversion brought about by the consecration and of feeding the soul 'in an objective sense' (1.15). Since these factors obstruct a determination of Christ's presence by the worth of the communicant or receptionism, Wyclif could not have committed himself irrevocably to this theory. On the theoretical level, he evidently had weaker convictions about what he embraced than what he rejected.

On the practical level, however, he was equally sure of both. Less indulgent towards unworthy priests than Thomas, he sets stringent standards for celebrants, who, as Stacey observes, 'must possess the three theological virtues and have three kinds of grace: provenient, co-operating and consummating'.[83] Unless a priest meets these requirements, his celebration of the eucharist will not result in valid communion. This severity is not gratuitous. A climate of anticlericalism contributed to it and Wyclif distinguished himself by his promotion of laymen's rights even before his notoriety as an opponent of transubstantiation. A further motive behind his antagonism to this doctrine was in fact his disapproval of the privileges it afforded clergymen and their abuse of these privileges. 'By what reason mayest thou say that thou makest thy maker?' he snaps in one of his sermons.[84] This taunt prefigures one of Voltaire's favourite strictures (see p.182). Wyclif seeks to reduce the prestige of celebrants by discarding the traditional opinion, confirmed by Thomas, that the eucharist automatically confers grace on the communicant. According to another tradition, which he endorses, the sacrament is a mere symbol of grace. Not only did he censure abuse of the eucharist, but also he promoted a dramatic reform, the celebration of the sacrament by worthy laymen: 'Every predestined layman is a priest' (4.21). Though daring, this idea was premature, for the friction between laymen and priests had as yet produced no flame. But it won him no friends either and, although his nominalist enemies were deviating from the orthodoxy of the day too, they were discreet, numerous and influential. He was condemned by five papal bulls (1377), expelled from Oxford (*ca.*1381) and, 43 years after his death, reburied in unhallowed ground by order of pope Martin v. Known as the Lollards,

---

[83] John Stacey, *John Wyclif and reform* (London 1964), pp.108-109.
[84] *Great sermons*, p.114.

the sect he had founded began to dwindle after his death and disappeared some fifty years later.

His writings nonetheless impressed the realists at the University of Prague and especially their eventual leader, John Hus. A priest of unimpeachable character and extraordinary zeal, Hus defended all that was orthodox in Wyclif and ignored the rest. Yet his enemies persisted in accusing him of Wyclif's heresies and of heresies they erroneously attributed to the Englishman. Among the accusations they repeated most often were remanence, which Wyclif had advocated, and the inability of a priest living in mortal sin to consecrate, which he had not advocated. The hatred inspired by Hus did not spring from a vigilant concern for orthodoxy, but rather the rivalry of nominalist philosophers and the resentment of corrupt clergymen whose privileges he attacked. He interpreted Augustine's mystic body as the true church, thus implying the exclusion of clergymen untouched by divine grace, such as pope John XXIII himself. Lured by the unkept promise of an opportunity to defend himself, he fell into the trap laid for him by his enemies at the Council of Constance. They imprisoned him and, unable to trick or coerce him into an admission of their allegations, they finally condemned him anyway. Once he had burned at the stake (1415), the dispute in which he had participated became a war.

The abuse which the Bohemians fighting in his name found most intolerable, however, had disturbed him far less: the prohibition of the cup in lay communion. Before Constance, several of his more radical fellow priests had restored the cup to their celebration of the eucharist. Faced with the opposition of conservative clergymen, they appealed to him for support, which he gave them, though cautiously. In justifying them by the words and example of Jesus at the Last Supper, he advised conciliation and the pursuit of approval by the Church. The Council nonetheless blamed him for the return to the lay cup, in which it saw a rebellion to be put down at all costs.

In contrast with Hus, Luther was undoubtedly a heretic from the Catholic point of view and, among other heresies, he tended to impanation which he had inherited from William of Ockham. He nonetheless resembles Wyclif and Hus by his insistence on the Bible as the definitive standard of faith, his demand for reform of the Church, his opposition to papal authority and his objections to elimination of the lay cup. No less zealous and outspoken than Hus, he enraged the hierarchy too, yet escaped their vengeance. By his time, dissidence had acquired the political power to protect him from the forces that had doomed Hus. A more resourceful theologian than the Bohemian, he changed his mind in the course of his career, which hinged on his break with the Church. First, the Augustinian monk attacked the corruption of his fellow Catholics and then the great reformer resisted the more radical opinions of other Protestant leaders.

In *The Babylonian capitivity of the Church* (1520), he condemned the priestly elaboration of the Last Supper he found in the mass. He objected to the accessories that cluttered the rite and distracted participants from the words of Christ, which he considered the very substance of the sacrament.[85] The custom of whispering these words so that the public could not hear them, as if to preserve them from contamination, offended him.[86] Nor did he approve of the exclusive right to the cup claimed by clergymen, for why should they have access to two species and laymen only one? And what is to prevent them from denying the rest of this sacrament or parts of others to laymen?[87] 'They are acting [. . .] contrary to the act, example and institution of Christ' (xxxvi.21). Since Matthew, Mark, Luke and Paul stipulate that Jesus gave both species to all his disciples, all Christians should be allowed to commune under both. According to Matthew,[88] Jesus even tells them all to drink and Mark reports that all did drink (see p.15), yet neither mentions the bread in this context. Luther infers that 'Both attach the note of universality to the cup, not to the bread, as though the Spirit foresaw this schism, by which some would be forbidden to partake of the cup' (xxxvi. 20). This is an allusion to the Bohemian schism over the lay cup after Hus's death. Luther sympathises with the Bohemians' defence of their

[85] 'We must be particularly careful to put aside whatever has been added to [the] original [. . .] institution [of the sacrament] by the zeal and devotion of men: such things as vestments, ornaments, chants, prayers, organs, candles and the whole pageantry of outward things. We must [. . .] set nothing before us but the very word of Christ by which he instituted the sacrament' (*The Babylonian captivity of the Church, Luther's works*, translated by A. T. W. Steinhäuser (Philadelphia 1959), xxxvi.36. Original text in Latin).

[86] 'What we deplore in this captivity is that nowadays they take every precaution that no layman should hear these words of Christ, as if they were too sacred to be delivered to the common people' (xxxvi.41).

[87] 'If [. . .] either kind may be withheld from the laity, then with equal right and reason a part of baptism or penance might also be taken away from them by this same authority of the church [. . .] If the church can withhold from the laity one kind, the wine, it can also withhold from them the other, the bread' (xxxvi.21-22).

[88] ' "Drink all of you from this," he said' (Mt.xxvi.27).

right to the cup and censures the decree against it by the Council of Constance: 'It was not the church which ordained these things, but the tyrants of the churches, without the consent of the church, which is the people of God' (xxxvi). The 'captivity' of the cup, in his opinion, evidences the general usurpation of power over the true Church, the body of the predestinate, by the clergy of Babylon, or Rome.[89]

Though less evident, a similar reason lies behind his opposition to the sacrificial interpretation of the eucharist. Christ did not offer himself in sacrifice at the Last Supper and, since he sacrificed himself on the cross, he does not want to be sacrificed again, but rather remembered: 'Wie seid Ihr denn so kühn, dass Ihr aus dem Gedächtnis ein Opfer macht?'[90] Unaware of eucharistic sacrifice in the ancient tradition, Luther assumed that the Church had again adulterated the primitive faith which he was determined to defend against such encroachments. He thought scripture the only unimpeachable source of theology and his exegesis of the institution narratives yielded allusions neither to sacrifice nor to good works: 'When he instituted this sacrament [...] at the Last Supper, Christ did not offer himself to God the Father, nor did he perform a good work on behalf of others' (xxxvi.52). Aware of a connection between the sacrificial conception of the eucharist and ancient Hebrew sacrifice, Luther draws another argument from the Old Testament. There were two kinds of sacrifice, he notes, one in which the participants offered the entire victim to God (holocaust) and another in which they shared it with him (communion sacrifice). The eucharist resembles neither: 'Warum essen und trinken wir [...] alles Brot und Wein und lassen Gott gar nichts davon?'[91] This objection to the eucharist as sacrifice does not seem to have occurred to the ancient proponents of the concept. Although Luther generally relegates such common sense to a subordinate role in his eucharistic theology, it furnishes him with an even more obvious objection: 'The same thing cannot be received and

---

[89] 'Your sister in Babylon, who is with you among the chosen, sends you greetings' (1 Peter v.13). 'Pierre a passé pour avoir été évêque de Rome; mais on sait assez qu'en ce temps-là, et longtemps après, il n'y eut aucun évêché particulier [...] Nous avons une lettre sous son nom, dans laquelle il dit qu'il est à Babylone: des canonistes judicieux ont prétendu que par Babylone on devait entendre Rome. Ainsi, supposé qu'il eût daté de Rome, on aurait pu conclure que la lettre avait été écrite à Babylone' ('Pierre', *Dictionnaire philosophique*, ed. Naves (Paris 1961) p.348).

[90] *The Abrogation of private mass* (1521), *D. Martin Luthers Werke* (Weimar 1883-), viii.493. All quotations in German will come from this edition. Note the abbreviation W.A.: Weimarer Ausgabe.

[91] *Vom Missbrauch der Messe* (1521), W.A. viii.515.

offered at the same time, nor can it be both given and accepted by the same person' (xxxvi.52).

To these tactical reasons, he adds one which he takes more seriously, the equation of eucharistic sacrifice with good works at a time when the sale of indulgences encouraged popular belief in the possibility of earning salvation piecemeal, a black market Pelagianism. He complains, 'dass man, [statt des Glaubens] an [. . .] äusserliche Werke, welche ein Sünder und Bube tun kann, gepredigt hat'.[92] The complaints and the implied object of the complaint reveal that Luther and his contemporaries had no greater insight into the profound significance of eucharistic sacrifice than Thomas. Jesus at the Last Supper, he believes, left a legacy to his Christian posterity. He sealed this testament, which promises the remission of sins, by his body and blood, tokens of salvation.[93] Luther derives this conception of the eucharist from his interpretation of *testament* in the title *New Testament* and he considers it essential for a proper understanding of the text. Counting celebrations of the eucharist as good works, he fears, exposes it more than any other factor to the ambition and corruption of the priesthood.

This practice had in fact resulted in the custom of private mass, a mass celebrated by a subsidised priest who himself served as the sole communicant. The custom tempted priests to market the eucharist and laymen to undertake the purchase of salvation by instalments. Sinners and rogues could accumulate private masses, while unscrupulous priests could pocket their money, thus degrading the eucharist to the status of commercial fraud. Luther deplored the power that the clergy had usurped by means of this abuse. 'Jedermann weiss, worauf [. . .] das ganze Reich der Pfaffen gegründet und gebaut ist,' he growls; among other elements, 'auf dem verkehrten und gottlosen Missbrauch des Sakraments.'[94] Like Hus and Wyclif, he opposes the popular inclination to attribute the prerogative of the Holy Spirit to priests: 'Kein Heiliger auf Erden, ja kein Engel im Himmel [kann] das Brot und Wein zu Christus Leib und Blut machen.'[95] God's word and God's word alone can cause the body and blood to be present in the eucharist. Luther

[92] *Vom Missbrauch*, W.A. viii.505.
[93] 'What we call the mass is a promise of the forgiveness of sins made to us by God, and such a promise as has been confirmed by the death of the Son of God. For the only difference between a promise and a testament is that the testament involves the death of the one who promises' (xxxvi.38).
[94] *Vom Missbrauch*, W.A. viii,520.
[95] *Deutsche Katechismus (Der Grosse Katechismus)* (1529), W.A. xxx, Part 1, p.224.

breaks with scholastic tradition by teaching that the faith of communicants and not the intention of the celebrant activates the power of this word. Even if an unbelieving celebrant follows the ritual prescribed by Jesus and repeats his words, believing communicants will obtain the real presence: '[Es] kann [. . .] nicht anders denn durch den Glauben empfangen werden.'[96] What happens, though, when the celebrant himself is the sole communicant? Luther suspects that priests celebrating private masses do not have enough faith to achieve the real presence, because they are preoccupied with earning money by the performance of a service. They are probably cheating the laymen who pay for this service on the assumption that Christ's body and blood will be present. The customer cannot tell whether they have the necessary faith, whether they are whispering the correct words or whether they succeed in consecrating the bread and wine. He 'muss also im Sack kaufen' (W.A. xxxviii.210), as Luther puts it in *Von der Winkelmesse* (1533). In this work he imagines the devil unmasking a celebrant of private masses: 'Du gottloser ungläubiger Pfaff [. . .] meinst, Christus habe es um Deinen Willen geordnet [. . .] seinen Leib und [sein] Blut wandeln [zu] lassen [. . .] Du schweigst dort im Winkel und frisst [das Abendmahl] allein [. . .] und [. . .] verkäufst es als Dein [überflüssiges] gutes Werk' (W.A. xxxviii.200). In a day when the devil had his due, Luther obviously enjoyed casting himself in this role and exploiting the opportunity to lavish his sarcasm on 'niche' priests. The necessary participation of believing communicants in any authentic celebration of the eucharist practically excludes private masses from this category. More explicitly, however, Luther affirms that no one can represent anyone else at mass, just as no one can believe on anyone else's behalf.[97]

His objections to such practical abuses as private mass often result in criticism of theoretical excesses. In penetrating the hypocrisy of niche priests, for instance, his spokesman the devil ranges from private mass to transubstantiation. Everyone knows, the devil testifies, that niche priests 'die grössten Betrüger und Verführer auf Erden sind, die den Christen eitel Brot und Wein [für] Christus Leib und Blut [. . .] halten' (*Von der Winkelmesse*, W.A. xxxviii.205). After youthful acceptance of transubstantiation, Luther began to oppose it in 1520,

[96] *Der Grosse Katechismus*, W.A. xxx, Part 1, p.226.
[97] 'Man [kann] für keinen anderen [. . .] Messe halten [. . .] Ich kann nicht für dich glauben' (*Vom Missbrauch*, W.A., viii.519-20).

without realising that it had become dogma.[98] Ignorant of its early development, he blames Thomas for deriving it from 'the pseudo philosophy of Aristotle'.[99] For 1200 years, he assumes, neither the Church nor the Fathers had any idea of it. He especially disapproves of its philosophical sophistication inaccessible to the ordinary layman, who does not know the difference between substance and accidents.[100] The implied destruction of substance according to Ockham's interpretation, which he accepted, worried him, and also the endless growth of Christ's body, an inevitable result as he saw it.[101] Transubstantiation, he thought, cannot withstand the test of reason and it either has no support in scripture, as he implies in one passage of the *Babylonian captivity*, or weakens the words of God, as he states in another.[102] It does not seem impossible to him, however, for he refuses to limit the power of the Almighty in any way. He disputes it rather on the grounds of necessity: 'In order for the divine nature to dwell in [the sacrament] it is not necessary for the human nature to be transubstantiated and the divine nature contained under the accidents of the human nature' (xxxvi.35).

Since we cannot know such things, he refuses to decide how this indwelling occurs. He nonetheless expresses a strong preference for the solution secretly held by his fellow nominalists Ockham and d'Ailly. He reproduces the latter's opinion: 'To hold that real bread and real wine, and not merely their accidents, are present on the altar, would [. . .] require fewer superfluous miracles – if only the Church had not decreed otherwise' (xxxvi.29). The bread and wine would subsist entirely and yet coexist with the whole body and blood of Christ. Luther suggests this coexistence by massing prepositions: 'Der Glaube vernimmt, dass "in" gleich so viel in dieser Sachen gilt als über, ausser,

---

[98] see Hartmut Hilgenfeld, *Mittelalterlich-traditionelle Elemente in Luthers Abendmahlsschriften* (Zurich 1971), p.407.

[99] xxxvi.31. 'This opinion of Thomas hangs [. . .] completely in the air without the support of Scripture or reason [. . .] Aristotle speaks of subject and accidents so very differently from St Thomas that it seems to me this great man is to be pitied not only for attempting to draw his opinions in matters of faith from Aristotle, but also for attempting to base them upon a man whom he did not understand' (xxxvi.36).

[100] 'Laymen have never become familiar with [the] fine-spun philosophy of substance and accidents, and could not grasp it if it were taught to them' (xxxvi.31).

[101] see Hilgenfeld, p.407.

[102] 'What is asserted without the Scriptures or proven revelation may be held as an opinion, but need not be believed' (xxxvi.29); 'It would [. . .] not be right to enfeeble the words of God [. . .] by depriving them of their meaning' (xxxvi.31).

65

unter, durch and wieder herdurch und allenthalben. Ach, was rede ich von so hohen Dingen, die doch unaussprechlich sind!'[103] As in the person of Christ, two different substances are united in a single being without fusion, but with exchange of attributes, so that Christ's body resembles bread and his blood, wine. To illustrate the idea, he borrows an example from the Fathers: 'In red-hot iron [. . .] the two substances, fire and iron, are so mingled that every part is both iron and fire' (xxxvi. 32). In further explanation of how Christ's body and blood can be in the bread and wine, he borrows a classification of existence in circumscriptive, definitive and repletive modes from his nominalist predecessors. The body and blood, in his opinion, are not only multipresent in the definitive sense, but also ubiquitous in the repletive or supernatural sense. The following description of the eucharist applies the circumscriptive mode to bread and wine, and the definitive mode to the body and blood of Christ: 'Der Ort ist wohl leiblich und begreiflich und hat seine Masse nach der Länge, Breite und Dicke, aber das, so drinnen ist, hat nicht gleiche Länge, Breite oder Dicke mit der Stätte, darin es ist, ja es hat gar keine Länge oder Breite' (*Vom Abendmahl*, W.A. xxvi.328). Circumscriptive bread and wine have dimensions and are perceptible to the senses, while definitive body and blood have none, but the latter occupy the same space as the former. Luther was convinced that the institution narratives do not support transubstantiation, but rather this version of impanation, which his followers would term consubstantiation. When Jesus says, 'This is my body', a sentence tending to confirm the exchange of attributes, 'the [Hebrew] language and common sense both prove that [*this*] points to the bread and not to the body' (xxxvi.34). Since the bread is therefore in the circumscriptive mode, the ubiquity of the body facilitates its consubstantiation with the bread.

Although Luther maintains the identity of the eucharistic and heavenly bodies, he qualifies this identity. The eucharistic body is the same in being and nature, he submits, but not in form and manner. The word of God, in his opinion, 'schafft was es lautet' (*Vom Abendmahl*, W.A. xxvi.283). It created the world, it made Mary pregnant and it does what it says in the eucharist. 'This is my body' and 'This is my blood' introduce Christ's entire body and blood into the sacrament

[103] *Vom Abendmahl Bekenntnis Christi* (1528), W.A. xxvi.341.

definitively without removing them from heaven.[104] Luther approves 'Berengar's' Capernaistic confession on the assumption that the chewing of Christ's flesh be understood as the effect of the bread communicating its attributes to the body united with it. On the strength of this conviction, he defied what he took for exaggerated vigilance against Capernaism among fellow Protestants: 'Wer dies Brot mit Zähnen oder Zungen zerdrückt, der zerdrückt mit den Zähnen und Zungen den Leib Christ' (*Vom Abendmahl*, W.A. xxvi.442). He nonetheless believed that one must commune spiritually as well as physically. A uniquely physical communion poisons the communicant[105] and a uniquely spiritual communion in the manner of certain Protestant opponents does not bring salvation.

Karlstadt, Luther's colleague at the University of Wittemberg, as well as Alsatian and Swiss theologians, particularly Zwingli in Zurich, were limiting Christ's body in the eucharist to a spiritual presence. While each had his own interpretation of 'This is my body' and 'This is my blood', they all amounted to metaphor according to Luther. Zwingli had come to the conclusion that the Aramaic equivalent of *is* in these sentences really meant *represents* (as indeed it might have), for he also took the presence of Christ's body in heaven very seriously. Luther, on the other hand, insisted on the text of the Vulgate and accused Zwingli of confusing representation with being. Faithful to the spirit of the Reformation, however, both agreed that the Bible should serve as the court of final appeal.

In an attempt to reconcile them, the Marburg Disputation of 1529 registered a consensus on every point except one. The fifteenth article regrets that they do not concur on whether 'der wahre Leib und Blut Christi leiblich im Brot und Wein sei'.[106] Common sense convinced Zwingli that it was not, while faith persuaded Luther that it was. The conflict resulted from contrasting conceptions of body (Köhler, p.30):

Zwingli – Was im Raum ist, ist ein Körper.
Luther – Das ist schon wahr: was vom Raum umschlossen ist, ist ein Körper,

---

[104] Luther stresses that the point of faith is to believe what is difficult to believe: 'Es ist schwer zu glauben, dass ein Leib [. . .] zugleich im Himmel und im Abendmahl [sei]' (*Dass diese Wort Christi 'Das ist mein Leib' noch fest stehen, wider die Schwärmgeister* (1527), W.A. xxiii.161).

[105] 'Ja ich habe wohl mehr gesagt, nämlich, dass Christus Leib leiblich essen ohne Geist und Glauben Gift und Tod sei' (*Vom Abendmahl*, W.A. xxvi.292).

[106] Walther Köhler, ed., *Das Marburger Religiongespräch* (Leipzig 1929), p.170.

aber es folgt daraus nicht das Umgekehrte: was ein Körper ist, muss auch vom Raum umschlossen sein.

Thus Luther rejects the limitation of body to what men can perceive by their senses and promotes a kind of bodily existence known only to faith. In writings from this period, he complains that Zwingli and company deny all modes of presence more subtle than 'Brot im Korbe und Wein im Becher'. He likewise derides the 'golden Stuhl'[107] to which they confine Christ in heaven. Nor does he have any patience with Zwingli's objection that, if Christ's body were in several places at one time, ours would be too. The nominalist has no use for such 'mathematics'. As far as he is concerned, Christ's body and blood are not only multipresent in the definitive sense, but also ubiquitous in the repletive sense.

The foregoing discussion neither exhausts the details nor covers the entire evolution of his eucharistic doctrine, too vast an undertaking for the present study. It does attempt to review his solutions to the major problems besetting eucharistic theology throughout the Middle Ages, the problems of content and mutation. For some Protestants, his theology of the eucharist would become faith. For others, the tendency championed by Zwingli would develop into a rival family of doctrines. Calvin would later contribute his own version, a compromise between the other two. Luther's influence on the eucharist in Catholic dogma, on the other hand, was mostly negative, for it merely provoked a reactionary consolidation of tradition.

In 1547, two years after Luther's death, the Council of Trent began to examine a list of eucharistic propositions extracted from his works and from those of other Protestant leaders. According to custom, first the theologians and then the prelates discussed them, but before the latter could reach any decisions, an epidemic disrupted the council. Although, with the approval of pope Paul III, some of the prelates continued their deliberations in Bologna, the emperor Charles V angrily disapproved, because he could exercise little influence there. Unrecognised by him, the eight canons they agreed to, which condemned eucharistic heresies held by Protestants, remained a dead letter. When the council reopened in Trent (1551), it officially ignored the work accomplished at Bologna, which nonetheless facilitated understanding between prelates who had been there. Since the lay cup subsisted in parts

[107] *Dass diese Wort*, W.A. xxiii.145, 131.

of the empire, such as Bohemia, the council postponed consideration of this volatile issue.

At the end of the thirteenth session, however, it ratified a decree in eight chapters and eleven canons on other eucharistic matters. In reaction to Zwingli and his allies, chapter one reaffirms the real presence. It also claims that Christ can sit 'at the right hand of the Father in heaven, according to the natural mode of [existence]' (Denz. n.874), and yet be present at the same time in the eucharist wherever it is celebrated. Canon one anathematises anyone denying 'that in the [. . .] Eucharist are contained truly, really and substantially the body and blood together with the soul and divinity of [. . .] Christ' (Denz. n.883). Chapter three includes a description of horizontal and vertical concomitance (Denz. n.876):

The body [is] under the species of bread and the blood under the species of wine by the force of the words [of consecration]; but the body itself [is] under the species of wine and the blood under the species of bread, and the soul under both by the force of [. . .] natural [concomitance] and the divinity, furthermore, on account of the [hypostatic] union [. . .] with his body and soul.

Canon three condemns anyone disbelieving the presence of 'the whole Christ' (Denz. n.885) under both species, for suspicions that demand for the lay cup sprang from this error lingered in the minds of the more conservative prelates. Chapter four offers a brief definition of transubstantiation and approves the use of this word. Aimed at Luther, canon two, which explains the difference between transubstantiation and consubstantiation, curses anyone rejecting the former and advocating the latter. Chapter five and canon six exonerate the eucharistic ritual of idolatry. Chapter eight founds the exclusive right of clergymen to administer the sacrament on apostolic succession, while canon ten condemns opposition to clerical self-administration as in private mass. One may commune either spiritually or both spiritually and physically, according to chapter eight, but not physically alone. Canon eight censures those who like Zwingli admit spiritual manducation alone. This decree therefore answers Luther in particular, but also Zwingli and others, yet it typically refuses them the honour of mentioning their names.

Early the next year, the Protestant princes of Germany, in a league with the French against the emperor, captured nearby Innsbruck. Suspended, the council reconvened ten years later and only then did it return to the question of the lay cup. There was much sentiment in favour of renewing the permission to commune under both species in Bohemia, a concession which had ended the Hussite schism there, and of extending this privilege to German states threatened by Protestantism. Fearful of losing their control over the proceedings, however, the presiding papal legates decided again to postpone the impending controversy over whether, to whom and under what conditions the lay cup would be granted. Instead, they obtained approval of a decree on related matters of dogmatic principle at the end of the twenty-first session. Chapter one covers bad faith with bluster: 'Laymen and clerics not officiating are bound by no divine law to receive the Eucharist under both species [...] Communion under one species suffices [...] for salvation' (Denz. n.930). Canon one damns the contrary opinion. Chapter two affirms the right of the Church to 'determine or change whatever she may judge to be more expedient for the benefit of those who receive' (Denz. n.931) the sacrament. Canon two attacks those who accuse the Church of injustice or error in restricting laymen to communion under the species of bread alone.

The prelates finally considered the renewal and extension of the right to commune under both species in the twenty-second session. National rivalries immediately embittered the debate between conservatives under orders from Philip II, who had inherited the western half of the empire, and liberals supported by German princes, including Ferdinand who had inherited the eastern half. Several factions in favour of intermediate solutions split the council further. The legates could not even assemble a majority by revealing that Pius IV himself supported concession of the lay cup. After much bickering and many manoeuvres, by Ferdinand in particular, they effected a compromise by leaving the decision to the pope. Later, Pius granted the privilege of the cup to the countries that wanted it in return for Ferdinand's help in closing the council, which had been moving towards a reduction in papal power. Within fifty years, however, the privilege was withdrawn from all the countries that had received it, including Bohemia, the last to lose it.

During the same session, the council gave even more attention to the sacrificial aspect of the mass. Luther's attack on this principle, neglected since Augustine, stirred the defenders of orthodoxy to a determined resistance. Discussion of seven articles, most of them extracted from his works, had already begun in Bologna and continued during the second and third periods at Trent. In preparation for the twenty-second session (1562), one committee submitted a short decree on discipline and another, a longer one on doctrine. Little more than a benign exhortation, the disciplinary decree reflects fear of offending fellow clergymen rather than zeal for reform of notorious abuses. Among 'the things [. . .] to be avoided', it notes irreverence, covetousness and superstition. The doctrinal decree, on the other hand, makes no concessions to the Protestants. 'Such is the nature of man', remarks chapter five, 'that he cannot easily without external means be raised to meditation on divine things' (Denz. n.943). Reverence therefore requires a softer voice in reciting the more sacred parts of the liturgy, such as the consecration formula in the eucharist. Canon nine condemns the condemnation of this practice. Chapter five approves such paraphernalia as 'lights, incense [and] vestments' (Denz. n.943) on the pretext that 'the minds of the faithful [are] excited by these visible signs of religion and piety to the contemplation of the most sublime matters which lie hidden in this sacrifice'. (Denz. n.943). Canon seven anathematises the Lutheran strictures in this area. In chapter six, one encounters a curious attempt to clear private mass of Luther's charge that it allows no participation by communicants. The council approves 'masses in which the priest alone [communes] partly because [. . .] the people [commune] spiritually, and partly, too, because they are celebrated by a public minister of the Church not only for himself, but for all the faithful' (Denz. n.944). Canon eight accordingly recriminates opposition to these masses. Yet this confidence in the interest of bystanders and the sincerity of celebrants does little to dispel Protestant suspicions of hypocrisy and simony. Canon one passes judgement on Luther's protest against counting the mass as a good work.

Having exposed the shortcomings of Old Testament sacrifice, chapter one proclaims Christ the self-sacrificing priest who transmitted his sacrificial function to the apostles at the Last Supper, hence the exclusive right of the Church to celebrate mass! Here one also finds references to passages in Hebrews, which in turn refer to others in Psalms and Genesis. These references attempt to prove Christ's descendance from the non-levitical priesthood of Melchisidech, a myth initiated by the author of Hebrews.[108] The latter, who was probably not thinking of the eucharist, neither understood nor cared to understand these Old Testament passages, which, in any case, contain no possible allusion to

[108] He.v.6-10, vii.1-17; see George Buchanan's commentary on these verses in his translation of *Hebrews, The Anchor Bible*, xxxvi (New York 1972).

the sacrament. He does not even mention the bread and wine blessed by the priest in Genesis. After the attribution of descendance from Melchisidech to Christ, the decree nonetheless attains a high degree of eloquence in explaining the relationship between Christ's self-sacrifice and the sacrifice of the eucharist (Denz. n.938):

Though [Christ] was about to offer himself once to God the Father upon the altar of the Cross [. . .] so that he might accomplish an eternal redemption for [all who were to be sanctioned] nevertheless, that his sacerdotal office might not come to an end with his death [. . .] at the Last Supper [. . .] so that he might leave to his beloved spouse the Church a visible sacrifice [. . .] whereby that bloody sacrifice once to be completed on the Cross might be represented, and the memory of it remain even to the end of the world [. . .] and its saving grace be applied to the remission of those sins which we daily commit [. . .] offered to God the Father his own body and blood under the species of bread and wine and under the symbols of those same things gave to the apostles (whom he then constituted priests of the New Testament), so that they might partake, and he commanded them and their successors in the priesthood in these words to make offering: 'Do this in commemoration of me' [. . .] as the Catholic Church has always understood and taught.

Thus the council reaffirms the patristic doctrine of eucharistic sacrifice. Although the Church continued to claim that Jesus himself had established the eucharist and ordained its earliest celebrants, the institution narratives, aside from their doubtful authenticity, do not justify this pretention. The fathers of Trent apparently expected 'Do this as a memorial of me' (Lk.xxii.19; 1 Co.xi.24) to silence the Protestant clamour for scriptural proof. They may well have intended canon two, which assaults the denial of their interpretation, as a final rebuke of Luther. None of these arguments is very convincing. On the other hand, Jesus's inauguration of a rite consisting of communion on his body and blood, however one may interpret this command, definitely suggests a connection between the rite and the forthcoming crucifixion to which he willingly submitted. While the decree does not rely on scriptural evidence, the institution narratives in the context of the Passion tend to substantiate the theory that the crucifixion and the eucharist (but not the mass) constitute one and the same sacrifice, the major thesis of the twenty-second session.

The eucharist continued to inspire controversy, some of which had begun before Trent and some of which began afterwards. In the seventeenth century, the Calvinists and the French Catholics rekindled the old disputes over the primitive authenticity of transubstantiation, the real presence, eucharistic sacrifice and the restriction of lay communicants to a single species. Meanwhile, new quarrels erupted: 1. Descartes's attempts to integrate transubstantiation and the real presence into his philosophy led to a conflict between his disciples and their enemies; 2. The Jansenists provoked the Jesuits by the publication of a work entitled *De la fréquente communion*. All of these controversies, in fact, embroiled the Jansenists and the Jesuits in further episodes of their continuing feud.

Snoeks begins his study of the polemic between the Calvinists and the French Catholics with cardinal Du Perron's *Traité du Saint-Sacrement* (1622), a reply to *De l'institution de l'eucharistie* (1598) by the Protestant Philippe de Plessis-Mornay.[109] Answering Du Perron in turn, the minister Edme Aubertin published several works. Later, during the peace imposed by pope Clement IX (1668-1702), the Jansenists sought to emphasise their orthodoxy by attacking the Calvinists, with whom the Jesuits insisted on comparing them. Thus the Jansenist Pierre Nicole refuted Aubertin in a preface to *L'Office du Saint-Sacrement* (1659), although the author, Antoine Le Maistre apparently, did not intend to provoke the Huguenots. The *Office* was a manual for the nuns of Port Royal, who communed every Thursday to repair the Protestant affront to eucharistic sacrifice. The work appeared in print without the preface, but the latter circulated in manuscript form, so that it eventually reached the Huguenot minister Jean Claude. Soon a rejoinder by Claude was circulating too.

To ignore this challenge might have exposed the Jansenists to further Jesuit accusations of sympathy with Protestantism, accusations which Calvinist polemicists usually exploited. Nor would still another reply in the polemical series initiated by de Plessis-Mornay be enough, perhaps, to prevent a renewal of the persecution which the Jansenists had suffered before Clement's peace. Realising the need for a major work based on thorough research and an original thesis, Nicole undertook *La Perpétuité de la foi de l'Eglise catholique touchant l'eucharistie* (1669-1674). Although he wrote most of the work himself, he selflessly attributed it to Antoine Arnauld, whose prestige as a theologian, he felt, would better serve the Jansenist cause. Nicole's method in the first

---

[109] Rémi Snoeks, *L'Argument de tradition dans la controverse eucharistique entre catholiques et réformés français au XVIIe siècle* (Louvain 1951).

volume, 'la méthode de prescription', seems extremely vulnerable today, but it impressed his contemporaries. The antagonism between Protestants and Catholics over fidelity to Christian origins had always thrived on ignorance of these origins, for the documentation was faulty and scant. Yet both parties thought Christianity a continuous and uniform tradition, which each accused the other of betraying. Nicole sought to terminate the series of unfounded mutual accusations by founding the authenticity of the Catholic eucharist on an opinion accepted by both sides. If all Christians agreed at any one time on eucharistic doctrine, he argues, this doctrine must be identical to the original belief, for no change could ever have escaped the vigilance of the faithful! Assuming, naively, that the Protestants could not honestly disagree with him, he interprets the condemnation of Berengar as the manifestation of a universal belief in the real presence. He observes that the Greek Church agrees with the Roman on this doctrine despite the schism, a point substantiated by many attestations in the third volume. The more conventional 'méthode de discussion' in the second volume merely contradicts Aubertin's attacks on the primitive authenticity of transubstantiation and the real presence by a review of Patristic sources.

Two preliminary editions of the *Perpétuité* had appeared in 1664 and 1665, hence the title of Claude's prompt reply, *Réponse aux deux traités intitulés Perpétuité* (etc.). As one might expect, he undermined 'la méthode de prescription' by insisting that, while the ancient Christians did not believe in transubstantiation and the real presence, the medieval Christians did. The faith had changed, despite the theory in the *Perpétuité*. Furthermore, transubstantiation and the real presence contradicted the evidence of the senses, natural reason and the New Testament. Although the *Réponse* involved Claude in a further exchange of polemic with Arnauld, neither would advance anything especially original.

On the pretext of defending the dogma against Claude, the Jesuit Jacques Nouet sought to avenge his humiliating defeat in a quarrel with Arnauld, which we shall discuss further on. In the *Présence de Jésus-Christ dans le très Saint-Sacrement* (1666), Nouet insinuates that, in contrast with the *Perpétuité*, his conventional defence of transubstantiation and the real presence was orthodox. He was showing Arnauld how to scold a heretic for relying on the senses and natural reason, for resorting to bad exegisis and a wrong interpretation of the Fathers, and for daring to claim that the faith of the Church had changed.

The last item implied that Arnauld was guilty of exposing the Church to this reproach. The other Catholic adversaries of the *Perpétuité* and Jansenism include the historian Louis de Maimbourg and the biblical scholar Richard Simon. Among the Protestant enemies of the work, one finds Jean Daillé, Mathieu de Laroque, Jacques Basnage and Pierre Allix. Laroque distinguished himself in polemic with Bossuet over the limitation of lay communion to a single species.

Bossuet's protégé Eusèbe Renaudot not only defended the *Perpétuité*, but also added a fourth and fifth volume to the work. The *Histoire des variations des églises protestantes* (1688) by Bossuet himself inflicted heavy damage on the Calvinist cause just three years after the revocation of the Edict of Nantes. The Huguenots in his opinion had inherited a eucharistic doctrine flawed from the beginning by Calvin's compromise between Lutheran consubstantiality and the uniquely spiritual communion of Zwingli.[110] He found that they wavered between a near tolerance of the real presence and the denial of any supernatural reality in the sacrament. Such variations seemed disgraceful then, and even to his Calvinist adversary Pierre Jurieu,[111] but later generations of Protestants rejected the ideal of undeviating orthodoxy. Nor did Bossuet's victory silence the Calvinist polemic against the eucharistic dogma of the Catholic Church, but the controversy no longer generated ideas or works of interest here.

When Descartes explained transubstantiation in terms of his philosophy, he made the most original contribution to eucharistic theology since Trent. His theory seems all the more valuable because he constantly stressed his intention of avoiding theological speculation, which he usually left to theologians. A devoted yet unzealous Catholic, he divorced reason, which interested him most, from faith, the province of clergymen in his view. In transubstantiation, however, he saw both an obstacle to the reconversion of the Protestants and an opportunity to illustrate his philosophy. Wary of involvement in theological controversy, he divulged his theory only on demand and after various

---

[110] 'Calvin, conformément à une conception des sacrements qui tend à séparer fortement le signe sensible de la réalité invisible, nie qu'il y ait autre chose dans le signe extérieur que le pain et le vin. Mais, par ailleurs, il enseigne que celui qui prend ces éléments matériels en esprit de foi, participe spirituellement à la substance du corps et du sang du Christ et reçoit ainsi, par l'action du Saint-Esprit, force et vigueur divines' (Snoeks, p.15).

[111] in his polemic against Bossuet and the Catholic Church, Jurieu concentrated on ecclesiology and neglected the eucharist.

precautions or on certain conditions. It answers two questions: how do the accidents of bread remain where bread itself has disappeared and how does the body of Christ assume the dimensions of this bread?

He solves the first problem in his 'Réponse aux quatrièmes objections', appended to the *Méditations* of 1641, these objections having been raised by Arnauld. As the latter had noted, Descartes denied the real existence of the accidents corresponding to sensations, which he attributed to direct or indirect contact with the objects they represented. He also denied that the three remaining accidents, figure, extension and mobility, could exist independently of the substance in which they inhered. Thus Arnauld found Descartes in partial conflict with the scholastic theory of transubstantiation, which prescribed the subsistence of all accidents after the disappearance of substance. 'Je prévois que les théologiens [s'en] offenseront',[112] he warns the philosopher. Descartes, who appreciated the Jansenist's concern, took the warning seriously in his *Réponse*. His treatment of certain accidents as modes inseparable from substance, he asserted, does not imply the inability of almighty God to separate them if he wishes. On the contrary, he had always believed that God could do an infinite number of things incomprehensible to us. This is evidently a strategic concession meant to persuade all Catholic theologians that the new philosophy did not necessarily threaten the scholasticism with which they were imbued.

Having taken this precaution, Descartes begins his explanation of the first phase in his theory by exposing his peculiar conception of *superficie*. Surface consists in the area of contact between adjacent bodies in an universe where bodies cannot penetrate each other and no vacuum is possible. Since the protrusions of one body necessarily fill the pores of the other, surface relief can be very irregular, as in the case of air and bread or flesh. Surface can also be very mobile, depending on the mobility of the adjacent bodies, air and wine or blood for instance. The degree of mobility in Descartes's physics determines whether a body is a solid, a liquid or a gas. Sensations derive from direct or indirect contact with surface mobility. When two bodies touch (according to the 'Réponse aux sixièmes objections'), the area of contact is a part of neither, but rather a mode of both 'qui demeurera toujours le même, quoique ces deux corps soient ôtés, pourvu seulement qu'on en substitue d'autres en leur place, qui soient précisément de la même grandeur

[112] quoted by Descartes, *Œuvres philosophiques* (Paris 1967-1973), ed. Ferdinand Alquié, ii.655. Further references to this edition will appear in parentheses after quotations.

The eucharist

et figure' (ii.875). The substances of Christ's body and blood replacing those of bread and wine in the eucharist conform to the relief of the surfaces which separate the latter from the surrounding air. The new substances assume the same degree of mobility, so that the surface continues to affect our senses in the same manner.[113]

After exposing this part of his theory in the 'Réponse aux quatrièmes objections', Descartes devotes several pages to a refutation of the corresponding scholastic position. Converting all the substance of bread and yet preserving something real in the bread seems contradictory to him: 'Encore qu'on nomme cela un accident, on le conçoit néanmoins comme une substance' (ii.701). Perhaps this very contradiction caused the defection of some who left the Roman Church. In editing Descartes's philosophical works, Alquié plausibly interprets this remark as an allusion to the substitution of consubstantiation for transubstantiation by the Lutherans (ii.701, n.2). Descartes is insinuating, in any case, that his theory may repair the damage done to the unity of the Church by the scholastics. God, he concedes, could in fact preserve the accidents of bread and wine after the conversion of their substances, thus adding a second miracle to the miracle of transubstantiation. This solution, however, not only offends human reason, but also violates a theological principle: 'Les paroles de la consécration n'opèrent rien que ce qu'elles signifient' (ii.702). In the final paragraph of his 'Réponse' to Arnauld, Descartes hopes that Catholic theologians will eventually repudiate the scholastic opinion 'comme peu sûre en la foi, éloignée de la raison et du tout incompréhensible' and replace it by his own 'comme certaine et indubitable' (ii.704). No wonder father Mersenne removed these pages from the manuscript before publishing the *Méditations* on Descartes's behalf!

Several years later (2 May 1644), Descartes wrote to the Jesuit Mesland, who had published an abridgement of this work, that he (Descartes) had kept part of his theory to himself. He had not explained 'l'extension de Jésus-Christ [dans le] Saint-Sacrement' (iii.75), because he had no obligation to do so, he generally refrained from theological speculation and the Council of Trent had stipulated that words can scarcely express

[113] in a letter to Mersenne in March of 1642, Descartes denies any similarity between his theory and Wyclif's. If the fathers at the Council of Constance had shared his opinion, he affirms, they would have condemned Wyclif anyway: 'En niant que la substance du pain et du vin demeure pour être le sujet des accidents, ils n'ont point, pour cela, déterminé que ces accidents fussent réels' (ii.925). Nor did the other councils, he adds. His posthumous detractors would accuse him of what amounts to remenance.

9999999999999999999999999999999999999999999999999999999999999999999999999999999999999999999999

the manner of Christ's presence in the eucharist. If his philosophy were more familiar to the public, however, one (Descartes? Mesland?) could clarify this mystery in a way 'qui fermerait la bouche aux ennemis de notre religion' (iii.75). He was cultivating Mesland's curiosity by tempting him with the promise of a devastating argument against the Protestants. By 9 February 1645, he thought this curiosity great enough to merit satisfaction. In a letter to Mesland, he recapitulated the first part of his theory, repeated the motives for his reticence about the second and invited the Jesuit to share the secret with him on two conditions: if Mesland did not find it to be entirely orthodox, he must not reveal it to anyone; if he should reveal it, he must not mention Descartes's name. Perhaps the philosopher was expecting too much; perhaps on purpose.

In exposing the second part of his theory, he distinguishes between two kinds of body, a portion of matter and a human organism. In the first case, neither the quantity of matter nor the relationship between the components can change without a change of identity. In the second case, on the contrary, both can change without altering the identity, provided the body 'demeure joint et uni substantiellement à la même âme'.[114] An adult has the same body as when he was a child, even though it has grown in size and none of the original matter remains. This body does not change even with the amputation of an arm or leg. The unity and identity of a human body therefore depend uniquely on its soul.

In the ordinary nourishment of the human body, Descartes discovers a natural equivalent of transubstantiation. When one eats ordinary bread and drinks ordinary wine, the stomach dissolves them into particles which flow into the veins and mingle with the blood: 'Les petites parties de ce pain et de ce vin [...] se transsubstantient naturellement et deviennent parties de notre corps' (iii.549). Thus the first kind of body, a quantity of matter, becomes a part of the second kind, a human body; a spiritual unity may be said to absorb a material unity. Supernatural transubstantiation, on the other hand, merely substitutes a miracle for the digestive process in order to obtain a similar result. Reciting the consecration formula causes the soul of Christ to inform

---

[114] 'Quand nous parlons du corps d'un homme, nous n'entendons pas une partie déterminée de matière, ni qui ait une grandeur déterminée, mais seulement nous entendons toute la matière qui est ensemble unie avec l'âme de cet homme; en sorte que, bien que cette matière change, et que sa quantité augmente ou diminue, nous croyons toujours que c'est le même corps, *idem numero*, pendant qu'il demeure joint et uni substantiellement à la même âme' (iii.547).

the bread and wine on the altar, so that they become his human body. The spiritual unity of this body transcends the material division occasioned by transubstantiation in different places and at different times, everywhere in Christendom and ever since the Last Supper. Consequently, every piece of consecrated bread and every drop of consecrated wine are Christ's entire body informed by his unique soul. At this point, Descartes anticipates the consternation of Catholics who believe Christ's body to be materially intact in the eucharist. 'Tous les membres extérieurs, et leur quantité et matière,' he reassures them, 'ne sont point nécessaires à l'intégrité du corps humain, et ne sont en rien utiles ni convenables à ce sacrement' (iii.550). Impossible here, they would even imply a contradiction. Nor should their absence in any way detract from the veneration of the sacrament.

In his preoccupation with the dichotomy between material and spiritual unity, Descartes seems to have forgotten the unity of living organisms.[115] His eucharistic body lacks the biological organisation that Catholic communicants have always felt they have in common with the sacramental Christ. Bread and wine informed by Christ's soul do not remind them of the resurrected body enough to inspire belief in eternal life. Thus Descartes's theory of transubstantiation was bound to arouse the watchdogs of Catholic orthodoxy, and especially those who already resented his philosophy. Worse, it provided them with a dangerous argument against the orthodoxy of his metaphysics.

Mesland did not, in any case, deny them this opportunity for revenge. Despite Descartes's recommendations of caution and discretion, the letters containing his theory of transubstantiation circulated among his followers for years after his death in 1650. Needless to say, they raised a controversy involving a variety of reactions, which ranged from enthusiasm to outrage. While exposing his memory to censure by enemies, they divided the partisans of his philosophy into apologists and critics of his theory. The Calvinists, as usual, exploited the quarrel in their own interest. Hostile Catholics indicted him on charges of deviation from Catholicism and conformity with Calvinism. They accused him of assigning a body of bread to Christ, attacked the identity

---

[115] Alquié notes that Descartes exposes a different conception in the *Passions de l'âme* (1649): '[Il] reconnaît au corps humain une indivisibilité venant de la solidarité organique de toutes les parties qui le composent. Indépendamment de son union avec l'âme, le corps machine (chez l'homme comme chez l'animal) a donc une unité qui le différencie déjà des corps faits de matière inorganisée' (iii.549, n.1).

of body with extension and defended the independent existence of accidents. The most influential of these adversaries was the Jesuit Le Valois who, under the pseudonym of Louis de La Ville, published in 1680 the *Sentiments de m. Descartes . . . opposés à la doctrine de l'Eglise et conformes aux erreurs de Calvin*. This text reappeared two years later as the first of two parts in the anonymous *La Philosophie de m. Descartes contraire à la foi catholique*. In his preface, the editor and author explains that, since de La Ville exposes only one of Descartes's two major errors, he will censure the other one himself. De La Ville stipulates, in the first part, that a body cannot be really present without its essence. Descartes, he observes, considers extension the essence of body. Yet the philosopher believes Christ's body to be present in the eucharist without extension. De La Ville concludes that this theory implies a contradiction of the real presence in the manner of Calvin. According to the author of the second part, Descartes equates accidents to appearances existing only in the mind. But faith teaches us that the accidents of bread and wine continue to exist after the destruction of their substance in the eucharist. Accidents therefore enjoy a real existence and Descartes's theory 'ne peut du tout subsister avec ce que la foi nous enseigne' (p.55). Leibniz, who agreed with this verdict, insinuated that Descartes was not sincere in his distinction between truths of reason and faith. In substituting appearances for real accidents, the Frenchman reaffirmed an opinion which he knew Catholic theologians had rejected. But Leibniz may have been guilty of insincerity himself, for he was promoting his own theory of transubstantiation in the interest of reuniting the Lutheran and Catholic Churches.

Descartes's followers were so anxious to prove his orthodoxy that they obtained a statement from Christina, queen of Sweden, acknowledging his influence on her conversion. Some of them sought to adapt his theory of transubstantiation to the criteria on which the scholastics were condemning it. Proceeding by geometrical demonstration in the manner of Spinoza, Pierre Varignon claimed that every particle of consecrated bread becomes a miniature but complete human body united with Christ's soul.[116] Other Cartesians deplored such modi-

---

[116] 'Imaginons [. . .] chacune des parties sensibles [. . .] du pain comme un tout dont Dieu change la disposition la plus intime des moindres parties élémentaires qui le composent, de manière qu'au lieu de pain il en fasse de la chair, des os, des artères, des veines, du sang, en un mot [. . .] un petit corps organisé comme l'est ordinairement le corps humain' (*Démonstration de la possibilité de la présence réelle* in *Œuvres complètes de Malebranche*, xvii-1 (Bruxelles 1977), p.503).

fications and, while refraining from an endorsement of the theory, insisted on Descartes's orthodoxy.

This is Bossuet's position. After learning of the theory by hearsay, he wrote an 'Examen d'une nouvelle explication du mystère de l'Eucharistie' in 1674-1675, but did not publish it for fear of disturbing Clement's peace. 'Cette animation du pain et du vin', he objects, will not convert bread into the body sacrificed for us and wine into the blood shed for us. 'Ce pain aurait été crucifié [. . .] du vin serait sorti des veines du Sauveur [!]'[117] In communion, we must receive more than a body associated with Christ, we must receive the body substantially joined with the living Word of God, who endows us with eternal life. The new explanation does not state that we commune on the body that rose from the dead: 'C'est là, néanmoins, le fond du mystère.'[118] We receive the entire substance of the body united with the Word, yet neither the entire extension nor the entire quantity. 'Je ne m'en embarrasse pas,' Bossuet comments, 'puisque c'est par sa substance [. . .] que ce corps de Jésus-Christ [. . .] me sauve' (p.153). If someone should ask him how he conceives of such things, he would confidently reply that he cannot conceive of them, but he is convinced that God can do them. He has further objections to the new explanation. It suggests that Christ has two bodies, which is absurd. It implies that we receive his body because we partake of his soul, when just the opposite is true. It founds the unity of the body on its union with the soul, which is false since the body has its own organic unity. Loath to admit that Descartes, whom he admired, had originated this theory, Bossuet retreated to the philosopher's published works. Had not Descartes recommended the *Méditations*, which seemed orthodox to Bossuet, as the best presentation of his thought? 'Si dans quelque écrit particulier il a proposé ou hasardé autre chose, je ne m'en informe pas' (p.143). The 'Réponse aux quatrièmes objections' satisfied him that the philosopher adhered to eucharistic dogma, but the idea that extension cannot be separated from matter troubled him. The subsistence of this accident would imply the survival of substance after the consecration of the bread and the wine. Bossuet eludes the difficulty by referring to a precaution taken by the philosopher: Descartes 'reconnaît que Dieu a pu mettre dans le fond [des

[117] E. Levesque, ed., 'Introduction à un fragment de Bossuet', *Revue Bossuet* (1900), p.141.

[118] p.145. In the preceding sentence Bossuet actually wrote: 'Le même corps qui a été immolé pour nous et qui a été dans le tombeau, qui est ressuscité de mort à vie et auquel le Verbe est actuellement uni dans le ciel.

81

corps] quelque chose qu'on ne peut concevoir' (p.154).[119] Anxious to clear Descartes's name, Bossuet therefore takes liberties with his intentions by treating his precaution as if it were an outright concession. He continued to think wishfully until 1701 when he finally had an opportunity to read the letters to Mesland. This time, he faces the evidence: 'Elles se trouveront directement opposées à la doctrine catholique.'[120] Discounting again the importance of unpublished works, he approves the decision to withhold the letters from the press and advises Descartes's disciples to respect this decision. Unlike the 'Réponse', he complains, they imply that the substances of bread and wine subsist after the consecration.

The Calvinist participants in the controversy applauded Descartes's Roman heresy. They agreed with him on extension, but they agreed with his Catholic adversaries on the conflict between this opinion and dogma. The Huguenot exile Pierre Bayle and the Genevan minister Jacob Vernet even edited collections of polemical essays displaying the variety of reactions to his theory of transubstantiation. In the 'Avis au lecteur' of his anonymous *Recueil de pièces curieuses* (1684), Bayle claims to have selected 'quelques pièces qui méritaient bien de ne pas demeurer dans l'obscurité où on les a laissées'. Should anyone miss the point, he explains this neglect as follows: 'On a redouté le crédit de ceux qui pouvaient s'en scandaliser.'[121] He was obviously looking forward to such a scandal. In the meantime, however, he thought Cartesian, that is clear and distinct, reason should suffice to convince the Catholics of their eucharistic errors.[122] Thanks to the essays in his collection, several points were clear to him. The Council of Trent had decided that Christ's body is present wherever hostias are consecrated and that the elements of this sacramental body interpenetrate each other. De Valois proves this decision to be incompatible with Descartes's theory. Other Catholics (Bernier and 'P.M.') explain transubstantiation in a manner different from that of Trent. A (Protestant)

119 'De ce que j'ai dit que les modes ne peuvent pas être entendus sans quelque substance en laquelle ils résident, on ne doit pas inférer que j'aie nié que par la toute puissance de Dieu ils en puissent être séparés, parce que je tiens pour être très assuré et crois fermement que Dieu peut faire une infinité de choses que nous ne sommes pas capables d'entendre' (ii.694).
120 letter to Pastel in *Correspondance de Bossuet* (Paris 1909-1925), xi.254.
121 the pages are not numbered.
122 'Si les hommes se servaient des lumières claires et distinctes de la raison pour choisir une opinion plutôt qu'une autre, il n'en faudrait pas davantage pour convaincre tous les catholiques romains de leurs erreurs à l'égard de l'Eucharistie' ('Avis').

professor of Sedan demonstrates that matter cannot be penetrated and two objects cannot be equal when one is bigger than the other. Consequently, Trent is in error. Thus Bayle arbitrates the dispute!

A friend and enemy of Voltaire, Jacob Vernet attempts a more seductive arbitration in his *Recueil de pièces fugitives sur l'Eucharistie* (1730), a project evidently inspired by Bayle's example. In his 'Préface', Vernet sympathises with victims of the Roman 'point d'honneur de ne jamais revenir de ce [que l'Eglise] a une fois prononcé' (p.vi). When philosophers dare to investigate clearer principles of reason than those discovered by their predecessors, they are accused of violating dogma, and especially eucharistic dogma. Opponents of Descartes's theory raise two objections: he denies the reality of accidents and he defines matter as essentially extended and impenetrable; but the essays in the *Recueil* treat the second objection alone. Although Vernet tentatively assigns the first essay to Malebranche, it is really one of Descartes's letters to Mesland.[123] This mistake suggests that his presumption exceeded his competence and even that the controversy had deteriorated to the point of losing contact with its origin. The second essay in the *Recueil* is the one by Varignon, whom Vernet treats with contempt: '[Il] appelle cela *démontrer la possibilité de la présence réelle*. Mais c'est véritablement enfanter une chimère' (p.xxv). Yet Vernet's own solution, which he proposes in the anonymous fourth essay,[124] seems even more feeble. The substances of bread and wine survive, but Christ declares them a symbol and equivalence of his body and blood. 'Le pain et la coupe sont *changés, transmués, transélémentés* [. . .] par la vertu du Saint-Esprit' (p.187). No less slyly than naively, therefore, Vernet omits *transubstantiés*, the one word that might have attracted Catholic readers. As it stands, his rhetorical compromise was unlikely to tempt them. Still, his *Recueil* illustrates the Protestant exploitation of a Catholic dispute over a theory intended to facilitate the reconversion of the Protestants to Catholicism.

Intervention in the Catholic dispute over frequent communion did not appeal to Protestants. They probably realised that the Jansenists were using this pretext to strike a hidden blow against the Jesuits. How

---

[123] Malebranche, however, did participate in the controversy by answering de Valois.

[124] he correctly attributes the third essay, which supports Descartes, to a Catholic priest. It is the work of Le Courayer who, after an abortive attempt to reconcile Anglicanism and Catholicism, fled to England.

often should one commune? Every Sunday according to François de Sales in the *Introduction à la vie dévote* (1608).[125] Daily and fortnightly communion are exceptions to his rule. He reserves daily communion for an elite: 'La disposition requise pour une si fréquente communion devant être fort exquise, il n'est pas bon de le conseiller généralement' (p.193). He concedes the advisibility of fortnightly communion for subordinates of people shocked or troubled by sacramental assiduity, people in other words who resent the example of a greater piety than their own: '[Il sera] bon de condescendre en quelque sorte à leur infirmité' (p.195). During the seventeenth century, Brémond reports, French Catholics were following de Sales's recommendations: 'La cause de la communion fréquente était pleinement gagnée.'[126]

Known as 'les filles du Saint Sacrement', the nuns of Port Royal usually communed twice a week, on feast days as well and, some of them, even more often. Jansenist leaders, including Arnauld himself, urged their fellow sectarians to commune frequently, provided they deserved it by their piety. Yet Saint-Cyran, the founder of French Jansenism and the spiritual director of Port Royal, opposed this tendency and strove to slow the pace by requiring a thorough penitence before communion. During Lent in 1635, he even recommended abstinence. In volume iii of *La Cour sainte*, published that same year, the Jesuit Nicolas Caussin prescribed strict rules for penitence. Most of the Jesuits seem to have applied de Sales's teaching, despite the proselytic temptations of more frequent communion.

The project resulting in the publication of *De la fréquente communion* evolved from the shocking discovery that the Jesuit de Sesmaisons allowed his penitents to attend balls after communion. The imprisoned Saint-Cyran appealed to Arnauld who, with the collaboration of Saint-Cyran's nephew Martin de Barcos, composed a thick treatise in 1640-1641. It presents a massive array of Patristic quotations in support of two points: 1. A long and worthy penitence for every mortal sin should precede absolution and communion; 2. Frequent communion requires

---

[125] the saint had unusual faith in the effect of the sacrament: 'Si les fruits les plus tendres et sujets à corruption, comme sont les cerises, les abricots et les fraises, se conservent aisément toute l'année étant confits au sucre ou au miel: ce n'est pas merveille si nos cœurs, quoique frêles et imbéciles, sont préservés de la corruption du péché lorsqu'ils sont sucrés et emmiellés de la chair et du sang incorruptibles du Fils de Dieu' (Paris 1628, pp.191-92).

[126] Henri Brémond, *Histoire littéraire du sentiment religieux en France depuis la fin des guerres de religion*, ix (Paris 1968), p.73.

a truly pious life conditioned by a pure and total love of God and devoted to the accomplishment of his will. The authors advocate a return to the fourth and fifth-century practice, which they assume to have been ecumenical, of preparing for communion by several days of rigorous penitence. People who had committed mortal sins, they hinted, were banned from the sacrament for several years. They recall that the Council of Trent ordered confessors to test the sincerity of penitents before admitting them to communion. Ostensibly, they were trying to preserve the veneration of the sacrament from erosion through easy and familiar access. But they were really insinuating that the Jesuits neglected penitence and encouraged the abuse of frequent communion. Oblique allusions to them imply the favourite Jansenist accusation of laxism.[127]

When *La fréquente*, as it was called then, appeared in 1643 with the approbations of four archbishops, twelve bishops and twenty doctors of theology, the Jesuits led by Nouet counterattacked. In a sermon against Arnauld, Nouet 'le traita de scorpion et l'appela un serpent ayant une langue à trois pointes'.[128] The publicity boosted sales, so that the first edition sold out in two weeks. Angered by Nouet's invective, the authors of the approbations, many of whom kept their distance from Jansenism, forced him to kneel bareheaded in public and retract, hence his grudge against Arnauld in the controversy with the Calvinists. The most effective reply was *De la pénitence publique et de la préparation à la communion* (1644) by the Jesuit scholar Denis Petau. 'Je ne sache personne', he remarks in the 'Préface', 'qui ne soit de l'avis de M. Arnauld qu'il faut se préparer à ce festin [. . .] avec un soin et une diligence extraordinaire.'[129] But Arnauld should not have written that it is permissible and even praiseworthy to abandon a current practice and return to an ancient one. The Church cannot be in error. The Council of Trent had established the present form of penitence and the attempt to replace it by a new one tended to schism. Yet these are routine objections. What really alarmed Petau was the prospect of a decline in the number of communicants: 'Qui pourra dorénavant prétendre de communier?'[130] Is anyone in this life virtuous and holy enough? No one except the

[127] 'La Compagnie', however, is not 'sournoisement visée à toutes les pages' as Brémond claims (p.78).
[128] Antoine Adam, *Du mysticisme à la révolte* (Paris 1968), p.166.
[129] the pages in the 'Préface' are not numbered.
[130] 5.7.11 (p.42). The pages in each book are numbered separately.

virgin Mary has ever been qualified, not even Paul and the other apostles! Although Petau was exaggerating for polemical effect, Arnauld had raised a very sensitive issue. The prosperity of the Church depended on the number of its communicants. Already dissatisfied with the previous statistics, Vincent de Paul complained that *La fréquente* was causing a decline. Though backed by impressive erudition, Petau's arguments did not put a stop to the success of *La fréquente*. Thus the Jesuits tried, as usual, to do in Rome what they could not do in Paris. Adam reveals that the pope secretly asked cardinal Mazarin, the French minister, to suggest that Arnauld and de Barcos take their case to Rome. Ever hostile to papal intervention, however, Parlement manifested its opposition and Mazarin let the matter drop. The Jesuits then sought to persuade the Roman Inquisition to condemn *La fréquente*, but they only obtained the censure of a few passages.

The contribution of the work to an eventual drop in the statistics so closely watched by 'Monsieur Vincent' is practically unquestionable. Yet relatively few Jansenists seem to have applied the doctrine of *La fréquente* in all its rigour before the eighteenth century, when remembrance of the author's polemical motive had faded. Though inclined to sympathy for the Jansenists, Bossuet urged his penitents, a pious elite, to commune very frequently. Among Brémond's many quotations to this effect, the following recalls Ambrose (see p.25): 'La communion journalière doit être votre soutien; dévorez, absorbez, engloutissez, saoûlez-vous' (*Correspondance*, v.197). His enemy Fénelon, a staunch ally of the Jesuits, agrees with him on frequent communion. Two letters, which Fénelon left in his papers after his death, contradict *La fréquente*. In one of these, he finds that persons who disapprove of daily communion are judging 'sur certains préjugés qu'elles tirent de l'ancienne pénitence'.[131] A Catholic who practises daily communion, he presumes, is not guilty of mortal sin and therefore does not have to undergo attrition before approaching the altar. Pure of conscience, he lives a pious life and submits in all sincerity to an experienced director who tolerates no laxity. The portrait seems optimistic for Tartuffe's generation. In his other letter, Fénelon asserts that a Catholic who '[vit] en bon laïque [...] peut et doit communier tous les jours s'il est libre' (v.727). He excepts people whose social obligations prevent them from taking proper precautions, a discreet echo of de

[131] Fénelon, *Œuvres complètes* (Paris 1850), v.176.

Sales and allusion, perhaps, to the court from which Bossuet had persuaded Louis XIV to banish him. In his only concession to *La fréquente*, he agrees that habitually self-indulgent sinners are unworthy of daily communion. His teaching tends to standardise the more frequent exception to de Sales's rule and Arnauld's, the less frequent exception.

Two years after the centennial of *La fréquente*, the Jesuit Jean Pichon went to the opposite extreme in *L'Esprit de Jésus-Christ et de l'Eglise sur la fréquente communion* (1745). Initially well received by enemies of Jansenism, the work nonetheless furnished the Jansenists with an inviting target, at which the editors of the clandestine *Nouvelles ecclésiastiques* aimed several issues. Church authorities and Pichon's superiors soon realised that his book tended to promote the very abuses censured by *La fréquente* and hence justify Arnauld's insinuations in retrospect.[132] They forced him to retract, to withdraw the unsold copies and, when he endeavoured to publish a revised edition, to abandon this project. By silencing his apology of eucharistic laxism, they terminated the dispute.

The dispute over frequent communion persisted therefore well into the eighteenth century, along with the controversy over Descartes's theory of transubstantiation and the polemic with the Calvinists over the Catholic eucharist. The Jansenists and the Jesuits continued to quarrel over communion but, after the promulgation of the bull Unigenitus in 1713, political allies began to support both parties, thus broadening the conflict, and, by 1731, a new issue had eclipsed the old ones, the refusal of last rites.

Unigenitus condemned 101 propositions extracted from the four-volume *Réflexions morales sur le Nouveau Testament* (1693) by the Jansenist Pasquier Quesnel. The latter had published a briefer preliminary edition under the title of *Morale de l'Evangile* in 1671. The work had enjoyed forty years of popularity and approval by the hierarchy when the Jesuits detected the massive heresy lurking between the pages. Louis XIV's exasperation over the failure of his attempts to extirpate Jansenism encouraged them to challenge a major source of Jansenist prestige. Backed by his influence, they proceeded against

---

132 'Enfin', urges Pichon, 'je voudrais qu'on dît à tout le monde: Communiez souvent. La communion fréquente est la force souveraine de la religion et par elle vous parviendrez à l'éternité bienheureuse' (p.362). It is the style rather than the content that conveys an impression of laxism.

the *Réflexions* in Rome, despite the reluctance of Clement XI to provoke the defenders of Gallican independence. Twenty-two months of royal pressure and Jesuit manipulation produced a bull that would confirm Clement's fears. On all levels of society, including the episcopal, the parlementary and the academic, the Gallicans joined forces with the Jansenists in opposition to Unigenitus, which raised the triple spectre of papal intervention, Jesuit hegemony and royal totalitarianism. Until Louis died two years later, however, the alliance proved ineffective and the *parlements* (high courts) were forced to ratify the bull as the law of church and state,[133] with reservations nonetheless.[134] The death of the tyrant interrupted the repression of dissidence, which he could not tolerate. A relative liberty of conscience under the regent brought the conflict over Unigenitus out in the open and the enemies of the bull publicly appealed to a future council, hence the name *appelants*. During the regency, they included the archbishop of Paris cardinal de Noailles, seven bishops, heavy majorities in the *parlements*, an influential fraction of the Sorbonne, a considerable portion of the minor clergy and many laymen. The movement prospered among the lower classes and varied in strength from province to province, being especially strong in Normandy, Champaign and the Ile de France (Paris). Known as *acceptants* or *constitutionnaires*,[135] the advocates of Unigenitus were more numerous and more influential in most places and on most levels. They could always count on the support of the hierarchy and usually on that of the crown. By 1730, they had reduced the number of appelant bishops to one [136] and completely purged the Sorbonne, but they could not curb parlementary powers.

[133] the status was confirmed three times, by the royal declaration of 1720, the *lit de justice* of 1730 and a decision by the Conseil d'Etat in 1755, not to mention papal confirmation by the letters *Pastoralis officii* of 1718 and the bref *Ex omnibus* of 1756. The *parlements* resisted all of these measures.

[134] they particularly resented the condemnation of proposition 91: 'La crainte d'une excommunication injuste ne doit jamais nous empêcher de faire notre devoir.' Here Gallican and Jansenist interests converged dramatically.

[135] Unigenitus was also called *la Constitution*.

[136] Charles de Caylus, bishop of Auxerre from 1704 until 1754, who purged his clergy of constitutionaries and created a haven for persecuted Jansenists. He took the recommendations in *La fréquente* very seriously: 'On refusait les sacrements non seulement aux ennemis, aux "molinistes", mais à bien d'autres personnes; il n'était pas rare d'attendre des années pour mériter d'être admis à communier et de revenir quatre on cinq fois au confessionnel avant de recevoir l'absolution' (Philippe Godard, *La Querelle des refus de sacrement, 1730-1765* (Paris 1937), p.117).

To curtail resistance to Unigenitus, a few constitutionary bishops had borrowed a tactic from Hardouin de Pérefixe, the archbishop of Paris under Louis xiv. Twice he had tried to force 'les filles du Saint Sacrement' to sign the *Formulaire*, a condemnation of Jansenism, by depriving them of communion. Twice they refused and, unable to administer to each other, they abstained from 1664 until 1669 and from 1706 until 1709, when Louis ordered them dispersed among other convents. Used against appelant convents in the eighteenth century, this tactic usually produced the same result.[137] Only a minority of appelants were nuns, however, and, since many qualified as celebrants, depriving them of communion was problematic, for they could administer to each other. Denied by one priest, an appelant could approach another; barred from the altar in one parish or diocese, he could go to another. Although constitutionary bishops rescinded the rights of the appelant priests in their dioceses to administer the sacraments, this measure did not affect former appelants and sympathetic or tolerant celebrants. The constitutionaries nonetheless discovered that dying appelants were more vulnerable, because they could seldom go and seek the sacraments they needed and because they needed them more urgently. Most sincere Catholics believed that access to heaven depended in some measure on viaticum (deathbed communión) and extreme unction. Insensitive to the anxiety they were inflicting on fellow-Christians, the constitutionaries hoped the danger of death without last rites might drive appelants to recant. Furthermore, if some died without them, the example might weaken the resolve of others. Like most such schemes, however, this one did not account for a basic human reflex, obstinacy under the threat of coercion. In many cases, moreover, the appelants were as guilty of deliberate provocation as the acceptants were of arrogant abuse.

The earliest case reported by Godard occurred in 1721 when Fleuriau d'Armenonville, the bishop of Orleans, exhorted a dying canon to abandon his opposition to Unigenitus. The canon refused and Fleuriau let him die without last rites. Such incidents soon began to proliferate and especially in his diocese. In 1731, a dying woman named Dupleix, who had opposed the bull, requested last rites from one of his priests.

---

[137] '[on voit] des communautés religieuses entières attendre les sacrements jusqu'à ce qu'elles se soumettent: vingt-huit religieuses du carmel de Toulouse, dix-neuf du carmel de Lectoure restent pendant dix ans sans communion [. . .] Les ursulines de Châlons-sur-Marne subissent un sort semblable [. . .] Parfois la censure produit plus d'effet: les visitandines de Castellane cessent leur résistance en 1727, trois d'entre elles étant mortes sans sacrements' (Godard, p.32).

When the latter asked her whether she accepted Unigenitus, she pretended not to know what he was talking about, but she assured him
she remained faithful to the religion of her ancestors. Deprived of last
rites, she managed to complain to the *lieutenant criminel* of Orleans and
appeal to the Parlement de Paris before she died. Having heard the case,
the Grand' Chambre of Parlement declared that priests had no right to
ask questions about acceptance of Unigenitus, and enjoined Fleuriau to
cancel his policy. But the Conseil du roi reversed this decision, thus
provoking the anger of the public, who suspected the bishops of trying
to extend their power. Parlement protested to Louis xv and, when he
ignored them, they protested again, though in vain.

This was the first time Parlement had intervened in a case involving
the refusal of last rites, thus Dupleix versus Fleuriau set a precedent and
established a pattern. The *parlements* would justify their intervention in
such affairs by citing their jurisdiction over the maintenance of public
order, the enforcement of royal edicts and canon law, and the preser-
vation of the Gallican Church's independence. While ever anxious to
emphasise their loyalty to the crown, they constantly encroached on
the prerogative of the king as well as that of the bishops and archbishops,
whose excesses and ambitions they opposed. Though divided over
tactics and the degree of severity necessary, the prelates, who convened
in the Assemblée Générale du Clergé Français, almost unanimously
opposed parlementary interference with sacramental policy. They
not only insisted that they had exclusive jurisdiction in the area, but
they also founded their claim on a royal edict of 1695.[138] A vacillating
king, Louis xv usually favoured them, both by conviction and in order
to sustain their indulgence for his sexual appetite. When he lacked
funds, however, he immediately and shamelessly shifted his favour to
the parlements. Never did he make a serious attempt to disentangle the
overlapping jurisdictions and confine each power to its own. Yet he
alone was in a position to arbitrate a dispute that threatened the *ancien
régime* as much as any other.

The Rivotte affair of 1737 presents an interesting variation in the
pattern of conflict. The dean of Saint Aimé in Douai, which belonged
to the parlementary jurisdiction of Paris, denied a request for last rights
by canon Rivotte, a Jansenist. He also refused to allow burial in hallowed
ground, so that Rivotte was laid to rest in the chapter garden with his

[138] patent letters recognising their right to regulate the confessional powers of priests
below the rank of curate.

face turned upward towards the church. Not for long, however, for his colleagues had him exhumed and reburied, face down, in the cemetery for still-born children. Horrified, his niece complained to Parlement, thus adding still another such case to an overloaded docket and reinitiating a tedious process.

The intensity of the conflict surged to an even higher level in 1747 when Christophe de Beaumont became archbishop of Paris. The champion of Unigenitus compensated for a slight deficiency in humanity and intelligence by an abundance of zeal and obstinacy. Convinced that appelant priests were subverting his diocese by their use of the sacraments, he resorted to *billets de confession*. Carlo Borromeo, the archbishop of Milan, had required confession certificates three days in advance of Easter communion, a policy approved by the Milan councils of 1565 and 1582. In 1665, the Assemblée générale had introduced them in France to prevent profanation of the sacraments by the Protestants. De Noailles, the pro-Jansenist archbishop of Paris, had used them against the Jesuits, a precedent savoured by the pro-Jesuit Beaumont. The latter did not require confession certificates for ordinary communion, but rather for viaticum and extreme unction. At first glance, his policy seems stricter in principle than in practice. Before receiving last rites, the penitent was supposed to produce a certificate proving that he had confessed to a *prêtre approuvé*, a priest who had the archbishop's written permission to dispense the sacraments.[139] Most dying penitents, however, were merely asked to name their confessor and, if they named an authorised priest, they received last rites without further ado. Confession certificates as such, therefore, had a greater ideological than pragmatic impact on the public mind. Questioning a dying appelant was nonetheless more perfidious than asking him for a certificate, because it forced him to choose between damning himself by a lie and damning himself by an acknowledgement of the truth.

Between 1749 and 1752, the new tactic caused a series of major incidents, most of which involved Bouettin, the curate of Saint Etienne du Mont in Paris. Having replaced a Jansenist curate, he inspired much hatred by his persecution of appelants. In 1749, he received a request for last rites from Charles Coffin, a prominent Jansenist who had publicly appealed to a future council in 1718. Asked for the name of his

[139] 'Beaumont se réservait d'approuver individuellement ceux qui s'adresseraient à lui pour déclarer leur soumission à la bulle et apposer leur signature pure et simple au bas du Formulaire' (Emile Régnault, *Christophe de Beaumont* (Paris 1882), i.161).

confessor, Coffin would only say that he was an authorised priest,[140] and he had no confession certificate. Bouettin having refused last rites, Coffin died without them, but the curate dared not oppose his burial in Saint Jean de Beauvais. The principal of the Collège de Beauvais, a former rector of the university and the official hymnographer of the Church of Paris, Coffin was the most distinguished victim of sacramental persecution in the eighteenth century. He enjoyed the esteem of *les gens de robe*, the judicial nobility, who sent their offspring to his college. The entire city including Bouettin, scoffed the *Nouvelles ecclésiastiques*, sang Coffin's faith in church with Beaumont's approval. Either four or ten thousand people followed his funeral procession, depending as usual on whom we should believe. The attendance in any case, which irritated the authorities in Paris and Versailles, struck Beaumont as insubordination.

Coffin's nephew was more of a rake than a Jansenist, but he hoped to inherit the estates of two elderly aunts who resembled his uncle. A counsellor in the Châtelet, he organised the publication of four memoirs by forty-one lawyers urging him to report Bouettin to Parlement. This he did, yet the Conseil du roi condemned the memoirs on the excuse that they were disturbing the peace and ordered all proceedings in the matter dropped. Eighteen months later, the nephew himself was dangerously ill and Bouettin refused his request for last rites because he had no confession certificate. Three times Parlement enjoined the curate to administer them and three times he refused. Summoned before the court, he testified that he owed the archbishop exclusive obedience. The judges found him so insolent that they sentenced him on the spot to a fine of three livres and two days of confinement in the Conciergerie. Summoned in turn, Beaumont refused to obey and denied Parlement's jurisdiction in the matter, but he did agree to let young Coffin confess to a former Jansenist.[141] Thus the nephew finally received last rites from Bouettin, who embraced him and conducted his funeral service a few days later. Parlement had meanwhile sent its official representatives, *les gens du roi*, to complain of Beaumont's behaviour. Yet the king expressed his irritation over the punishment inflicted on Bouettin and lectured them on Parlement's subordination to him and the respect it

[140] so that Beaumont would not know whom to punish. See n.141.
[141] Pierre Guéret, who had probably confessed his uncle too.

owed his Church. Insulted, Parlement sent Louis a remonstrance, which he ignored.[142]

Encouraged by his victory, Beaumont and several bishops who had been imitating him[143] redoubled their efforts on the assumption that the king would continue to support them. Soon Bouettin had denied last rites to a Jansenist priest named Lemaire for refusing to name his confessor or furnish a confession certificate. Lemaire appealed to Parlement, which enjoined Bouettin to administer to him and complained to the archbishop. The latter retorted that Bouettin was only obeying his orders. But Parlement also invited Beaumont to sit with its Grand' Chambre in his capacity as duke of Saint Cloud, a title belonging to the see of Paris. Unable to enforce a summons, the judges were obviously trying to lure him into an interrogation, but Beaumont, who was no fool, declined on the pretext of insufficient time. Frustrated, Parlement met from six in the evening until one in the morning, an unprecedented session, in order to avoid interference by the Conseil. It levied a three-livre fine on Bouettin, ordered the administration of last rites to Lemaire within twenty-four hours and enjoined Beaumont to prevent further refusals. The Conseil nullified this decision and Louis told the *gens du roi*, 'Je suis fort mécontent de mon parlement.'[144] Yet Parlement sent them back to inform him of Lemaire's predicament. Having received them cordially this time, Louis dispatched a Capuchin[145] to confess the dying priest and administer last rites, but Lemaire died several hours before he arrived. Sensitive to Louis's sudden change of attitude, Parlement issued a warrant for the arrest of Bouettin, who fled. Although the Conseil annulled the warrant and forbade further prosecution of the case, Parlement remonstrated and the king, reversing himself, consented to the removal of Bouettin. For the first time, moreover, he acknowledged the jurisdiction of the secular courts over refusal of last rites. Now it was Parlement's turn to believe victory within its grasp. It prohibited curates from withholding the sacraments for failure to present a confession certificate or name a confessor. The Conseil offered rhetorical rather than substantial resistance. Published, distributed and posted by the thousands, the parlementary injunction appeared in the *Gazette de France* and even on the courtyard walls of

---

[142] several years later (1755), Elizabeth Coffin was refused last rites.
[143] particularly Belzunce, bishop of Marseilles.
[144] Jacques Parguez, *La Bulle Unigenitus et le jansénisme politique* (Paris 1936), p.127.
[145] Clément, a distinguished preacher.

the arch-episcopal palace. 'Voilà mon billet de confession!' people gloated (Godard, p.76). And Louis did nothing.

In December of 1752,[146] attention shifted from Saint Etienne to Saint Médard, the scene of Jansenist convulsions twenty years before. The curate, a constitutionary, denied requests for last rites from Thècle and Perpétue, nuns in the Jansenist convent of Sainte Agathe, which served a boarding school. Thècle died without them, but Perpétue survived her apoplexy and appealed to Parlement. Summoned, the curate fled, leaving his two vicars to explain that he had acted on the archbishop's orders. When Parlement tried to force the other priests to administer to Perpétue, they abandoned the church, so that no one remained to celebrate Sunday mass. Enjoined to provide for her, Beaumont replied, 'L'administration des sacrements est un ministère que je ne tiens que de Dieu seul' (Parguez, p.132). Once he had rejected a second injunction, Parlement ordered his property seized and tried to convoke the peers and the king. Louis prohibited this assembly, annulled the seizure of Beaumont's property and forbade further prosecution of the case. On the request of three archbishops and sixteen bishops, he also nullified the parlementary injunction outlawing refusal of last rites for failure to present a confession certificate or name one's confessor. In a notarised statement, Perpétue declared that she would soon be well enough to commune in church and asked Parlement to drop its proceedings on her behalf. Her opinion no longer mattered, however, for Louis signed a *lettre de cachet* on Christmas Eve evicting her from her convent and confining her in Port Royal, which had long since been packed with constitutionary nuns. He also ordered the pupils of Sainte Agathe dismissed and the nuns dispersed among the convents.

Early the next year, an angry Parlement confronted him with 'les Grandes Remonstrances', which provoked its exile to Pontoise and a futile attempt to replace it by a Chambre Royale. The judicial profession refused to collaborate with the new court, the Châtelet daringly assumed the prosecution of refusals and the royal treasury began to suffer, hence the triumphant return of Parlement in 1754. In recalling the judges, Louis imposed silence on both sides, yet he assigned enforcement of this

---

[146] engrossed in the publication of the *Siècle de Louis XIV*, Voltaire had written to d'Argental from Prussia on 5 August. Addressing himself to 'Messieurs', he taunts: 'Tâchez [. . .] de ne point avoir des siflets universels pour vos querelles ridicules qui vous couvrent de plus de honte aux yeux de tous vos voisins, que les chef d'œuvres du temps de Louis 14 ne vous ont acquis de gloire' (Best.D4970).

silence to Parlement. After puzzling over his ambiguous declaration, the judges decided to interpret the silence as incumbent upon priests charged with the administration of last rites. Thus the declaration inspired many Jansenist pamphlets agreeing with the necessity for this silence and inaugurated a period of judicial retaliation against refusals, as numerous as ever.[147] Louis had in fact shifted his favour to Parlement, for he not only exiled a few stubborn prelates including Beaumont, but also, on the advice, perhaps, of pope Benedict XIV, obtained the suspension of confession certificates from the Assemblée when it met in 1755. At this meeting, the *Feuillants*, who considered resistance to Unigenitus a grave sin, disagreed with the *Théatins*, who considered it a mortal sin. Both sides nonetheless appealed to the pope and the Assemblée voted a generous *don gratuit*[148] to ensure Louis's co-operation. Benedict XIV responded in 1756 by the *bref Ex omnibus*, which confirmed the right of the Church to refuse last rites for appealing against Unigenitus, but recommended interrogation of the penitent to determine his eligibility for them. The silence of the *bref* on the question of confession certificates apparently implied disapproval. When the king forced Parlement to ratify *Ex omnibus* by a *lit de justice*,[149] the period of parlementary favour had obviously come to an end.

Beaumont and others had retreated to a tactical moderation during this period, but not Montmorency-Laval, the young bishop of Orleans. His chapter refused last rites to canon de Cougniou, a Jansenist appelant. De Cougniou complained to the *lieutenant criminel* of Orleans and, before long, Parlement had intervened. Enjoined to administer to him, his fellow canons argued that the royal declaration of 1754 applied only to laymen, thus de Cougniou died without last rites. According to Godard, Parlement and the lieutenant issued a total of seventeen writs, levied 15 000 livres in fines and banished four canons for life. Parlement even ordered a mass in memory of de Cougniou celebrated in perpetuity and a marble slab with an inscription of this writ placed in the church.

---

[147] for the period 1752-1754, Godard estimates from 40 to 50 complaints received by Parlement and 60 cases prosecuted under its jurisdiction, of which about one third concerned the city of Paris. Yet Parlement, he notes, was not in session during the customary vacation periods and the fifteen-month exile to Pontoise. He believes this estimate conservative.

[148] a voluntary contribution to the royal treasury intended to dissuade the king from levying taxes on the Church.

[149] a ceremony of intervention in Parlement by the crown to compel the ratification of a law against its will.

When Montmorency-Laval removed the curate for obeying the writ, Parlement restored the curate and persuaded the king to transfer the bishop to the see of Condom. Before he left, however, Montmorency-Laval retaliated by revoking the sacramental powers of all the priests in the diocese.

In greater or lesser conformity with Paris, the provincial *parlements* were embroiled in similar disputes with prelates whose dioceses lay within their jurisdictions. The Parlement de Provence was the most active of these and the severest of all in punishing offenders. It required them to kneel before it and sentenced one priest to be whipped and branded with the fleur-de-lis. Particularly hostile to Unigenitus, the Parlement de Normandie had refused to ratify the bull until the government resorted to force. In 1753, the clergy of Verneuil, a town in its jurisdiction, denied last rites to three consecutive appelants and, every time the local *bailliage* or the parlement in Rouen intervened, the Conseil overturned the decision. On one occasion, the parlement dared to insist that two of its annulled acts remain in force. It finally decided to adjourn its proceedings against the clergy of Verneuil, enjoin the bishop of Evreux to put a stop to the refusals and send a remonstrance to the king. When the bishop ignored the injunction, it issued a summons and levied a fine of 6000 livres. Under orders from the king, however, the marquis de Fougères arrived with an escort of officers from the Royal Dragoons and struck all mention of the Verneuil case from the parlementary registers. The judges nonetheless declared their persistence in adhering to their principles, so that the marquis returned with three *huissiers* from Versailles and three brigades of Royal Dragoons. Although the king suspended the more subversive members of the Rouen parlement and the *bailliage* of Verneuil, the agitation continued until 1754. It would be useless to mention all the other prominent cases involving provincial *parlements* here.

The suppression of the Jesuits in the early sixties eclipsed the refusal of last rites as the central issue, but the familiar incidents and disputes persisted. Beaumont's persecution of the Ursulines in Saint Cloud shows that an end to the war over the sacraments was not yet in sight. Before naming a new superior, he inquired into the nuns' attitude towards Unigenitus and, displeased with the results, deprived them of access to the sacraments. When sister Saint-François asked for last rites, Beurré, the convent chaplain, offered to administer them provided she sign a copy of Unigenitus and a statement censuring Parlement. Though

watched, she managed to smuggle a request to Parlement that Beurré
be forced to give her the sacraments. The chaplain refused and, threatened with arrest, fled. Parlement enjoined Lafont, the dean of the local
chapter, to replace him. After a week of resistance, Lafont consented,
but the new superior kept the door locked. The *lieutenant criminel* had it
forced open, so that sister Saint-François received last rites in time. The
Assemblée protested to the king, who ordered the convent closed and
the nuns dispersed among other convents.

On the behalf of the Ursulines, Parlement intervened for the last time
in 1764, when it sent Louis a general indictment of the archbishop.
Although the king exiled Beaumont four times [150] for his obstinacy,
the refusals continued until 1781 when the champion of Unigenitus died.
Three years earlier, he had tried and failed to keep Voltaire from being
buried in hallowed ground, for he was also a great enemy of the *philosophes*. Yet Voltaire's attacks on the eucharist did far less damage than
Beaumont's abuse of the sacrament in his crusade against resistance to
the bull. The use of last rites as bait for an ideological trap could only
undermine confidence in them and the priests who administered them.
Cruelty in persecuting 'heretics' condemned by chicanery hardly
honoured the Church. Thus the constitutionaries who participated in the
refusal of last rites contributed to a decline of faith in communion, but
so did the appelants and their judicial allies who deliberately provoked
them. As Louis xv dissipated the power his great grandfather had concentrated in the royal government, the prelates and the magistrates
encroached on his prerogative. The power of a nation flows from the
consent of its people and, since the king was neglecting them, the
hierarchy and the magistrates fought for their allegiance.

Despite the quarrels of the seventeenth and eighteenth centuries,
eucharistic dogma had not changed very much since Trent. At the
Collège de Louis-le-Grand, Voltaire learned practically the same doctrine as the one codified by the great council. This doctrine was both an
intellectual monument and a somewhat incoherent amalgam of the
vicissitudes which had fashioned it, as he would later demonstrate.
The long assimilation of cultic notions and metaphysical ideas not only
enriched the ancient tradition of sacrifice, but also distorted it. The
concept of sacrament, in particular, stemmed from that of sacrifice and,

[150] 1752, 1754, 1758 and 1764.

for several centuries, overshadowed it. After the emergence of primitive Hebrew sacrifice from foreign sources, the evolution of the cult through its Hebrew, Jewish, Platonic and scholastic phases presents variations of an amplitude that shatters the illusions of permanence sustained by Bossuet.[151] Even when one narrows the scope of investigation to development from Jesus to Trent, the contrast between his humble observance of Jewish rites and the arrogant sophistication of the great council is enormous. The contradictions between his fraternal dinner with the disciples and the disputes conditioning the evolution of the dogma from Paschase to Trent ruin the claim of a common purpose, not to mention the possibility of a divine symphony. Nor can one fairly credit the complacent assumption that the most valuable opinions always emerged victorious to the greater glory of the final product. On the contrary, excellence usually succumbed to mediocrity, originality to conformity and sincerity to hypocrisy or cynicism. Ambrose eventually overshadowed Augustine, Paschase soon eclipsed Ratramn, Lanfranc and Guitmund triumphed over Berengar, d'Ailly and company took their revenge on Hus and the memory of Wyclif and, unable to crush Luther, the Church tried to obliterate his theology by conciliar decree. Though one may cite gifted defenders of the majority opinion, none made a more significant contribution than Thomas, who merely ordered and clarified existing theology rather than develop it. Most of the great minds are on the wrong side in the history of eucharistic dogma, which reveals little evidence of divine inspiration, guidance or manipulation. Hopefully God remained aloof from so sordid a business! Human appetites motivated almost every major event in the evolution of the dogma, which itself reflects the all too human concerns of the men who contributed to it. Whenever a conflict between reason and faith arose, faith received massive support from the clergy whose authority it enhanced. How ironic that Augustine's followers, Ratramn, Berengar, Wyclif – Luther is an exception – and Zwingli should have subjected the eucharist to empirical analysis! They gave Voltaire his cue by insisting that after consecration, the sensual appearances of bread and wine prove their continuing presence and that the eucharistic body of Christ could not be the same as the one in heaven, a common-

---

[151] 'Quatre ou cinq faits authentiques [. . .] font voir notre religion aussi ancienne que le monde. Ils montrent [. . .] qu'elle n'a point d'autre auteur que celui qui a fondé l'univers' (*Discours sur l'histoire universelle* (Paris 1966), p.340. Bossuet published the first edition of the *Discours* in 1681).

sense tradition inaugurated by Augustine himself. Yet the great Father had consistently sacrificed reason to faith just as Ambrose and his followers had, Paschase, Lanfranc and Guitmund. These proponents of faith owed their triumph less to intellectual power and theological acumen than the weight of clerical numbers, political pressures and popular superstition.

Yet the unedifying history of eucharistic dogma did not particularly detract from the prestige it enjoyed among French Catholics in the seventeenth century and even the early decades of the eighteenth. Nor did the feuding with the Protestants over transubstantiation and between Catholic factions over Descartes's theory and frequent communion have an immediate impact on faith in the sacrament. Apparently, however, they did have a cumulative effect which, together with the flagrant abuse of last rites, caused an accelerating decline. The statistics derived from recent studies of eighteenth-century wills reveal that the symptoms of Catholic faith associated with the prospect of an eventual death began to decrease towards 1720 in Paris and 1750 in Provence.[152] It seems reasonable to assume that similar studies of other regions and studies of communion statistics on a similar scale would confirm the general trend established by Chaunu and Vovelle. To what extent did the *philosophes* and Voltaire in particular contribute to this trend? Except for the intellectual elite, the decline in Provence affected all levels of literate intelligence more or less uniformly.[153] Since one would expect greater influence by the *philosophes* on the upper levels, their influence appears to have been indirect rather than direct in this province and perhaps in others as well. The number of sincere Catholic communicants, in any case, probably shrank from a heavy majority to a large minority, which reached the limits of its regression under the Revolution. This faithful core, which ignored or despised Voltaire and the *philosophes*, continued to appreciate the metaphysical rewards of communion. They continued to participate wholeheartedly in Christ's self-sacrifice and commune on his body and blood, thus incorporating themselves into the Church whose authority they welcomed. Nor did celebrants generally distract them by cupidity or ambition after the

[152] Michel Vovelle, *Piété baroque et déchristianisation en Provence aux XVIIe et XVIIIe siècles* (Paris 1973); Pierre Chaunu, *La Mort à Paris (XVIe, XVIIe, XVIIIe siècles)* (Paris 1978).

[153] 'Il ne semble [. . .] pas y avoir, en dessous des élites cultivées du moins, corrélation directe entre l'évolution de la pratique et l'accès à la culture' (Vovelle, p.607).

99

reform of discipline under the Counterreformation. Ironically, the feuding between Catholic factions, the persecution of the Protestants and the polemic of the *philosophes* damaged the superstructure of the Church more than its foundations. Even Jean Meslier, secretly an atheist, administered the eucharist until his death in 1729 and communion sustained the faith of his parishioners, whatever suspicions they may have had of his sincerity. Thus the wishes of the retrospectively orthodox theologians from Ambrose on proved entirely sound, however suspect their underlying motives.

The dogma they produced satisfied a need experienced by nearly all men, including Voltaire himself. Essentially, it sprang and continued to spring from the natural reliance on faith for the solution of a problem which reason, depending ultimately as it does on the senses, could not solve: the problem of communicating with the source of self-conscious life. Seldom if ever, nonetheless, did the tradition flow freely from this source without the interference of less spontaneous interests, particularly those of the priest and the ruler, often the same man. The inextricable fusion of ambition with dedication to one's fellow men and the unceasing instability of a motivation divided between concerns for this world and the next complicate evaluation. But the decisive role of selfish and wordly passions in founding the basic elements of the dogma and in consolidating it against revolt cannot be denied. To cover these passions with the convenient mystery of God's will was unacceptable to the eighteenth century. The relative permanence and universality of the historical result did not reveal a divine origin, but rather the effect of a valuable illusion. It was valuable because the assimilation of the life-giving substance and participation in the redeeming sacrifice encouraged a great many people to live this life well in hopes of obtaining a better one.

2

Voltaire and the eucharist

ALTHOUGH we have little knowledge of Voltaire's childhood, his father's Jansenist inclinations suggest that he received his first communion at an age when children could commune properly, but without any insight into the meaning of the eucharist. Trained rather than educated, they could probably see little more to the rite than a solemn and regular duty which adults expected of them. Anxious to pack the upper echelons of society with loyal Catholic alumni, Jesuits like those who taught Voltaire at Louis-le-Grand did everything they could to encourage this devotional routine. A habit contracted before the awakening of critical reason and rewarded by the approval of adults does not often stimulate thought in an adolescent. At the most, we might expect impertinent blasphemy or pranks at the expense of so sacrosanct a rite, but we hear of none. Nor is there even any evidence that, when the young satirist began to attack other dogmas, the eucharist drew his fire too.

The earliest example of such satire may well be an exercise in English composition written in 1726 during his exile in England.[1] The Small Leningrad Notebook contains an anecdote about a French 'parson' playing piquet with his 'whore', as Voltaire specifies. Meanwhile, many

[1] during the Jansenist convulsions, he had investigated a miracle that involved the sacrament. In 1725, a woman named Lafosse, who had been suffering from a haemorrhage for twenty years, was healed when she followed a procession bearing the eucharist. An appelant priest had consecrated the hostia and, according to the Jansenists, the miracle proved the real presence. Voltaire wrote to the présidente de Bernières that he had visited mme Lafosse several times and that she had visited him. Impressed by his assiduity, cardinal de Noailles invited him to a Te Deum celebrating the miracle, but the deist's language reveals that he hardly took the miracle seriously. 'Je sers Dieu et le diable tout à la fois,' he commented. 'Pour comble (ou d'honneur ou de ridicule)', he remarks, Noailles had mentioned him (though not by name) in a publication concerning the miracle. In the *Siècle de Louis XIV* (1752), he took a few liberties with the facts: 'Le Saint Sacrement [. . .] guérit en vain la femme Lafosse [. . .] au bout de trois mois, et en la rendant aveugle' (M.xv.61). Augustin Gazier protests that she was still alive and healthy in 1751. See *Histoire générale du mouvement janséniste* (Paris 1923), i.276-77.

'devotious' women are waiting before the altar on their 'kneels'. Called 'to administer God', the priest kisses his whore and leaves with his box of communion wafers, into which he has inadvertently dropped some of the ivory counters used in the game. While 'distributing God in wafers', he gives an old woman one of these counters. 'This old jade, having received her portion of God', finds that she cannot swallow it. 'She endeavours to chaw it in vain', and complains to the priest, 'I believe you gave me God the Father, so he is tough and hard.'[2]

At first, Voltaire characteristically ignores the distinction between the persons in the trinity, which he treats as a unity. The notion of administering God himself instead of the eucharist reflects both the presumption of a whoremongering celebrant and the superstition of communicants. The distribution of God in the form of wafers not only reinforces these impressions, but also emphasises the absurdity of the belief that a small object can enclose the entire deity. The portion of God, which recalls Berengar's caricature of Lanfranc's doctrine (see p.44), subjects the spiritual content to the laws governing the material of the container. The old jade restores the distinction between the trinitarian persons by her assumption that God the Father, popularly thought to contrast with the others by his severity, would be hard to chew. The anecdote therefore consists in a series of situations, each of which successively exposes the immaterial to a ridicule implied by its dependence on the material. In each case, common sense refuses to exempt the imperceptible from its judgements of the perceptible, in other words, from the empirical laws of nature. Voltaire's irony resides in the various affronts to God's impregnable dignity, a contradiction implying that eucharistic mystery is illusory and fraudulent. It is a pity that he did not see fit to share his humour with his English public.

In the English edition of the *Henriade* (1728),[3] he inserted a more subtle passage describing the future Henry IV's conversion to Catholicism as if this prince had been moved by divine inspiration and not the desire to rule over a Catholic kingdom. Yet Voltaire's epic versification of this about-face, which involves the eucharist, betrays conflicting intentions on his part:

---

[2] *Notebooks*, ed. Theodore Besterman, *The Complete Works of Voltaire* [hereafter Voltaire] 81-82 (Genève 1968), i,57. A condensed version of this story appears in i.363, in the Leningrad notebooks (1735-1750).

[3] published in England, but untranslated.

Le Christ de nos péchés victime renaissante,
De ses élus chéris nourriture vivante,
Descend sur les autels à ses yeux éperdus,
Et lui découvre un Dieu sous un pain qui n'est plus.
Son cœur obéissant se soumet, s'abandonne
A ces mystères dont son esprit s'étonne.[4]

Did he really expect us to take the schema of transubstantiation in the fourth line seriously? We can scarcely knit our brows over the discovery of God in a piece of bread no longer there. As for the second hemistich in the second line, living food insinuates worse than cannibalism, since cannibals, like the Oreillons in *Candide*, usually put their victims to death before eating them.[5] Voltaire must have had a pious painting in mind when he composed line three. One might hesitate between *rapture* and *bewilderment* in translating *éperdus*, but only until the last line where such sacred mysteries astonish Henry. Astonishment and bewilderment convey either belief or scepticism depending on the inclination of the reader. Looking both ways like Janus, Voltaire was trying to cater to the tastes of both the authorities from whom he craved recognition and his fellow freethinkers eager to applaud his satire. His hypocritical piety nonetheless detracts from his commonsense detection of cannibalism in the real presence and trivially blasphemous magic in transubstantiation.

He no longer finds himself at cross-purposes in discussing communion with the Quaker in the first *Letter concerning the English nation*. Here satire manifestly predominates, but satire of whom? Because of his good sense, the old Quaker ranks high in dignity among characters sketched by Voltaire. When asked what kind of communion Quakers have, he answers that they have nothing of the kind Voltaire has in mind: '"How![6] no communion?" says I. "Only that spiritual one" replied he,[7] "of hearts."'[8] The protest against this omission, the

---

[4] *Henriade*, ed. O. R. Taylor (Voltaire 2), p.617.

[5] 'Candide, apercevant la chaudière et les broches, s'écria: "Nous allons certainement être rôtis ou bouillis"' (René Pomeau, ed., *Candide* (Paris 1959), p.145).

[6] 'Quoi!' in the French version. Gustave Lanson, ed., *Lettres philosophiques* (Paris 1924), i.5. For the original English version, see n.8.

[7] the mixed tenses, 'says I' and 'replied he,' are apparently an oversight corrected in the French translation. See n.10.

[8] *Letters concerning the English nation* (New York 1974), p.5. Harcourt Brown demonstrates that most of the letters, among them the first, were composed in English: 'The composition of the *Letters concerning the English nation*', *The Age of Enlightenment* (London 1967), pp.15-34.

condescension towards the Quaker's efforts to justify it by scripture and the following remark about the Quaker's inspiration are ironical genuflexions for the benefit of orthodox Christians. The Quaker cited 'his texts of Scripture and preached a most eloquent sermon against [communion] as though he had been inspired' (p.5). His imaginary inspiration, as Voltaire describes it, evokes the enthusiastic tendencies of eighteenth-century Jansenism. Among the 101 propositions condemned by Unigenitus were several exhortations for laymen to read the Bible.[9] But how does the Bible disprove the validity of communion? The Quaker 'harangued [. . .] to prove that the sacraments were merely of human invention and that the word *sacrament* was not once mentioned in the gospel' (p.5). Voltaire's gallicised English may be awkward, but it is no less captivating and incisive for that. In reporting the character of Andrew Pitt, whom he had interviewed at Hampstead, he breathed permanent life into the old man. Even when he translated this passage into French for the *Lettres philosophiques,* he managed to preserve the colour of his original English.[10] The Quaker's rejection of communion as a human invention unsupported by scripture could scarcely fail to excite the curiosity of a French public accustomed to appeals from warring religious factions ever since the sixteenth century.

Not until 1738 would this public see the original version of the thirteenth *Lettre philosophique,* the only one rejected by the censor Rothelin in 1734. Composed in French, this text includes a series of paragraphs confronting Catholic explanations of natural phenomena with contradictory scientific discoveries. The following is one of these: 'Le mystère [. . .] de l'Eucharistie [a] beau être [contraire] aux démonstrations connues, [il n'en est] pas moins [révéré] chez les philosophes catholiques qui savent que les objets de la raison et de la foi sont de différente nature' (i.201). The laconic final clause is an ironical echo of the apologetic cliché giving faith priority over reason. It winks at the common sense of readers aware that research into the nature of matter tends to sap faith in the eucharistic dogma. Transubstantiation, which looks suspiciously like a manipulation of convenient abstractions in the scholastic mind, seemed absurd to sensualists following Locke, to

---

[9] for instance, n.80: 'Lectio Sacrae Scripturae est pro omnibus' (Parguez, p.199).

[10] here is the dialogue already quoted in English: 'A l'égard de la communion, lui dis-je, comment en usez-vous? – Nous n'en usons point, dit-il. – Quoi! point de communion? – Non, point d'autre que celle des cœurs' (i.4-5).

whom Voltaire devoted the thirteenth letter in both its preliminary and final versions.

In the previous year when he was arranging to publish the *Letters* in England, he wrote to Formont the story of mme de Fontaine-Martel's death. Although his relations with her do not appear to have gone beyond friendship, he had been living in her house for some time. She became ill and he had to tell her that she was going to die: 'Elle ne voulait point entendre parler des cérémonies du départ; mais j'étais obligé d'honneur à la faire mourir dans les règles.'[11] He brought her a priest, whom he qualifies as half Jansenist and half politician. Having confessed her, the priest was ready to administer last rites: 'Quand ce comédien de Saint-Eustache lui demanda tout haut si elle n'était pas bien persuadée que son Dieu [. . .] était dans l'Eucharistie, elle répondit, "ah, oui!" d'un ton qui m'eût fait pouffer de rire dans des circonstances moins lugubres.' Thus Voltaire applauds her courage and her sarcasm for what he considers superstition. He does not particularly mourn her, however, for she refused to leave anything to her servants. Evidently, his friendship with her depended at least in part on a shared common-sense rejection of dogma such as the real presence.

To this scant harvest of polemic against the eucharist before 1754, one might add a page in the deist *Extrait* of Meslier's atheist *Mémoire*[12] which Voltaire published in 1762 and dated 1742. His enthusiasm for Meslier began in the Cirey period, when he collaborated with mme Du Châtelet in a methodical scrutiny of the Bible. He may also have begun his research on the history of eucharistic dogma in preparation for the *Essai sur les mœurs*, but none of this activity resulted in publication then. Only in Colmar would he, already an old man, realise the potential of the eucharist for antichristian propaganda.

The sporadic and yet intensive research that produced the *Siècle de Louis XIV* began in 1732[13] and the research that produced the *Essai*

---

[11] 27 January 1733; Best.D563. Unless otherwise stated, correspondence is quoted from *Correspondence and related documents*, ed. Theodore Besterman [hereafter Best.D], Voltaire 85-135 (Geneva, Banbury, Oxford 1968-1977).

[12] 'Suivant leurs principes, [les Christicoles] n'ont qu'à dire seulement quatre paroles sur telle quantité de verres de vin, ou de ces petites images de pâte, ils en feront autant de dieux, y en eût-il des millions. Quelle folie! [. . .] C'est ouvrir une porte spacieuse à toutes sortes d'idolâtries [. . .] Et que sont donc nos dieux, que nous tenons enfermés dans des boîtes de peur des souris?' (M.xxiv.335).

[13] according to Voltaire's letter to Thieriot on 13 May, Best.D488.

sur les mœurs, a branch that outgrew the trunk, in 1741.[14] The historical activity, which characterised both the Cirey period and Voltaire's unhappy sojourns in Versailles and Potsdam, continued during his stay in Colmar and well into the Genevan years. His study of Church history at Potsdam must have awakened many a memory of his Jesuit schooling and particularly when he delved into the rites controversy in China to prepare the final chapter of the *Siècle*.

The 'Disputes sur les cérémonies chinoises' treat of the conflict between the Jesuits and the missionaries of other Catholic orders during the seventeenth and early eighteenth centuries. The Jesuits had arrived first, obtained imperial favour and converted many Chinese to Christianity. The validity of these conversions nonetheless depended on a comparison of Confucianism with Christianity, a comparison which, in their opinion, demonstrated belief in the same God and justified tolerance of the traditional Chinese rites their converts continued to observe.[15] In discussing these rites, Voltaire correctly distinguishes between the family cult and the cult in honour of Confucius practised by the intellectual class, but he would never admit the fact that this class tended to agnostic materialism. These cults, which resembled each other, were ancient in origin, especially the ancestral cult. Rowbotham describes them both as follows:

fasting in preparation, testing the victim, burial of the hair and blood, pouring of the wine over the effigy, prostrations, offering of final supplications claiming benefits for the worship offered, offering of wine and flesh before the altar [. . .] prayers and chants.[16]

The use of wine, flesh and blood could scarcely have failed to remind Jesuit missionaries of the eucharist. The challenge to their syncretic

---

[14] according to Voltaire's letter to Frederick on 1 June, Best.D2493.

[15] Matteo Ricci, the founder of the Jesuit mission, reached Peking in 1610. He advanced three arguments in favour of toleration: 1. The rites celebrated social virtue and they had originated in a climate of monotheism; 2. The scholarly aristocracy used the cult of Confucius as an antidote to popular superstition; 3. Interviews with Chinese who practiced the rites had yielded no evidence of idolatry or superstition. Even after other orders had established missions in China, the Jesuits controlled four-fifths of the Christian communities there and nearly all of their converts practiced the rites. They anticipated that Chinese Christians would eventually abandon the rites. Benedict XIV put an end to the ensuing controversy in 1742 by *Ex quo singulari*, which declared the distinction between civic duty and superstition to be practically impossible for the Chinese mind. According to Basil Guy, Chinese 'sacrifice [. . .] in many ways resembles the ritual of the mass' (*The French image of China before and after Voltaire*, Studies on Voltaire 21 (Genève 1963), p.273).

[16] Arnold Rowbotham, *Missionary and mandarin* (Berkeley 1942), p.131.

ingenuity must have been tempting, and yet they wisely avoided this trap.

Other aspects of these rites caught Voltaire's eye. He noted that the worshippers prostrated themselves in keeping with the oriental custom of greeting a superior. The Romans, who had found this custom everywhere they went in Asia, 'l'appelèrent autrefois adorer'. In the Confucian cult, Voltaire also observed, mandarins 'égorgent [...] des animaux dont on fait ensuite des repas' (M.xv.77). It is interesting that the sacrificial aspect of the cult similar to the Hebrew communion meal should attract his attention. Perhaps he owed his curiosity to Tournemine, the teacher at Louis-le-Grand who had the greatest influence on him and one whom the discoveries of Jesuit colleagues in China fascinated.[17] Yet Voltaire elaborated on neither of these remarks, as he probably would have later in more polemical works. Instead, he asked a series of questions designed both to reassure pious readers of his detachment and invite fellow freethinkers to find the answers he knew they would find. The device is more successful than the one he had used for this purpose in the *Henriade*: 'Ces cérémonies sont-elles idolâtriques? sont-elles purement civiles? reconnaît-on ses pères et Confutzée pour des dieux? sont-ils même invoqués seulement comme nos saints? est-ce enfin un usage politique dont quelques Chinois superstitieux abusent?' (M.xv.77). Westerners could decide these questions, he comments, only with difficulty in China and not at all in Europe. He himself avoids giving or appearing to give any answers for them in the rest of this chapter. His own opinion appears in the chapter on Chinese religion in the *Essai sur les mœurs*, a chapter based on the same research. Here he attributes the rites controversy to western prejudices: 'Une génuflexion, qui n'est chez [les Chinois] qu'une révérence ordinaire [...] a paru un acte d'adoration [aux Européens]' (i.222). He therefore agreed with the Jesuits that the rites were merely civic in nature and one can easily ascertain the answers he would have given to the other questions he left unanswered. Neither did he, for instance, consider the rites idolatrous nor did he see any resemblance between them and the veneration of saints, a subordinate form of worship which he did consider idolatrous.

---

[17] in 'Voltaire, sinophile', *Publications of the Modern Language Association* 47 (1932), pp.1050-65, Rowbotham remarks that Tournemine corresponded with Joachim Bouret, one of the most learned Jesuits at the court of Peking.

In the following paragraphs of the chapter in the *Siècle*, sympathy with the Jesuit position emerges and, on the next page, opposition to their enemies.[18] At the end of the *Siècle*, the chapter has the effect of demonstrating how rigorism, rivalry and ignorance had spoiled a great opportunity for Christianity and European culture as epitomised by Louis xiv, even though the latter's name is nowhere to be found. This public lesson taught by history nonetheless overshadows a private lesson retained by the writer. While one could never hope to eradicate religious practices rooted in an ancient tradition, one might be able to drain them of their superstitious content by instituting them as a routine civic duty. Why might one not, for instance, follow the example of the king in conforming to a national custom and thus substitute loyalty to him for the supernatural significance of the rite? Perhaps Voltaire even suspected, as well he might, that many of the courtiers he had known at Versailles were taking Easter communion in this very spirit. The ideas may well have dawned on him during his study of the rites controversy in preparation for the 'Disputes sur les cérémonies chinoises' in 1751.[19]

Having escaped Frederick ii's spite in 1753, he found the road home to Paris blocked by Louis xv's spite. In hopes of appeasing his own king, he settled temporarily in Colmar and undertook a sycophantic letter campaign to convince him of his docility and loyalty. Would he eventually have succeeded? Perhaps. He had many influential friends and Louis the Beloved had seldom distinguished himself by his will-power. Responsibility, in any case, for the failure of the campaign lies at least partly with Voltaire himself, who could not resist the temptation of an opportunity to publish a work offensive to the pious. Some

[18] 'Les jésuites soutinrent la cause des Chinois et de leurs pratiques qu'il semblait qu'on ne pouvait proscrire sans fermer toute entrée à la religion chrétienne, dans un empire si jaloux de ses usages' (M.xv.77).

'Maigrot [. . .] ce Français évêque de la Chine, déclara non seulement les rites observés pour les morts superstitieux et idolâtres, mais il déclara les lettrés athées: c'était le sentiment de tous les rigoristes de France [. . .] Les jésuites [. . .] représentèrent à Rome qu'il paraissait assez incompatible que les Chinois fussent à la fois athées et idolâtres' (M.xv.78). Voltaire would later claim these intellectuals as deist allies.

[19] Fontius believes the work was done between January and March of this year. During this period, Voltaire obtained Hyacinthe d'Avrigny's *Mémoires chronologiques et dogmatiques pour servir à l'histoire ecclésiastique depuis 1600 jusqu'en 1716* (1720, 1739) in 4 vols. He returned two volumes in March. Fontius describes this work as the 'Hauptquelle für die abschliessenden Religionskapitel' (Martin Fontius, *Voltaire in Berlin* (Berlin 1966), p.107).

of the circumstances involved in the publication by the Huguenot Néaulme, based in the Hague and Berlin, of the *Abrégé de l'histoire générale* (1753), an early version of the *Essai sur les mœurs*, remain obscure.[20] But Fontius proves that, despite Voltaire's protestations to the contrary, he knew of Néaulme's project in advance and even collaborated with him to an undetermined extent. Since the appearance of the work in print could scarcely have taken him by surprise, the consternation in his letters of late 1753[21] could only have come from finding his name on the title page. Néaulme was using the name to sell the book, though at the author's expense and certainly without his permission. The Church and the pious faction in the government, whose waning powers no longer fully supported their pretensions, usually did not feel strong enough to retaliate against an author who denied responsibility for an offensive work. When his name appeared on the title page, however, they thought he was flaunting this relative weakness and they reacted by an angry determination to punish him. The *Abrégé* therefore caused a storm of protest and pious courtiers promptly brought to it Louis's attention. Thus the king told his mistress, mme de Pompadour, whom Voltaire had asked to intercede on his behalf, that he did not want him to return to Paris.[22]

Though discouraged, Voltaire did not despair. He wrote many letters repudiating the *Abrégé* and sought to publish denials of responsibility for it in periodicals. He even engaged notaries to confirm the dissimilarity between the printed text, taken from an early manuscript, and a recent manuscript presenting a more advanced version of the work. He gave the act they drew up maximum circulation, so that a copy soon reached the king, but to no avail. The violation of the taboo against signing subversive works seems to have provided Louis, who did not trust him anyway, with a pretext to keep him away from Paris.

[20] despite Fontius's considerable contribution in *Voltaire* (see pp.121-50), the following mysteries are intact: Which of several stolen manuscripts did Néaulme print? What exactly was the process of transmission? What role did Voltaire's bitter, yet almost insignificant enemy Rousset de Missy play? And most important of all, to what extent did Voltaire collaborate with Néaulme?

[21] to d'Argental on 21 December: 'Jean Néaulme me coupe la gorge' (Best.D5596).

[22] another mystery concerning Néaulme's publication of the *Abrégé* is the author of a sentence inserted in the initial paragraph: 'Les historiens, semblables en cela aux rois, sacrifient le genre humain à un seul homme.' Louis must have resented this sentence and Frederick, despite Fontius's arguments to the contrary, may possibly have ordered this insertion, for Néaulme was his printer.

Even more than the failure of his plea for royal forgiveness, the threat of excommunication and imprisonment drove Voltaire to impugn the accuracy and fidelity of the *Abrégé*. The lightning in the distance suddenly struck at his doorstep when the Jesuit Mérat preached a sermon against him in Colmar. On the request of Kroust (director of the Jesuit school in Colmar, the rector of the local Jesuit college, Menoux, whom Voltaire had met at the court of Stanislas, had sent Mérat from Nancy. Mérat also reported Voltaire to the prince-bishop of Basel residing in Porrentruy and 'ce Porentru', as Voltaire called him,[23] alerted the Attorney-General of the Strasbourg *parlement*. But Voltaire persuaded the minister comte d'Argenson, a schoolmate at Louis-le-Grand, to block the proceedings against him. He also complained to Menoux about Mérat and, although Menoux was more interested in trying to convert him by stressing his age and illness, Mérat eventually paid Voltaire a peace-making visit and was later reassigned. The writer must have felt relieved at this point, but certainly not serene. In contrast with the teachers at Louis-le-Grand and the missionaries in China, he found the Jesuits in Northeastern France intolerant and aggressive. In a letter to the marquis d'Argens, a former colleague at Potsdam, he had described Colmar as half-German, half-French and entirely Iroquois, in other words, half barbarian, half civilised and entirely savage. In fact, the *Lettres juives*, published by d'Argens earlier that year, had been burned there 'en bonne compagnie': 'Un brave iroquois jésuite, nommé Aubert, prêcha si vivement contre Bayle et contre vous[24] que sept personnes chargées du sacrifice apportèrent chacune leur Bayle et le brûlèrent dans la place publique.'[25] Voltaire asks d'Argens to send him the Bayle dictionary in Frederick's palace so that he may burn that one too. Surely the king will consent! Having witnessed the burning of his own *Akakia* in Berlin, Voltaire facetiously substituted the burning of authors for that of books as if this substitution were an accomplished fact. Despite his merry nonchalance here and elsewhere,[26] this burnt offering of books by freethinkers living and dead – for he considered Bayle a freethinker – gave him pause after Mérat's sermon.

[23] to d'Argental, 24 February 1754 (Best.D5691).
[24] d'Argens borrowed most of his material from Bayle.
[25] 3 March 1754 (Best.D5705).
[26] in letters to count d'Argenson on 20 February (Best.D5682) and d'Argental on 24 February, he tells the same story, but without mentioning d'Argens's book.

Two further aspects of his stay in Colmar conditioned the communion of 1754, his illness or hypochondria and the hoax of his death. How seriously must we take the routine complaints about his health in the correspondence? While approaching his sixtieth birthday, he was enduring a particularly discouraging and even humiliating period in his life. He had often been ill, once almost fatally, and had watched several close friends die.[27] Increasingly, he kept to his bed or bedroom where he nonetheless continued to work as hard as ever. Poor health had become more a habit than a reality, a habit no doubt half-consciously cultivated and exploited. He took overdoses of medicine in a day when pharmacology was not very advanced and the various diagnoses of his ailments stimulated a morbid curiosity. He actually bragged to his correspondents that he had not left his room for six months, a boast that became a refrain. Most of them paid little attention to this talk, but Menoux, in his haste to snatch the devil's most promising soul, was ready to administer last rites a little too early. Voltaire would remember this clerical vice. He needed the Jesuit's cooperation too urgently to think of duping Menoux, but another correspondent, whose identity remains unknown, inspired a hoax that illustrates his remarkable serenity about death. He identifies the man merely as 'un vieux baron de Lorraine, dévot comme un sot'.[28] Here is what happened: 'Retiré dans son château, [il] s'est avisé de m'écrire sans me connaître une douzaine de lettres pour me convertir. J'ai pris enfin le parti de les lui renvoyer, en lui mandant que j'étais mort.'[29] The news found its way into a number of contemporary periodicals and, according to Kieffer, friends and enemies, from January until March of 1754, thought he was dead.[30] The incident, to say the least, reveals a rare sense of humour.

By Easter of that year (14 April), his plight had eased somewhat, but the future seemed as yet to hold little promise for him. Since Louis, despite Voltaire's efforts, had not relented, a return to Paris was out

[27] he nearly died of smallpox in 1723 and his friend de Maisons did die of this disease. He also attended the deaths of the actress Adrienne Lecouvreur (1730), his friends mme de Fontaine-Martel (1733) and mme Du Châtelet (1747).

[28] to the Duchess of Saxe-Gotha, 12 January (Best.D5622).

[29] to mme Denis, 9 January (Best.D5621).

[30] 'Le bruit court que de Voltaire est mort,' the Neveu tells Bertin's other guests in Denis Diderot, *Le Neveu de Rameau* (Paris 1950), p.33. Jean Fabre, the editor of this edition, notes (p.172, n.120): 'Le bruit en avait couru, en effet, à trois reprises: à la fin de 1753, à l'automne 1760 [. . .] au printemps 1762 [. . .] Voltaire s'en amusait fort, y voyait un excellent moyen de propagande et l'occasion de jouer un mauvais tour aux gens trop expressés de l'enterrer.'

of the question. Although the local threat of retaliation had receded, his appetite for publication would sooner or later give the Alsatian Jesuits and the bishop of Porrentruy another opportunity. Where was he to go? Discreet inquiries had revealed that Frederick no longer extended his hospitality to him, and so there was no avenue of retreat in that direction. The count de Tressan, a false friend, persuaded Stanislas that permission for him to reside in Lorraine would offend Frederick. The Supreme Council of Bern, in 1752, had declined when he offered to dedicate one of his tragedies to them, an inhospitable gesture. Only later would he receive enthusiastic invitations from Geneva[31] and Lausanne. Time seemed to be closing in on him, for nothing encouraged him to look forward to another twenty-four years of activity. The professional playwright and amateur actor conceived the need for action dramatic enough to extricate himself from his predicament.

Nor did his eventual act occur to him on the spur of the moment. On 24 February, he had written to d'Argental to console him: 'On dit que vous étes malade comme moi [. . .] Voici le temps de profiter de voïes du salut que Le Clergé ouvre à tous Les fidèles' (Best.D5691). He devoted the rest of the letter to a humorous exposition of pious repression in Alsace, including the aforementioned burning of Bayle's dictionary. As one might have expected, therefore, the context does not authorise the usual interpretation of *salut* and *fidèles*. On the contrary, salvation means escape from pious retaliation in this life, and the faithful are freethinkers like Voltaire and the 'cher ange' to whom he is writing. Although he does not identify the *voies de salut*, he must have had the sacraments in mind. The Jesuits of Louis-le-Grand could hardly have failed to acquaint him with their unceasing availability. By Easter of 1754, their most illustrious and embarrassing alumnus must have realised that some of the Company and Menoux in particular coveted the prestige of a brilliant conversion more than the profound conviction of a beloved disciple. In a letter to countess de Lutzelbourg on 13 March, he made an ironical promise to bring her his 'billet de confession' after Easter. The absurdity of trying to enforce belief in dogma by legal documentation was an invitation to Voltaire, who made a career of mocking subservience to such pious tyranny. In March or April, he wrote a second letter to 'mon cher diable' the marquis d'Argens, in which he ridicules Maupertuis's return to Catholicism after years of

[31] alerted by Vernet, who was editing the *Histoire générale*, the brothers Cramer wrote to him for the first time on 15 April.

free thought: 'Je conçois qu'un diable aille à la messe quand il est en terre papale comme Nancy ou Colmar, mais vous devez gémir lorsqu'un enfant de Belzébuth va à la messe par hypocrisie et par vanité' (Best. D5756). Since Berlin was in a Protestant land, he could find no better motive for his enemy's uncharacteristic devotion than vanity and hypocrisy. This judgement is probably unfair,[32] but it shows that some time before Easter[33] he wanted d'Argens to distinguish between what Maupertuis was doing and what he himself was going to do. Thus attending mass in a Protestant country disgraces a freethinker, but not in a Catholic one.

Voltaire's secretary Collini reveals what happened at Easter.[34] The writer had told him that he was going to commune with him. A Capuchin monk appeared and the secretary left them alone in the bedroom. At church the next day, Voltaire and Collini took communion side by side and the secretary stole a glance: Voltaire 'présentait sa langue et fixait ses yeux bien ouverts sur la physionomie du prêtre. Je connaissais ces regards-là' (Collini, p.128). Noyes is right to observe that Catholic communicants receive the communion wafer directly on the tongue, but his attempts to establish Voltaire's sincerity convince almost no one. Artists have captured the mischievous sparkle to which Collini is referring.[35] Neither this look nor the circumstances lend any

[32] Maupertuis was deeply troubled by this time and who is to say that his return to Catholicism was not sincere?

[33] unless he had already taken communion and intended this letter to prepare d'Argens for the news whenever and however it should reach him. But this discretion seems unnecessary with d'Argens.

[34] friends in Paris, Collini testifies, had been informed that Voltaire would be expected to commune and spies were watching him to see if he would comply. It seems likely that he was being watched, but not for this purpose. No allusion to such an expectation appears in the correspondence (Côme-Alexandre Collini, *Mon Séjour auprès de Voltaire* (Paris 1970), p.127).

[35] according to Louis Gielly, three artists were especially successful in portraying Voltaire: the painters Largillière and La Tour, and the sculptor Houdon (*Voltaire: documents iconographiques* (Geneva 1948)). Gielly agrees with Georges Pascal on Largillière's portrait of Voltaire at the age of twenty-four: 'des yeux pétillants de finesse et d'esprit' (Gielly, pp.10-11); 'ces yeux pétillants d'esprit': Pascal, *Largillière* (Paris 1928), p.36. Extant copies of La Tour's pastel (1736) made a different impression on Alfred Leroy: 'Les yeux illuminent une physionomie où les vicissitudes de l'existence ont laissé leur empreinte' (*Quentin de La Tour et la société française du XVIIIe siècle* (Paris 1953), p.64). H. H. Arnison shows that Houdon endowed his statues of Voltaire with extraordinary vitality by the following technique: 'He cut out the entire iris, bored a deeper hole for the pupil and, by allowing a small fragment of the material to overhang the iris, established an illusionistic effect of light and shadow that made the eye actually appear to move' (p.20). The sculptor derived many variants and copies, including the chefs-d'œuvre

support to the hypothesis of a heartfelt, but unacknowledged, belief in the eucharist. Afterwards, Collini adds, the unlikely communicant sent twelve bottles of a good wine and a loin of veal to the Capuchin monastery, a fitting reward for having confessed a devil!

Two days later (16 April), Voltaire wrote one letter to mme Denis and another to d'Argental. He had no more loyal or sympathetic friend than d'Argental, yet he told him nothing of his communion. He did include his version of the incident in his letter to his niece, after an allusion to a poem by Gentil-Bernard (Best.D5779):

Colmar est une singulière petite ville. On est venu me faire des compliments en cérémonie sur ce que j'avais fait mes pâques. Je m'étais confessé dans mon lit au gardien des capucins. Voicy ma confession: 'Il y a six mois que je suis malade, sans sortir de ma chambre. Je n'ay pas eu de grandes tentations et mes péchez se réduisent à avoir été fort en colère contre un jésuitte.' 'Ah si ce n'est que contre un jésuitte', m'a dit le capucin, 'il n'y a pas grand mal.' Il m'a donné un beau billet de confession. J'en ay un encore plus beau de communion. Je serai sauvé, mais dans ce monde je veux une bonne édition de mes ouvrages.

This nonchalant transition to a desire he would have us believe unrequited in his lifetime slyly invites mme Denis to look upon his communion as a routine event. Not this communion, he is insinuating, but the compliments by the locals deserve her curiosity. As we have seen, he had already announced the confession certificate and his salvation, though apparently not to mme Denis. Whatever he and the Capuchin actually told each other, the joke at the expense of the Jesuits was clever enough to distract attention from his equivocal participation in the primary sacrament of the Church. Before another letter to his niece on 5 May, he did not mention this startling act in any other extant correspondence and, even there, his nonchalance and brevity appear calculated (Best.D5803):

Vous ne m'avez pas cru aparemment, quand je vous ay dit qu'il y a bientôt sept mois que je passe ma vie en robe de chambre, que je ne mange point de viande, et que je ne suis sorti qu'une seule fois pour faire mes pâques. Avec du jeûne et des sacrements, je ne conçois pas comment il y a de méchantes gens qui ne me regardent pas comme un bon crétien.

Here again, he was trying to integrate his communion into the routine to which he had accustomed mme Denis and the Parisian friends with

in the Comédie-Française and the Hermitage in Leningrad, from a single study of Voltaire shortly before his death (*The Sculptures of Houdon* (London 1975)).

whom she shared his letters. While six months in his bedroom were stretching to seven, he substituted the sacrament for the meat eliminated from his diet. His ironical incomprehension of how the unkind could suspect his Christianity seems less a complaint about pious reaction to his deed, as Kieffer assumes,[36] than a remark intended to delight his fellow devils who should know when to slap their sides. Obviously, he had not sought to provoke such a reaction and there is little evidence that the Easter of 1754 caused anything like the twin scandals of 1768 and 1769.

Except for the naive hospitality offered him that summer by Calmet, abbot of Senones, it availed him nothing, because it did not change Louis's mind and the invitations from Geneva and Lausanne opened an escape route to the south. It is a pity that he had no further opportunity to test the local Jesuits by taking sacraments. What would they have done about this subversion of the formalism they taught and the exemplification they sought? What subtle counterattack would these disciplined troops have used against so wicked a manœuvre? This we will never know. Emerging from the Colmar ordeal unscathed, Voltaire had learned a few valuable lessons. In age, illness and approaching death, the poet and actor no longer saw merely an edifying or convenient role, but also a tactical advantage. The antichristian polemicist realised that a notorious freethinker could degrade the sacraments simply by participating in them and thus demonstrate their absurdity for the benefit of the natural light. The deist historian may even have thought that he had found a way to influence the manners to which he was devoting his *Essai* and provoke a decisive mutation in them. The sacramental formalism preached by the Jesuits and the civic edification they claimed for the Chinese rites form a most intriguing background to the communion of 1754. After all, it made good sense to commune in a Catholic country.

The communion in Colmar had not distracted Voltaire from the composition of a third volume for the *Essai sur l'histoire générale*, the re-entitled and corrected *Abrégé*, and all three volumes reappeared in 1754. After revising this text, supplementing it and incorporating the *Siècle* in it, he published another edition under the same title in his complete works printed by the Cramers in 1756. He continued to re-edit

[36] 'Il se plaint à sa nièce de l'animosité qui règne contre lui' (Kieffer, 'De la vie', p.107).

the text and in the quarto edition of his complete works, printed by Gabriel Cramer in 1769, he re-entitled it again as the *Essai sur les mœurs et l'esprit des nations et sur les principaux faits de l'histoire depuis Charlemagne jusqu'à Louis XIII*. He now excluded the *Siècle* and included the *Philosophie de l'histoire* (1765) as an introduction re-entitled 'Discours préliminaire'.

First published in the *Abrégé*, chapter 21 on the 'Rites religieux du temps de Charlemagne' betokens a passing interest in the eucharist. Voltaire notes that all communicants received both species under Charlemagne, that the Greek church conserved this practice and that it continued in the Roman church until the thirteenth century. At the end of the paragraph in which this statement occurs, he concludes, 'Toutes ces pratiques changèrent selon la conjoncture des temps, et selon la prudence des pasteurs, ou selon le caprice, comme tout change.'[36a] He seems to have intended the equivocal combination of *et* and *ou* to camouflage his insinuation that the hazards of history and priestly expedient, rather than divine influence, caused modifications in the sacraments.

Likewise published in 1753, chapter 45 treats the earliest eucharistic controversies, that of the ninth century, which Voltaire sets in the tenth, and that of the eleventh century. He warns his readers against the assumption that 'du temps de Clovis [465-511] [...] on fut parfaitement instruit dans les Alpes du dogme de la transubstantiation' (i.484). Before undertaking to found this warning on fact, he tries to explain why no earlier controversy had occurred. Together with predestination, he supposes, the relations between the persons of the trinity and between the two natures in Christ preoccupied the Platonic imagination of Hellenistic Christians in the early centuries. He reinforces this solid and precise reason by another nearly as solid, but vague (i.485):

Si du pain et du vin sont changés en la seconde personne de la Trinité, et par conséquent en Dieu, si on mange et on boit cette seconde personne réellement ou par la foi: cette question [...] était d'un autre genre, qui ne paraissait pas soumis à la philosophie de ce temps.

No doubt, but why? He does not say. Perhaps the Platonic belief that matter merely approaches the reality of thought offered obvious solutions to these problems. The Platonist mind had little difficulty in converting and assimilating ideas, but Voltairian common sense could hardly accept an ephemeral status for the material objects perceived

---

[36a] *Essai sur les mœurs*, ed. René Pomeau (Paris 1963), i.360.

by the senses, since it depends on them for knowledge. Impatient with Platonism, which he blamed for much of the mysticism he found in Christianity, Voltaire was probably content to dismiss it as incompatible with eucharistic speculation.

He understood that the dispute between Paschase and Ratramn concerned the real presence, but he found the position defended by Ratramn and others, among whom he included John the Scot (see p.39), obscure: '[Ils] avaient écrit sur ce mystère d'une manière à faire penser qu'ils ne croyaient pas ce qu'on appela depuis la réelle présence' (i.485). In 1753, he supported this assertion by a quotation from Ratramn's *On the body*: 'C'est le corps de Jésus-Christ qui est vu, reçu, et mangé, non par les sens corporels, mais par les yeux de l'esprit fidèle.'[37] Actually, this Augustinian thought suits Paschase as well as Ratramn. In 1761, Voltaire added two more quotations from the same work: 'Il n'y a aucun changement dans le pain et dans le vin; ils ne sont donc que ce qu'ils étaient auparavant.'[38] 'Le pain appelé corps, et le vin appelé sang, sont une figure, parce que c'est un mystère.'[39] The second quotation does not distinguish Ratramn from Paschase either, but the first, on the contrary, indicates the bone of contention between them. Other passages in Ratramn puzzled Voltaire because they seemed to contradict these or even support the real presence. The reality of Christ's bodily presence in the sacrament, on one hand, and the difference between the sacramental and the heavenly bodies, on the other, must have confused him. Voltairian reason could not attain the reconciliation of these propositions through the Platonic reality of ideas. The proper interpretation of Ratramn's *Body* is, moreover, controversial even today. Instead of trying to untie the knot, Voltaire cut it in 1761: 'De quelque manière qu'il s'entendît et qu'on l'entendît, on écrivit contre lui' (i.486). Ratramn's criticism of the eucharist apparently distracted him from Paschase's opinion, which would nonetheless prevail. To Paschase, he merely attributes the introduction of the real presence, an error, and he inserts a standard quotation from his *Body* (see p.31).

He introduces his discussion of the dispute between Paschase and Ratramn by referring to a manuscript in the Bodleian Library at Oxford.

---

[37] i.485; 'Id est Christi corpus ostenditur quod non sensibus carnis, sed animi fidelis contuitu vel aspicitur, vel accipitur, vel comeditur' (Ratramn, ix).

[38] i.485; '*Si ergo nihil est hic permutatum, non est aliud quam ante fuit*' (Ratramn, xiii).

[39] i.486; 'Quod panis qui corpus Christi, et calix, qui sanguis Christi appellatur, figura sit, quia misterium' (Ratramn, xcvii).

Here is part of his quotation from this document: 'Le corps dans lequel Jésus-Christ souffrit, et le corps eucharistique sont entièrement différents. Le premier était composé de chair et d'os animés par une âme raisonnable; mais ce que nous nommons eucharistie n'a ni sang, ni os, ni âme' (i.485). This tenth-century text, he infers, suggests that, in many English churches at that time, 'on croyait qu'on ne mangeait et qu'on ne buvait Dieu que spirituellement' (i.485). The remark is naive in that all western churches taught the presence of a body not only spiritual but also real. This spiritual presence, in other words, did not, according to the prevailing opinion, contradict the reality of the presence as he implies. Voltairian good sense could not comprehend the Platonic compatibility between a spiritual and a real presence. But Voltaire's quotation is more radical than his comment, since it distinguishes between the sacramental and the heavenly bodies. He did not realise that Aelfric the Grammarian (*ca.* 950-1020), who wrote the paschal homily from which this passage came, had borrowed the distinction from Ratramn. Ratramn had few such disciples, and few churches in England or elsewhere adopted his doctrine, as Voltaire would have us believe. This insinuation illustrates the danger of commonsense judgement where evidence is sparse.

Voltaire committed another error when he accredited the legend of a Stercorian heresy resulting from the dispute between Paschase and Ratramn. The Stercoranists, he wrote in 1761, 'prétendirent qu'on digérait le pain et le vin sacrés, et [que ceux-ci] suivaient le sort ordinaire des aliments' (i.486). Yet, according to Gaudel,[40] these heretics never existed. The continuing sensual appearances of bread and wine after consecration, much emphasised by Ratramn, worried Paschasian theologians. Unaware of the later distinction between subject and accidents, they found themselves obliged to dismiss these appearances as a mere illusion. In their zeal to protect this vulnerable position, they reacted to commonsense interpretations of these appearances with accusations of Stercoranism. They even managed to convince themselves that heretics of this persuasion actually existed and this conviction became an obsession. The legend thus propagated came down to Voltaire who accepted it uncritically. Although he had no reason to doubt the precedent set by the alleged Stercoranists, he did not elaborate in the *Essai*, but merely exposed the reasoning attributed to them. Only later would a jocular obscenity at the expense of the eucharist evolve.

[40] A. Gaudel, 'Stercoranisme', *Dictionnaire de théologie catholique*.

The space allotted to Berengar from 1753 on implies that Voltaire thought he had found a kindred spirit in him. Enthusiastically, he introduces him as one who had written and taught that 'le corps véritable de Jésus-Christ n'est point et ne peut être sous les apparences du pain et du vin' (i.486). In Berengar's assault on Paschasian metabolism, he finds several commonsense arguments in which he takes delight: what causes indigestion when overeaten can only be food; what inebriates when drunk in excessive quantities is a real liquid; there can be no whiteness without a white object and no roundness without a round object;[41] it is impossible for one body to be in a thousand places at the same time. All of these arguments and especially the last would serve his polemical purposes. After this summary of Berengar's critical position, he produces a quotation from Lanfranc claiming that the body born of the Virgin is the same in substance as the eucharistic body, though not in form. The Church concurred with this opinion, he observes: 'Bérenger n'avait raisonné qu'en philosophe. Il s'agissait [. . .] d'un mystère que l'Eglise reconnaissait comme incompréhensible [. . .] Il devait donc [. . .] soumettre sa raison comme elle, disait-on' (i.487). In noting the discipline inflicted on Berengar, he remarks, 'cette rétraction forcée ne fit que graver plus avant ses sentiments dans son cœur' (i.487). He also mentions the temporal preoccupations contributing to Berengar's humiliations, a further source of embarrassment for the Church. Ratramn and Berengar's tendency continued, he asserts, and reappeared among the Vaudois, the Albigeois, the Hussites and the Protestants.

In 1761, he inserted in the text a general statement which serves as a partial conclusion to this account of the first two eucharistic controversies: 'Dans toutes les disputes qui ont animé les chrétiens les uns contre les autres depuis la naissance de l'Eglise, Rome s'est toujours décidée pour l'opinion qui soumettait le plus l'esprit humain, et qui anéantissait le plus le raisonnement' (i.487). When one allows for typical stylistic exaggerations, *toutes*, *toujours* and *le plus* twice,[42] this remark has the ring of truth. The arbitrary preference of mysterious to reasonable solutions of doctrinal problems definitely exposed the

[41] a scholastic commonplace. Apparently, the specific whiteness and roundness of a human body are meant, for communion wafers are white and round.

[42] Jeanne Monty describes his use of the indefinite pronoun *tout* as 'un tic verbal, par lequel s'exprime, d'une manière inconsciente peut-être, la personnalité de l'auteur. Pour Voltaire il n'existe pas de milieu entre la superstition et la sagesse, l'intolérance et la tolérance', *Etude sur le style polémique de Voltaire: Le Dictionnaire philosophique*, Studies on Voltaire 44 (1966), p.39.

Church to the accusations of enhancing its prestige and expanding its power over the faithful by its claim to competence in the supernatural sphere. In the same addition of 1761, Voltaire illustrates this criticism by testifying to the psychological effect of the real presence on the communicant, which he had almost certainly experienced as a child (i.488):

La croyance d'un dieu réellement présent dans l'eucharistie, passant dans la bouche et dans l'estomac d'un communiant, le remplissait d'une terreur religieuse. Quel respect ne devait-on pas avoir pour ceux qui changeaient d'un mot le pain en dieu, et surtout pour le chef d'une religion qui opérait un tel prodige!

It is difficult not to see irony in this testimony and perhaps bitter irony, for deception of children often produces resentment in adults. Voltaire, moreover, has already begun to exploit the Stercorian theory of digesting the divinity for satiric purposes. Such a reduction to the absurd, he realised, forces a decision between resignation and revolt, and he knew he could rely on a revolt by most of his contemporaries. 'Quand la simple raison humaine combattit ces mystères', he hints, 'elle affaiblit l'objet de sa vénération' (i.488). Too great a number of priests working the miracle constantly, he adds, trivialise it, thus banality exposes transubstantiation and the real presence to the corrosive effect of reason.

The *Essai* returns to the eucharist in chapter 73 (1753), which concerns Wyclif, Hus and Jerome of Prague. Voltaire finds that Wyclif renewed Berengar's criticism and 'soutint qu'il ne faut rien croire d'impossible et de contradictoire, qu'un accident ne peut subsister sans sujet' (i.698). This language evokes Wyclif's protest against the subsistence of bread and wine accidents after their substances have become those of Christ's body and blood. The contradiction between sensual appearances and the absence of the corresponding substance appeals to Voltaire's empirically conditioned mind: 'Le pain et le vin de l'eucharistie demeurent du pain et du vin' (i.698). Between the two passages quoted, he inserted in 1761 an echo of Berengar he found in Wyclif: 'Un même corps ne peut être à la fois, tout entier, en cent mille endroits' (i.698). This objection to the miraculous distribution of a body remaining whole in heaven would proliferate in his works. Having said little about Wyclif, he neglects the role of Wyclif's eucharistic doctrines in the Hus affair, which he nonetheless relates in some detail. He does say that Hus rejected Wyclif's doctrine and adopted only his hostility to abuses of Church power. In reality, Hus went further, approving all that was orthodox in the English theologian.

Chapter 128 on Luther, which first appeared in 1756, reveals no great sympathy with him either. Voltaire suspected the self-generating passion that transformed a monk protesting against abuses into the founder of a rebellious church. The campaign against private masses struck him as demagogy: Luther 'se déchaîna contre les messes privées, et il fut d'autant plus applaudi qu'il se récriait contre la vente publique de ces messes' (ii.219). The violence conveyed by the verbs *se déchaîner* and *se récrier* suggests that Voltaire thought Luther's outrage excessive. The phlegmatic sentences following explain that the celebration of private masses began in the thirteenth century (an error),[43] that they afforded a meagre pittance to mendicant friars and poor priests, and that the people pay for them just as they pay for anything else, in other words, willingly. Voltaire thus insinuates that Luther was capitalising on an unreasonable pretext.

The tone changes, however, when he turns to the Lutheran rebuke of transubstantiation. He welcomes the observation that the doctrine appears neither in scripture nor in the Fathers. His presentation of a claim by Luther's partisans implies approval: 'La doctrine qui fait évanouir la substance du pain et du vin, et qui en conserve la forme, n'avait été universellement établie dans l'Eglise que du temps de Grégoire VII [le Grand]' (ii.219). He reproduces their opinion that the development of this theory had begun with the work of Paschase, when in reality, it goes back at least to Ambrose. Luther himself, he reports, retained part of the mystery and rejected the rest. Since Voltaire had referred to transubstantiation in his opening sentence, however, he might have avoided ambiguity here by stating that Luther dropped this doctrine and kept the real presence. The reformer, he continues, 'avoue que le corps de Jésus-Christ est dans les espèces consacrées; mais il y est, dit-il, comme le feu est dans le fer enflammé: le fer et le feu subsistent ensemble' (ii.219). This ancient simile naturally appealed to his empirical bent. He also cites three prepositions used by Luther to convey the mysterious incorporation of Christ's body and blood in the bread and wine: 'dedans, dessus, et dessous, *in, cum,*[44] *sub*' (ii.219). Despite such

---

[43] according to 'Stipends' in the *New Catholic encyclopedia* (Toronto 1967), private masses may have been celebrated in the sixth century, but certainly in the eighth. They were common by the eleventh century.

[44] *dessus* oversimplifies *cum*. See pp.65-66

temptations as the ambiguity of these prepositions, Voltaire curiously refrains from ironical comment on Luther's eucharistic revolt. The wish to be taken seriously as a historian may have motivated this restraint. Yet he may also have been relying on the ironical contrast between the sober context and the intrinsic absurdity of concepts remote from human experience and, therefore, without resonance in the common understanding.

In 1769, on the other hand, he added an openly ironical conclusion comparing the Lutheran with the Calvinist and the Catholic interpretations: 'Tandis que ceux qu'on appelait *papistes* mangeaient Dieu sans pain, les luthériens mangeaient du pain, et Dieu. Les calvinistes vinrent bientôt après, qui mangèrent le pain, et qui ne mangèrent point Dieu' (ii.219). Trinitarian and eucharistic dogmas justify this satirical synecdoche substituting God for Christ's bodily presence in the sacrament. The triple distinction between various combinations of eating bread, a natural food, and God, an unnatural food, exposes the first two sects to ridicule and the third as well, though to a lesser extent. The irony of this conclusion tends to contaminate the entire passage on the Lutheran alteration of eucharistic theology. The reader can scarcely avoid the impression that Voltaire classes it with other instances of quibbling over abstractions inaccessible to common sense. We will see more of these enumerations.

Though he devoted part of the next chapter (129), likewise published in 1756, to Zwingli, he omitted the Marburg Colloquium which had opposed the reformer from Zurich to Luther. Yet he did give a synopsis of Zwingli's eucharistic doctrine. More radical than Luther, Zwingli rejected both impanation and invination: 'Il n'admet point que Dieu entrât dans le pain et dans le vin, moins encore que tout le corps de Jésus-Christ fût tout entier dans chaque parcelle et dans chaque goutte' (ii.226). The presence of the whole body in every piece of bread and drop of wine varies the refrain of a single body in a thousand different places. Voltaire apparently felt that the remark was enough to indicate the continuing rejection of eucharistic mysteries on empirical grounds during the Reformation, even though Luther retained some of them. Satisfied with this point, apparently, he dropped the subject.

Among the sixteen chapters he added in 1761 was one (172) on the Council of Trent. For once, he openly acknowledged the source he preferred, Paolo Sarpi's *Istoria del concilio tridentino* (1619). In this work he found the account of a dispute over the eucharist between Franciscans and Dominicans during the proceedings: 'Les cordeliers soutiennent que le corps de Dieu [...] passe d'un lieu à un autre; et les jacobins affirment [...] qu'il est fait en un instant du pain transsubstantié' (ii.506). While this sentence condenses three paragraphs in the *Istoria*,[45] it gives prominence to a minor incident which Sarpi keeps in perspective. The degree and accuracy of the condensation deserve praise, but not the isolation and emphasis of this particular dispute. Voltaire appears to have selected it for special treatment, because disagreement between rival orders of the Church weakens confidence in the disputed doctrine and because their incompatible interpretations of transubstantiation imply that speculation beyond the limits of experience results in contradiction. His reduction of the dispute to terms which common sense can grasp also strips it of the linguistic envelope protecting theological debate from scrutiny by the uninitiated. Since his presentation of the conflicting arguments exposes the futility of the quarrel from an empirical viewpoint, he did not really need to reveal his ironical intentions.

In his restatement of the council's decision on concomitance, he resorted to less subtle tongue-in-cheek humour. When read for the first time, the passage leaves one with a misleading impression of restraint: 'Le corps et le sang sont ensemble dans chaque espèce par concomitance, tout entiers, reproduits en un instant dans chaque parcelle et dans chaque goutte, auxquelles on doit un culte de latrie' (ii.506). But the conciliar decree neither mentions pieces of bread and drops of wine nor stipulates a cult of latria for these material things (see p.69). The first point reduces concomitance to empirical absurdity and the second implies a crude idolatry which the council never intended. The worship of pieces and drops recalls, no doubt intentionally, the passages in earlier chapters of the *Essai* registering protests by Berengar, Wyclif and Zwingli over the distribution of Christ's body. Voltaire is insinuating that the Church, faced with the challenge of Protestantism, entrenched itself even more deeply in its obscurantism. Despite its claim to divine inspiration, it spurned common sense.

The dispute over the lay cup at Trent drew further irony from the author of the *Essai*. The reasons given by the opponents of concession seemed feeble to him: 'La manne du désert, figure de l'eucharistie, avait été mangée sans boire [...] Jonathas ne but point en mangeant son miel [...] Jésus-Christ, en donnant le pain aux apôtres, les traita en

[45] those beginning with the following phrases: 'Quando si venne ad esprimere', 'Volevano in somma le dominicani' and 'Li francescani desideravano che' (Bari 1935).

laïques, et [. . .] il les fit prêtres en leur donnant du vin' (ii.510). The
trivial *manger sans boire* ridicules the tenuous parallel between the
manna of Exodus[46] and the bread of the eucharist initially drawn by
Paul.[47] Jonathan unknowingly broke the fast imposed by Saul, his
father, when he dipped a stick in a honeycomb and ate a 'mouthful of
honey' (1 Samuel ii.9): the connection with the eucharist is even more
remote. The final argument would qualify as the most ludicrous of the
three, if Voltaire had not simplified it abusively. The enemies of the
lay cup actually argued that Jesus had only shared bread with the two
followers he met on the road to Emmaus, while he had distributed both
bread and wine to his disciples at the Last Supper. Nothing in the
Emmaus episode, other than the routine Jewish custom of breaking
bread, authorises a eucharistic interpretation, but they insisted that Jesus
was treating the disciples as priests and the two followers as laymen.[48]
Though wishful, this thinking is not as devious as Voltaire insinuates.
His simplification amplifies the bias of the prelates opposed to the lay
cup, thus adjusting it to common sense.

In chapter 196, added in 1756, he foreshadows future propaganda
against the eucharist while discussing the extinction of Christianity
in Japan. Towards the end, he notes offhand that bread and wine had
been unknown to more than half the world before the sixteenth century
and to much of America and Africa even in his own day. 'Il faut y porter
ces nourritures', he comments, 'pour y célébrer les mystères de notre
religion' (ii.798). This statement of fact in a part of the *Essai* devoted
to Christian proselytism in Asia undermines the claim to catholicity
upon which missionaries predicated their efforts. How could the
eucharist have universal significance when its essential ingredients are

[46] Exodus xvi.14-15: 'When the coating of dew lifted, there on the surface of the
desert was a thing delicate, powdery, as fine as hoar-frost on the ground [. . .] "That",
said Moses to them, "is the bread Yahweh gives you to eat." '

[47] 1 Corinthians x.3: 'All [Israel] ate the same spiritual food' in the time of Moses. One
also finds in the *Concili Tridentini actorum*, 7.4.1, p.174 (30 Sept. 1551): 'Manna enim
ante data in deserto sola edebatur.' Genesis xvi relates the appearance of the manna and
Genesis xvii, the water flowing from the rock struck by Moses. The text implies an interval
between the first and second miracles.

[48] 'Man setzt sich natürlich auch mit den Abendmahlsberichten des Neuen Testamentes
auseinander und erweitert die in den früheren Konzilsdebatten vorgebrachten Argmuente:
Wenn Christus beim letzten Abendmahl die Apostel unter beiden Gestalten kommuni-
zierte, wollte er nicht die Kirche dazu verpflichten [. . .] der Kelch war nur für die Apostel
bestimmt, nicht für die Laien; die Emmausjünger empfingen nur die Brotsgestalt [. . .]
Es liegt auf der Hand, dass keines dieser Argumente wirklich befriedigte' (Hubert Jedin,
Geschichte des Konzils von Trient (Freiburg 1970), iv.161).

unavailable in so many countries? Voltaire refrains from an explicit answer to this question in his historical works, but the first part of the *Histoire de l'empire de Russie* (1759) takes a step further in the same direction. Here he tells how peoples conquered by the Russians resisted their attempts to convert them to Greek Orthodoxy: 'Une de leurs grandes objections était que ce culte ne pouvait être fait pour eux, puisque le vin et le pain sont nécessaires à nos mystères, et qu'ils ne peuvent avoir ni pain ni vin dans leurs pays' (M.xvi.414): This remark sets the stage for irony in his polemical works over the exportation of a supposedly universal sacrament to lands whose agriculture cannot even supply its material requirements.

The modest amount of space given the eucharist in this comprehensive history of manners, composed before and after the communion of 1754, reveals that Voltaire still had not fully recognised its potential as a polemical issue. Among the theologians who made a major contribution to the development of the dogma after Charlemagne, he omits Guitmund and Thomas altogether, and merely touches on the points raised by the others who happened to catch his rapid eye. He also badly neglects the eucharistic implications of Hus's story and ignores the Marburg Colloquium, though neither Luther's nor Zwingli's opinions escape him entirely. But his remarks show that he had explored the history of the dogma enough to know where he could attack when the opportunity came. He may, in fact, have had this intention, along with other, more obvious ones, in undertaking the studies preliminary to the *Essai*. In the future, the knowledge he had acquired would furnish him with most of the basic elements he needed to assault the sacrament. Despite the restraint he found necessary because of his historiographical ambitions, he develops, and at times no doubt unwittingly, the tactics he would perfect later on. Though usually implied and not expressed, three habitual arguments emerge from an analysis of the treatment he gives the eucharist in the *Essai*: 1. the tardy development of doctrines considered to be permanent standards of orthodoxy; 2. the persistent opposition of sincere, intelligent and reasonable theologians; 3. the Church's policy of exalting obscurantism and resisting common sense in the interest of a selfish priesthood.

He did not immediately exploit the polemical possibilities he had found in his study of eucharistic history. Recent events, which he had already ridiculed in the Colmar correspondence, offered a more tempting target in the late fifties and early sixties. As we have seen, he made fun of the confession certificate he had received on the eve of his Easter communion in 1754.

An episode concerning the refusal of last rites occurs in the earliest known version of *Candide*, the La Vallière manuscript written before October of 1758. Arriving in Paris, in chapter 22, Candide and Martin encounter a crowd loudly mourning twelve dead men in their coffins. A bystander asks them, 'Est-ce que vous ne savez pas quel impôt on a mis depuis peu sur les morts?' Despite Candide's lack of curiosity, the man explains: 'On présente aux mourants depuis quelques mois des billets payables au porteur pour l'autre monde, que tout homme à l'agonie doit signer, et s'il ne signe pas il n'est point enterré, (p.174). The acceptance of Unigenitus which the constitutionaries demanded of dying appelants amounts to a tax levied on a decent burial and confession certificates, to a check assuring payment in the form of last rites.[49] The deliberately inappropriate vocabulary alerts common sense to the inadequacy, absurdity and tyranny of such transactions where death is concerned. The crowd mourning the twelve Jansenists is only the second of three horrors greeting Candide and Martin in Paris, the other two being the spectacle of Jansenist convulsions and the tumult following the incident in which Damiens nicked Louis XV with a small knife.[50] In this early draft of *Candide*, Voltaire manifestly wanted to persuade his readers that Paris was the kind of place where such things happen.

Even without this episode, the definitive version of chapter 22, a spiteful caricature of Parisian life, reflects the bitter frustrations of an exile who sorely loved his native city. Another episode about confession certificates illustrates this point. Candide comes down with a minor illness, which doctors promptly transform into a major one. Assuming him to be on his deathbed, 'un habitué du quartier vint avec douceur lui demander un billet payable au porteur pour l'autre monde' (p.175). Voltaire does not immediately identify this visitor, because that would spoil the financial interest of his joke, but nearly all of his eighteenth-century readers must have recognised him at once as a constitutionary. A victim for slightly less than twenty-one chapters, Candide has the good sense to refuse his co-operation and ignore the pleas of pious

[49] Régnault states that confession certificates were called, ironically, 'billets de banque pour l'autre monde' (*Christophe de Beaumont*, i.214).

[50] Godard believes that the agitation over refusals of last rites in the Palais de justice caused Damiens to act (*La Querelle des refus de sacrement*, p.102).

bystanders recommending this fashion. A man of even more bitter experience, his companion Martin is in a mood to throw the priest out of the window. When the priest swears that Candide will not receive a decent burial, one of Voltaire's more obsessive preoccupations, Martin threatens to bury the intruder. In the ensuing fracas, Martin evicts the priest, thus causing a scandal. Perhaps Voltaire would have liked to see Beaumont evicted from Paris in similar fashion. Just as the priest, an uninvited and presumptuous stranger, makes trouble in Candide's lodgings, the archbishop, the unwelcome and arrogant representative of a foreign power, was making trouble in Voltaire's native city. Consequently, he may well have imagined a small-scale equivalent of Beaumont's act accomplished by a subordinate of the archbishop eager to obey his orders. This parallel exposed the archbishop to disapproval above which the dignity of his office would normally have elevated him. Voltaire seems especially to have resented Beaumont's interference in what he regarded as the natural right to a decent burial. He had never forgiven the Church for its responsibility in the barbarous treatment of Adrienne Lecouvreur's body, which he recalls in a sarcastic remark further on.[51]

His attitude is more cautious, on the other hand, in a text on this subject in the 1763 edition of the *Essai sur l'histoire générale*, one that eventually became a part of chapter 36 in the *Précis du siècle de Louis XV* (1768). Here he assumes that Beaumont and Belzunce, bishop of Marseilles, had recourse to confession certificates in an effort to distract the government from plans to tax Church property. Aware of hostility to Unigenitus, he says, they deliberately exacerbated it in order to create a public disturbance. Thus every dying Catholic in their dioceses had to produce a confession certificate before receiving last rites: 'Il fallait que ces billets fussent signés par des prêtres adhérents à la bulle, sans quoi point d'extrême onction, point de viatique; on refusait sans pitié ces deux consolations aux appelants et à ceux qui se confessaient à des appelants' (M.xv.377). Voltaire's sympathy with the appelants in this context seems surprisingly mild and one of his comments shows why: 'C'étaient des insectes sortis du cadavre du molinisme et du

---

[51] 'A Paris on [...] respecte [les actrices] quand elles sont belles, et on les jette à la voirie quand elles sont mortes' (p.177).

jansénisme, qui, en bourdonnant dans la ville, piquaient tous les cito-yens' (M.xv.377). While he had declared war on the Jesuits in 1759,[52] he had never trusted the Jansenists and he trusted them even less after 1762 when they began to destroy the French branch of the Jesuit order.[53] Seeing the balance of power tip to Jansenism did not inspire pity for Jansenist victims of Beaumont's blackmail. In the three-way struggle between the archbishop, the Parlement of Paris with its Jansenist sym-pathies, and the crown, Voltaire sides with Louis xv against Parlement and Beaumont.

He nonetheless describes the predicament of innocent victims, such as the two dying nuns[54] who 'craignaient d'être damnées si elles rece-vaient cette bulle en mourant [et] craignaient d'être damnées aussi en manquant d'extrême onction' (M.xv.379). When Parlement asked Beaumont to spare the nuns, he replied, 'selon sa coutume, qu'il ne devait compte qu'à Dieu [et] son temporel fut sais'.[55] Voltaire did not realise that Louis had preve~ted Parlement from carrying out its threat to seize the archbishop's property.[56] *Selon sa coutume* almost certainly means 'in keeping with his habitual cynicism' and the seizure, in Vol-taire's opinion, was an appropriate answer to his claim of independence. In the 1769 edition of his complete works, Voltaire qualified the measures taken to make the Church honour its civic responsibilities in this affair by inserting a sentence reminiscent of his earlier descriptions of battles: 'La justice [faisait] communier les malades la baïonnette au bout du fusil.'[57] Among the examples in the original text, he presents the case of a dying Jansenist canon at the cathedral of Orleans. Despite a twelve thousand franc fine inflicted on his fellow canons and a communion organised 'comme pour une exécution' (M.xv.383), the poor man died without last rites.[58] Voltaire's morbid irony does not elicit sympathy for the Jansenist, but rather censure of the other canons for neglect of their civic responsibility. The threat of taxation, he says, provoked

[52] in his *Relation de la maladie . . . du jésuite Berthier* (1759-1760), according to John Pappas, 'La rupture entre Voltaire et les jésuites', *Lettres romanes* 13 (1959), pp.366-70.

[53] in his *The Jansenists and the expulsion of the Jesuits from France (1757-1765)* (New Haven 1975), Dale Van Kley concludes, 'Not only did the Jansenists rail at the Jesuit order [. . .] but they destroyed it' (p.237).

[54] Thècle and Perpétue in the convent of Sainte-Agathe. See p.94.

[55] M.xv.379-80. See above, p.94.

[56] according to Godard, p.81, and Parguez, p.131.

[57] 'Dès que le canon des Suédois eut fait brèche aux retranchements, ils s'avancèrent la baïonnette au bout du fusil' (M.xvi.174).

[58] de Cougniou. See p.95.

at least one reprisal against a member of Parlement, which was considering the measure: 'Un conseiller du parlement, malade à sa campagne [. . .] demanda les sacrements; un curé les lui refusa comme à un ennemi de l'Eglise, et le laissa mourir sans cette cérémonie.'[59] This event, which he relates without comment, tends to confirm his erroneous contention that fear of taxation and not Jansenism motivated the refusal of last rites. In general, his account of the affair in the *Précis* merely hints at the opinion of a very opinionated writer.

To assess the full extent of his hostility to the refusal of last rites, one must yet consult his fifth *Remarque pour servir de supplément à l'Essai sur les mœurs* (1763). Borrowing Montesquieu's technique in the *Lettres persanes* (1721), he imagines 'un brame philosophe [qui] arrive de l'Inde en Europe' (ii.908). This Hindu's Voltairian curiosity about religious manners results in the discovery of 'un écrit qui insulte au bon sens' and 'je ne sais quels billets [qui] mettent tout en rumeur' (ii.909). In a footnote, Voltaire identifies these items as Unigenitus and confession certificates, which 'l'Europe a regardés comme les deux plus impertinentes productions de ce siècle' (ii.909). The French *impertinent* has the connotation, lacking in the English cognate, of 'contre le bon sens'.[60] Here Voltaire, who lost no love on the Jansenists, seems less concerned with the injustice than the absurdity of requiring a political self-condemnation as a condition for the satisfaction of a religious need.

His opinion of confession certificates varies from playful jokes in the Colmar correspondence to angry protest in *Candide* and from detachment in the *Précis* to annoyance in the fifth remark. His hostility to Jansenists, the exclusive victims, and his belief in the necessary relativity of truth in all public statements, printed, written or declared, seem to have kept him from attacking the certificates more aggressively. As for refusal of last rites, *Candide* recriminates the intrusion of the Church in a matter that does not concern it and the fifth remark censures the unreasonable behaviour of the clergy. The letters from Colmar ridicule the solemnification of a trivial routine, while the *Précis* simply tells how, in Voltaire's mistaken view, Parlement had tried to force the Church to live up to its fiscal responsibilities. Common experience brings Voltaire

[59] M.xv.385. Was Voltaire thinking of the following case related by Godard? 'Une ordonnance du lieutenant général de Bayeux est annulée par le Conseil [du Roi] le 26 mai 1739: L'officier avait enjoint au curé de la paroisse de Saint-Sauveur d'administrer le procureur du roi retenu chez lui par la maladie, et menacé de l'assigner en cas de refus pour en expliquer les motifs' (p.213).

[60] *Larousse du XXe siècle* (Paris 1932).

to expect the Church to provide for the decent disposal of the dead and he accordingly regards this routine service as an obligation and not a privilege. To his mind, in fact, this is one of the ways in which the Church justifies its existence.

He not only concerned himself with last rites during this period, but also the eucharist itself. The bankruptcy of the Jesuit La Valette, which eventually led to the dissolution of the Society in France, provided him with an opportunity to pursue this matter. In the *Lettre de Charles Gouju à ses frères* (1761)[61] he poses as the cousin of a man ruined by La Valette. In view of the conflicts between the Jesuit's Christian responsibility and his commercial speculation, Gouju asks his brothers to decide the following question: 'Je vous demande [si les jésuites] pensent vraiment tenir Dieu dans leurs mains à la messe, lorsqu'ils nous pillent au sortir de la sainte table.'[62] This is the first time that Voltaire attacked the doctrine of intention directly.[63] Would a celebrant who believes he holds the transubstantiated body and blood of God the Son in his own hands dare to betray that very divinity? Reason eliminates the possibility of such a self-condemnation, thus hypocrisy alone can reconcile commercial fraud with the celebration of the mass. In an earlier paragraph, Gouju 'demande à tout homme qui fait usage de sa raison' (p.148) whether La Valette believed in Christianity when, after taking the vow of poverty, he did six million francs of business. Obviously not, according to Voltaire. Since such celebrants do not believe in transubstantiation, they can have no intention of transubstantiating and the dogma itself invalidates communion taken from them. Voltaire must have realised, moreover, that this logic ruins the Church's attempts to guarantee the presence of Christ's body and blood after consecration, however unworthy the celebrant.

Another argument against the eucharist appears in a letter to Damilaville on 9 March 1762 (Best.D10367). The notes with which he had

[61] 'J'accouche, j'accouche, tenez, voilà des Gouju', he wrote to d'Argental on 11 October 1761 (Best.D10069).

[62] *Facéties*, ed. Jean Macary (Paris 1973), p.148.

[63] according to the Council of Trent, a sacrament is effective only if the minister intends to '*faire au moins ce que fait l'Eglise*' (Session vii, canon 11). The ensuing debate over the necessity for a profound and conscious intention was resolved in 1690, when Alexander viii condemned the following proposition advanced by Farvaques: 'Valide est le baptême conféré par un ministre qui observe tout le rite extérieur et garde la forme du sacrement, mais dit fermement à part soi: Je n'ai pas l'intention de faire ce que fait l'église.' A. Thouvenin concludes: 'Il est nécessaire enfin que l'intention soit *absolue*' ('Intention', *Dictionnaire de théologie catholique*, viii.2272, 2277).

loaded his deist tragedy *Olympie* ('O! l'impie'),[64] he affirms, disclose that 'notre sainte religion a tout pris de l'ancienne, jusqu'à la confession et à la communion à laquelle nous avons seulement ajouté avec le temps la transsubstantiation'. Unfortunately, none of the thirteen notes ('une douzaine' (Best.D10399)) that have come down to us traces communion back to Judaism or cites the tardy development of transubstantiation.

In the campaign to rehabilitate Jean Calas, broken on the wheel in 1762, his knowledge of eucharistic history provided him with a few useful arguments. His *Mémoire de Donat Calas* (1762), which he attributed to Jean's son, defends the fidelity of Protestantism to Christian traditions abandoned by Catholicism. Anxious to avoid offence to Catholic readers, 'Donat' admits he may have been misinformed when he learned that Ratramn 'écrivait en cent endroits de son livre en faisant parler Jésus-Christ même: "Ne croyez pas que ce soit corporellement que vous mangiez ma chair et buviez mon sang" (M.xxiv.383). Voltaire could not have found a hundred passages where Ratramn assigns such words to Christ, because there is only one of them: 'Tamquam diceret [Christus]: Non ergo carnem meam vel sanguinem meum vobis corporaliter comedendam vel bibendum [. . .] putetis' (xxx). On the other hand, Ratramn negates corporeal and affirms spiritual communion many times in his short treatise, thus Voltaire does not drastically misrepresent him. In his continuation of the same sentence, however, he makes a wild claim: 'On chantait dans la plupart des églises cette homélie conservée dans plusieurs bibliothèques: "Nous recevons le corps et le sang de Jésus-Christ, non corporellement, mais spirituellement" (M.xxiv.383). This pseudo-quotation condenses a much larger sentence in Aelfric's Paschal Homily imitating Ratramn,[65] which was almost certainly chanted nowhere since he intended it to be preached. Nor could it have been read in many churches, because he wrote it in Saxon and Ratramn had little popularity in the tenth century. Yet the entire Church did believe in the principle expressed, on which Paschase was in agreement with Ratramn. In the *Traité sur la tolérance*, printed the next year, Voltaire defends the right to agree with Ratramn against

---

[64] Voltaire to d'Alembert on 18 January 1763 (Best.D10922). *Olympie* was first published in 1763.

[65] '[Jesus] did not command the body with which he was invested to be eaten, nor the blood to be drunk which he shed for us; but he meant by that speech the holy housel, which is spiritually his body and his blood' (*The Sermones Catholici or Homilies of Aelfric*, translated by Benjamin Thorpe (London 1846), ii.275).

Paschase and with Berengar against John the Scot, a slip of the pen for Lanfranc, without being hanged or forfeiting the right to inherit from his father. The Barbare in the dialogue of chapter 16 demands, among other conditions, that the Mourant be 'tout à l'heure du sentiment de Lanfranc contre Bérenger' (M.xxv.91), if he wants to leave his property to his survivors. In both cases, Voltaire is referring to the partial confiscation of Jean Calas's property by officials giving his Protestantism as a legal pretext.[66] Accustomed to accepting the priority of the religious tradition followed as proof of its purity, his readers could scarcely fail to understand that he was challenging the authenticity of Catholic dogma.

The rehabilitation of Calas did not prevent him from prosecuting the infamous in general. In the 'Catéchisme de l'honnête homme' (1763), the honest man finds the deification of onions no more insane than the belief that 'un morceau de pâte [peut être] changé en autant de dieux que de miettes'.[67] But the persecution of people who do not believe in the latter absurdity absolutely horrifies him. While promoting tolerance, therefore, Voltaire exposes concomitance to scepticism in the manner of Berengar. In the same year, Rousseau made a comparable attack on the real presence and transubstantiation in his published letter to Beaumont.[68] Although Rousseau had written to Voltaire, 'Je ne vous aime pas, Monsieur' (17 June 1760), Voltaire delighted, albeit ironically, in what Rousseau dared to tell the archbishop:

Il luy prouve que le tout est plus petit que la partie chez les papistes, il prétend qu'il est très vraisemblable que christ en instituant la divine eucaristie mangea de son pain béni, et qu'alors il est visible qu'il mit sa tête dans sa bouche. Mais nous répondons à cela que la tête dans le pain n'était pas plus grosse qu'une tête d'épingle.[69]

D'Alembert, to whom he sent this letter (1 May 1763), would understand that Voltaire thought Rousseau a little naive to attack Beaumont in

[66] '[Parlement] declares [Calas's] goods confiscated and acquired by those whom it may concern, substraction made of the third part of them for his wife and children [...] and for the expenses of those who exposed them' ('Procès-verbal of the execution of Jean Calas, père' in Edna Nixon, *Voltaire and the Calas case* (New York 1961), p.100).

[67] *Dictionnaire philosophique*, ed. Raymond Naves [hereafter *Dict.*], p.135 (Paris 1961).

[68] *Jean-Jacques Rousseau, citoyen de Genève, à Christophe de Beaumont, archevêque de Paris* (1762).

[69] Best.D11182. Rousseau is answering Beaumont's objection to a passage in *Emile* where 'l'inspiré' declares, 'Je vous apprends de la part de Dieu que c'est la partie qui est plus grande que le tout' (*Œuvres complètes* (Paris 1969), iv.614).

print and include his name in the title of the work. But d'Alembert would also understand that Voltaire agreed with Rousseau's analysis and that the final remark simply carries this analysis to an extreme. *Nous* are of course freethinkers who sabotage the real presence by explaining it to common sense. Christ's body present in the piece of bread he may have eaten at the Last Supper had to be smaller than his mouth, since his disciples ate similar pieces of bread containing it. Thus the whole was smaller than one of its parts. Rousseau and Voltaire ignore the spiritual interpretation of this bodily presence in dogma, a contradiction in terms from their viewpoint.

The second question of 'Religion' (1764) in the *Portatif* indicates that the ancient Egyptian worship of onions continued to intrigue Voltaire. He attributes the persistence of such a cult, despite the progress of reason in Egypt, to priests and the superstitious. 'Quiconque eût reproché à certains Egyptiens de manger leurs dieux', he remarks, 'eût été mangé lui-même' (*Dict.*, p.363). He then implies that, according to Juvenal, an Egyptian 'tué et mangé tout cru' (*Dict.*, p.363) was being punished for this presumption.[70] Having defined the Catholic eucharist as eating God many times, he could rely on his readers to recognise the parallel with that sacrament. Not that Christians ate people who accused them of eating God, but Catholics had at least massacred Protestants for refusing to accept, among other dogmas, transubstantiation and the real presence.[71]

The divinity student in the *Questions sur les miracles* (1765) writes to his professor (Vernet?) that his German baron (Frederick) ascribes the same effect to the same cause. The dispute over how one should celebrate Easter, the baron observes, has caused more bloodshed than the quarrels between Austria and France, between the Guelphs and the Ghibellines and between the red and white roses. Allusions to war and mass execution in the context show that he is thinking of the struggle between the Catholics and the Protestants. This turmoil, he believes,

[70] in his edition of Voltaire's *Taureau blanc*, Pomeau suggests Juvenal, *Satire* xv, as a souce of Voltaire's fascination with deified onions in Egypt: 'Porrum et caepe nefas violare et frangere morsu' (Paris 1956), p.93 n.64.

[71] 'De la Chine' in the *Portatif* contains the following passage: 'La religion des lettrés [. . .] est admirable. Point de superstition, point de légendes absurdes, point de ces dogmes qui insultent à la raison et à la nature, et auxquels des bonzes donnent mille sens différents, parce qu'ils n'en ont aucun. Le culte le plus simple leur a paru le meilleur depuis quarante siècles [. . .] Ils se contentent d'adorer un Dieu avec tous les sages de la terre, tandis qu'en Europe on se partage entre Thomas et Bonaventure, entre Calvin et Luther, entre Jansénius et Molina' (*Dict.*, pp.108-109).

stems from an obvious contradiction: 'Dieu, quand il était sur la terre, a fait la pâque en mangeant un agneau cuit dans des laitues; et la moitié de l'Europe, depuis plus de huit siècles, croit faire la pâque en mangeant Jésus-Christ lui-même en chair et en os' (*Facéties*, p.238). Needless to say, he means the Catholic half of Europe and he is referring to the tenth century when he believed Paschase had written his *Body*. The eating of Christ in flesh and bone is an ironical caricature of the more reasonable Jewish custom of eating the paschal lamb and suggests cannibalism or self-delusion. While supporting the commonsense objection to the real presence by Calvinists here, Voltaire exploits a discrepancy in the Protestant position at the end of the letter. After assuring his confidentially unitarian professor of his trinitarian orthodoxy, the divinity student demonstrates his embarrassing zeal by declaring that he would even admit '(Dieu me pardonne!) le miracle de la transsubstantiation si le saint concile de Nicée et le modéré saint Athanase l'avaient enseigné' (p.243). Thus Voltaire inaugurates an argument injurious to both the Protestant and the Catholic viewpoint. Do the corrupt councils and the fanatic theologians of antiquity enjoy greater authority than the corrupt councils and fanatic theologians of the Middle Ages? The ironical repetition of *saint* reminds Voltaire's readers that, according to him, reason rejects all such authority.

Other letters in the *Questions* deride Rousseau's ill-fated communion in Môtiers.[72] Voltairian humour lurks behind the Swiss formality and solemnity of a letter from Beaudinet to Covelle. The Genevan ministers, says Beaudinet, sent letters and tracts against Rousseau to Montmolin, the minister of Môtiers who had admitted him to communion. They charitably accused him of having had conversations, during his youth, with a Savoyard vicar or, in other words, of having published his theist *Profession de foi du vicaire savoyard* in *Emile* (1762). Threatened with excommunication by Montmolin, 'M. Rousseau prétendait qu'un entretien avec un vicaire savoyard n'était pas une raison pour être excommunié de la manducation spirituelle' (p.273). Rousseau appealed to George Keith, the governor of Neuchâtel, who recommended him to the king, and Frederick took the communicant under his protection. 'Sauvegarde rarement efficace,' comments Beaudinet-Voltaire. Despite Frederick's promise, Montmolin's parishioners stoned Rousseau out of town. Voltaire has a measure of satire for everyone and everything

[72] in the territory of Neuchâtel which then belonged to Prussia.

represented here. Beaudinet has no more sense of humour than the other French-speaking Swiss in the *Miracles*. Montmolin, his fellow ministers and his parishioners prove to be as intolerant as Catholics. Rousseau pays the price Voltaire believed he deserved for his naive provocation of religious authorities, but Voltaire may also have resented his greater courage in facing Catholic intolerance of free thought. The subject of a farce, communion itself inspires nothing better than the superstitious betrayal of theism by Rousseau and the bigotry of his Christian persecutors.

In the next letter of the *Questions*, Montmolin tells his version of the story to his Catholic colleague Needham, but, with Voltaire pulling the strings, he flatters himself no more than Beaudinet flattered him.[73] To justify his excommunication of Rousseau, he enumerates all the different kinds of communion Rousseau has taken over the years, that is to say, all the different kinds of Christianity he has embraced (p.275):

Il avait d'abord communié dans la ville de Genève [. . .] sous les deux espèces du pain levé; ensuite il alla communier, avec du pain azyme, sans boire, chez les Savoyards, qui sont tous de profonds théologiens; puis il revint à Genève communier avec pain et vin, puis il alla en France où il eut le malheur de ne point communier du tout, et il fut près de mourir d'inanition. Enfin il me demanda la sainte cène [. . .] d'une manière si pressante que je pris le parti de lui jeter des pierres pour l'écarter de ma table.

Calvinism, in which Rousseau was brought up in Geneva, prescribed communion on both bread and wine. When he ran away to Savoy and converted to Catholicism by expedient, he communed on bread alone as all Catholic laymen did. Montmolin-Voltaire inverts the chronology of his confessional evolution by having him return to Geneva and Calvinism before his long residence in the region of Paris. There, his Christianity 'nearly starved' under the influence of deist and atheist philosophes. Returning to Geneva, he re-embraced the faith of his forefathers in a spirit of patriotism and, in Môtiers, he continued to commune, when allowed, in the Calvinist manner. If one reconstitutes the chronology of Rousseau's conversions, even in the absence of the innuendoes by Voltaire's satiric puppet Montmolin, they tend to implicate him in an unconscionable vacillation. Indeed, one finds him shifting from one kind of communion to another so frequently that

[73] 'Je procédai bravement à [. . .] excommunier [Jean-Jacques]' (p.275).

his reputation suffers. Actually, Rousseau's religion of the heart rele-
gated them all to a status somewhat like that of the civic ceremony
which Voltaire himself inclined to confer on them and especially when
Rousseau returned to Geneva from Paris. Again, however, Voltaire
is not only aiming at Rousseau, but also at communion itself. Rousseau's
experience illustrates a point Voltaire had borrowed from French
literary tradition and used against Christianity, the regional variation of
custom.[74] Every time Rousseau moved from one country to another,
according to Montmolin-Voltaire, he changed his manner of communing. Since national tradition determines the form of the custom, the
latter obeys human and not universal or, as the deist sees it, divine laws.
Eighteenth-century reason interprets Rousseau's eucharistic variations
as proof that men and by no means God instituted communion.

Needham's tardy participation in the *Questions* gives Voltaire the
opportunity to expose a Catholic figure directly to Calvinist criticism
of the Catholic eucharist. Beaudinet's narration of the questioning
undergone by the Jesuit in Neuchâtel includes a paragraph in which
Voltaire's caricature of Needham brazenly acknowledges the worst that
Calvinist ears could hear, 'qu'il célébrait sa synaxe tous les dimanches,
qu'il faisait l'*hocus pocus* avec une dextérité merveilleuse; il se vanta de
faire Théon, et même des milliers de Théoi: de quoi toute l'assemblée
frémit' (p.293). The derivation of the English *hocus pocus* from Jesus's
words, 'Hoc est corpus meum', in the Vulgate version of the institution
narrative is folk etymology,[75] whether Voltaire knew it or not. The
celebrant says the words during the elevation of the hostia in order to
transubstantiate it. Substituting *hocus pocus* for them in the language
assigned to Needham punctures the dignity of both the priest and the
sacrament. In this context, *hocus pocus* conveys English Protestant
contempt for the magic or superstition of the mass. Since Voltaire puts
it in the mouth of Needham, whom he insisted on calling an Irishman,
he may have known that he was an Englishman. Perhaps Catholicism
seemed as un-English to him as it did to many Englishmen! Other
words in the quotation are French equivalents of ancient Greek words:
synaxe means mass, *Théon*, god and *Théoi*, gods. Voltaire is merely
using these exotic terms to add an element of mystery to his usual

[74] Pascal, for example: 'Vérité au-deçà des Pyrénées, erreur au-delà' (*Pensées*, ed.
Louis Lafuma (Paris 1962), n.60); and Montaigne: 'Quelle vérité que ces montagnes
bornent, qui est mensonge au monde qui se tient au-delà' (*Essais* (Paris 1950), p.653).
[75] see 'Hocus pocus', *Oxford dictionary of English etymology* (Oxford 1966).

remarks about making God and distributing him in a thousand pieces. The shudder of Needham's Calvinist interrogators comically exaggerates the dangers of his testimony, which, though equally heretical from either a Catholic or a Protestant viewpoint, can do no harm, in Voltaire's opinion, and, in fact, does no harm according to this letter. While Voltairian reason condemns Needham here, it does not approve his interrogators.

These attacks on the eucharist in the early sixties demonstrate that Voltaire had finally recognised how vulnerable the primary sacrament of the Church was. While his objections to the refusal of last rites pertain to the abuse of Church power rather than viaticum in particular, the number and variety of passages on communion are significant. One cannot say, on the other hand, that he had given this satirical target a very high priority, for he devotes no work to it, large or small, and the title 'Transsubstantiation' does not appear in the *Portatif,* but only in the 1767 edition of the *Dictionnaire philosophique,* a much expanded version of the same work.

Voltaire's polemics against the eucharist in 1767 tended to rework earlier material and re-emphasise it. Passages from two small works illustrate each of these trends. One in the *Essai sur les dissensions des églises de Pologne* combines old and new criticisms of the sacrament. Here Voltaire pleads for mutual tolerance between the Protestants, the Roman Catholics and the Greek Orthodox of Poland. He advises ordinary men to live together in brotherhood and 'cultiver la raison et la justice, sans se persécuter pour des mystères qu'ils ne peuvent entendre' (M.xxvi.456). Only saints, on the other hand, can learn from revelation 'comment on mange le Fils en corps et en âme dans un pain qui est anéanti, sans manger ni le Père ni le Saint-Esprit; ou comment le corps et l'âme de Jésus sont incorporés au pain, ou comment on mange Jésus par la foi' (M.xxvi.456). An echo of 'un pain qui n'est plus' in the *Henriade* (see p.103), *pain anéanti* recalls substantial destruction in Duns Scotus and the cessation of substantial existence in William of Ockham (see p.54). Although Voltaire does not seem aware of their opinions, he may have arrived at the same conclusion by the same analysis. Empirical reason tells us that bread cannot be instantaneously converted into a human body. If Christ's body therefore replaces the bread of the eucharist, this bread must first be destroyed. But reason also tells us that the bread cannot be destroyed in this way, and so Voltaire is really insinuating the impossibility of transubstantiation. While this dogma characterises the Roman Catholics of Poland and elsewhere, the next two questions concern both them and the Greek Orthodox.[76] If the three persons in the Godhead are inseparable, how can the body and soul be incorporated into the bread of the eucharist? Again, good sense persuades us that they cannot. The final point in the quotation above refers to Calvinist Protestants, Polish or otherwise. Since eating is a physical act, how can one eat Jesus by faith? Since common sense can understand a spiritual meal only metaphorically, Voltaire is implying that this metaphor designates nothing more than speculative illusion.

The rogaton *Avis à tous les orientaux* also blends new ideas with the old, but one of the latter has become daringly specific. The author facetiously warns all orientals of a plot by a Christian sect calling itself Catholic to subjugate the entire world. This sect believes in a trinity of gods, one of whom has been hanged. The spokesman continues: 'Ils prétendent le ressusciter tous les jours avec des paroles; ils le mettent dans un morceau de pain; ils le mangent et le rendent avec les autres excréments' (*Facéties*, p.352). The oriental role serves as a prextext to simplify the dogma for the benefit of the natural light, which Voltaire assumed to shine most brilliantly in minds uncorrupted by the Judaic family of religions. His demystification of eucharistic sacrifice produces the daily resuscitation of a hanged God by means of uttered words. Transubstantiation and the real presence amount to the baking of an additional ingredient into bread. Thus the first two remarks in the quotation above are new, but the third merely renews the Stercorian argument by more explicit abuse of the real presence. Digested along with the eucharistic bread, Christ's body becomes just another kind of excrement, a word Voltaire had previously avoided.

In the same year he added to his *Examen important de milord Bolingbroke*[77] a new chapter containing familiar polemics against the eucharist. But one passage, at least, reinterprets older material in an interesting way. Here Voltaire praises the theologians who had dared to protest against medieval innovations, though without naming them as he had in the *Essai*. They knew 'que dans les premiers siècles de l'Eglise, on

[76] this church uses transubstantiation to describe the changing of bread and wine into Christ's body and blood, but without invoking the difference between substances and accidents. See 'Transubstantiation', *Encyclopedia of religion and ethics* (Edinburgh 1933).

[77] though published only that year, this work may well have been in existence ever since Ferney, according to Ira Wade, *The Intellectual development of Voltaire* (Princeton 1969), pp.550-56.

n'avait jamais prétendu changer du pain en dieu dans le souper du Seigneur; que cela ne ressemblait nullement à la communion de la messe; que les premiers chrétiens avaient eu les images en horreur' (M.xxvi.294). The final phrase reinforces the charge of adulterating the Last Supper by the implication of idolatry. Eucharistic idolatry would become an important theme in his polemics.

In the *Dîner du comte de Boulainvilliers*, he unleashes Fréret[78] in an assault on this very aspect of the sacrament. 'Oseriez-vous nier votre idolâtrie,' Fréret challenges father Couet, 'vous [. . .] qui adorez d'un culte de latrie un morceau de pâte que vous enfermez dans une boîte, de peur des souris?'[79] Only the intensity of Fréret's scorn renews this protest against the idolatrous implications of the medieval obsession. He charges Couet and his fellow priests with the Catholic extravagance of claiming to convert pieces of bread into God by means of a few Latin words: 'Toutes les miettes de cette pâte', they affirm, 'deviennent autant de dieux créateurs de l'univers' (*Dial.*, p.191). By casting God in his mightiest and most exclusive role, Fréret magnifies the absurdity of pretending to multiply him sacramentally. At this point, Voltaire introduces a passage developed from the notebook entry of 1726:

Un gueux qu'on aura fait prêtre, un moine sortant des bras d'une prostituée, vient pour douze sous, revêtu d'un habit de comédien, me marmotter en une langue étrangère ce que vous appelez une messe, fendre l'air en quatre avec trois doigts, se couber, se redresser, tourner à droite et à gauche, par devant et par derrière, et faire autant de dieux qu'il lui plaît, les boire et les manger, et les rendre ensuite à son pot de chambre.[80]

This day in the life of a celebrant begins when he rises from the bed he has shared with a prostitute and ends with his evening stool. Impure acts therefore precede and follow the celebration of a mercenary mass. The description of the ceremony breaks down into brief phrases of unequal length imitating his jerky movements and suggesting an automatic routine. Fréret jolts the sentence off to a start with an insult; drags the celebrant from the arms of a whore; depreciates his private mass to the value of twelve pennies; clothes him in a histrion's costume

[78] a famous scholar, Nicolas Fréret had died in 1749. Voltaire seems to have known that he and Boulainvilliers (died 1722) privately engaged in destructive criticism of Christianity. The Fréret in the *Dîner* is of course a Voltairian persona.

[79] *Dialogues et anecdotes philosophiques*, ed. R. Naves [hereafter *Dial.*] (Paris 1961), pp.190-91.

[80] *Dial*, p.191; see also p.101, above.

(an echo of mme de Fontaine-Martel's last rites); lavishes his contempt on his indifferent muttering of the Latin litany; on the impudence of splitting the air in four with three fingers; on his officious bendings, turnings, backings and advances; on the multiplication, eating and drinking of God and above all, on the final repository of Christ's body and blood. Thus Voltaire integrates his Stercorian objection to the real presence into a text systematically impugning the integrity of celebrants and mocking the mechanics of the mass. Except for *prêtre* and *messe*, he excludes any vocabulary capable of sustaining the dignity normally associated with these terms, but the context tends to corrupt them too. After this barrage, Couet, who had admired transubstantiation in the conversation before dinner,[81] slyly contradicts himself after dinner. Why then does Voltaire's cup suddenly run over? As lord of Ferney, he often witnessed the scene he is describing and knew the worst of the actors. He found it expedient to have an ex-Jesuit chaplain in his house (Adam) and a curate for the church he had built in the yard (Gros). He tolerated Christianity on his premises to encourage his vassals in their convenient worship of a retributive deity, but, judging from Fréret's diatribe, both the spectacle and its significance were beginning to annoy him. The celebration within his sight and hearing of a sacrament he found offensive to reason did not facilitate his expedient hypocrisy.

Some of the same elements reappear in 'Transsubstantiation', which he inserted in the *Dictionnaire philosophique* that year. A by-line at the end of the article ascribes it to a fictitious 'M. Guillaume, ministre protestant' (p.412), who, in fact, opposes the dogma from the Protestant viewpoint. 'Les protestants, et surtout les philosophes protestants,' Guillaume testifies, 'regardent la transsubstantiation comme le dernier terme de l'impudence des moines, et de l'imbécillité des laïques' (p.411). Why Voltaire thought Guillaume should blame the regular and leave the secular clergy unmentioned in this connection is not clear. He may have felt that only monks were sufficiently divorced from reality to imagine so unreasonable a doctrine. A Protestant minister, in any case, would have greater contempt for them than priests. The contrast between the monks' impudence and the laymen's imbecility, on the other hand, evokes a familiar Voltairian theme. From impudence one infers

[81] 'La consubstantialité [. . .] monsieur le comte, la transsubstantiation sont de si belles choses! Plût au ciel que Scipion, Cicéron et Marc-Aurèle eussent approfondi ces vérités!' (*Dial.*, p.185).

the presumption of legislating in the name of the creator and the ambition to dominate over other men by pretending to knowledge of divine mystery. Imbecility implies docility, superstition and abandonment of authority to self-appointed experts. Only the concurrence of these vices could have produced such a belief. Protestants, continues Guillaume, 'ne pensent même pas qu'il y ait un seul homme de bon sens qui, après y avoir réfléchi, ait pu l'embrasser sérieusement' (p.411). Transubstantiation not only violates good sense, but also contradicts the very laws which God has established to regulate the universe. How could God break his own laws? 'Dieu même ne pourrait pas faire cette opération, parce que c'est en effet anéantir Dieu que de supposer qu'il fait les contradictoires' (p.411). Voltaire's Newtonian deity persists in abhorring a contradiction. The affinity between a God of common sense and the unitarian divinity which the Genevan ministers practised but did not preach[82] further elucidates his attribution of 'Transsubstantiation' to a Calvinist ghost author. Having revealed the fundamental contradiction this dogma imposes on God, Guillaume lists the consequences incompatible with a reasonable deity (p.411):

Non seulement un dieu dans un pain, mais un dieu à la place du pain; cent mille miettes de pain devenues en un instant autant de dieux, cette foule innombrable de dieux ne faisant qu'un seul dieu; de la blancheur sans un corps blanc; de la rondeur sans un corps rond; du vin changé en sang, et qui a le goût du vin; du pain qui est changé en chair et en fibres, et qui a le goût du pain.

While we have seen a few of these items before, Voltaire has adroitly supplemented them with others. He reminds us that, even though God is in a hundred thousand bread crumbs, he remains one and the same God. He adopts the traditional objection to the difference in colour and shape between bread and the human body. Wine converted into blood, he protests, continues to taste like wine, and bread converted into flesh, like bread. In each case, common sense rejects the teaching of dogma. After Fréret, Guillaume finds the freedom of the celebrant from moral responsibility more offensive than all the rest (p.411):

On voit tous les jours, dans les pays catholiques, des prêtres, des moines qui, sortant d'un lit incestueux, et n'ayant pas encore lavé leurs mains souillées

---

[82] Voltaire's campaign to convert the Genevan ministers, many of whom privately professed unitarianism, to deism backfired when his lieutenant d'Alembert advertised their heresy in the article 'Genève' which appeared in volume vii of the *Encyclopédie* (1757).

d'impuretés, vont faire des dieux par centaines, mangent et boivent leur dieu, chient et pissent leur dieu.

The Reformation had attacked the cohabitation of clergymen with their 'sisters', 'cousins', and 'nieces', less useful to them as housekeepers, the usual excuse, than as concubines. Protestant clergymen like Guillaume were encouraged to marry for this very reason. Under the Counter-Reformation, the Church had tried to eliminate the abuse, but only among the lower clergy and not always successfully. Despite the objections of his bishop, Meslier was in no hurry to get rid of his youthful 'servant'[83] in the early eighteenth century. Later in the century, Adam, the ex-Jesuit in residence at Ferney, and the Capuchin Joseph, whom we shall be meeting again, each kept a concubine.[84] Guillaume's ironical suspicions, in fact, reflect Voltaire's observations. On the other hand, the accusation of celebrating mass with dirty hands after amorous activity, which Fréret also makes in the *Dîner*, is probably unfair. Standards of cleanliness had improved in the middle and upper classes,[85] as Voltaire's appeal to them in this passage shows, and the lower clergy, even in rural parishes, had attained the level of bourgeois life.[86] Such

[83] 'Le curé renverra sa cousine incessamment, qu'il retient sous le nom de servante et de parente [. . .] Meslier [. . .] a retenu malgré les défenses que nous avons réitérées [. . .] une jeune servante âgée d'environ 18 ans' (report of bishop de Mailly's visit of 18 June 1716, in Jean Deprun, Roland Desné and Albert Soboul, ed., *Œuvres complètes de Jean Meslier* (Paris 1970-1972), iii.419-20). This volume includes a document testifying to the death of de Mailly by syphilis (p.425). 'Que Meslier retienne une servante qui n'a pas l'âge canonique (fixé à 50 ans dans le diocèse de Reims)', comments Desné, 'n'est pas [. . .] un fait exceptionnel' (i.xxx).

[84] 'Voltaire vit seul à Ferney avec l'ex-jésuite Père Adam qui [. . .] pour se désennuyer a fait une maîtresse dans le village et va la voir tous les jours; Voltaire [. . .] le persécute sur ses amours et son hypocrisie, et se fait lire tous les jours pendant le dîner un acte du *Tartuffe* [de Molière], et y a ajouté les réflexions les plus mordantes contre ceux qui veulent concilier l'amour et la dévotion' (Dupan to Freudenreich on 5 Oct. 1768 in Commentary, Best.D15245). 'Un [. . .] capucin, nommé père Joseph [. . .] [témoignait] à [. . .] Voltaire un grand désir de s'instruire et d'acheter des livres, et lui demandait pour cela quelque argent: mais c'était pour avoir soin d'une fille à laquelle il avait fait un enfant. Mon maître en fut dupe assez longtemps' (Jean-Louis Wagnière, *Examen des Mémoires secrets . . . dits de Bachaumont*, in Sébastien Longchamp and Wagnière, *Mémoires sur Voltaire et sur ses ouvrages* [hereafter L.W.] (Paris 1826), i.199-200).

[85] 'Perhaps the first advertisement offering a house with a bathroom is one in a Paris paper in 1765. Soon after this, such advertisements are frequent, and there are also many *salles de bains portatives* that could be erected in a courtyard or garden' (Lawrence Wright, *Clean and decent* (London 1960), p.126).

[86] 'L'amélioration du niveau de vie du pasteur et un plus haut degré d'instruction l'ont élevé dans la hiérarchie sociale et l'ont placé à la campagne dans l'élite de la société rurale' (Jean Delumeau, *Le Catholicisme entre Luther et Voltaire* (Paris 1971), p.274).

squalor revolted them as much as Voltaire's other readers who, though unaware of germs, appreciated cleanliness as a social amenity. Yet a Calvinist minister might well have suspected the worst of Catholic priests in France, who were largely responsible for the persecution of the Huguenots. Holding the alleged divine body in filthy hands harmonises with the Stercorian digestion of that body and, however disgusting, both tend to degrade the sacrament. But Guillaume sees an even greater scandal in the wealth and power which the pope, in his opinion, had drawn from absurd and sacrilegious superstitions such as transubstantiation. This is the final judgement of the good sense cited early in the article.

Though merely a page in length, 'Transsubstantiation' qualifies as the first separate writing by Voltaire entirely devoted to the eucharist. Together with another scornful page assigned to Fréret in the *Dîner*, the anti-eucharistic material in the new chapter of the *Examen* and the scathing passages in the *Avis* to the orientals and the *Essai* on the Polish dissensions, it marks a turning point. Manifestly, Voltaire no longer envisaged the sacrament as an occasional opportunity for lighthearted irony at the expense of the institution sponsoring it. Now, on the contrary, he was attacking it deliberately, repeatedly and angrily. His irony approaches sarcasm and he indulges in obscenity, while his sense of humour, when it survives, is grim. No other element of the infamous flaunted his inability to stamp it out like the mass routinely celebrated on his premises. As he reached the age of seventy in November of 1767, his patience was wearing thin.

Did Voltaire intend the Easter communion of 1768 as a blow against the eucharist? After 1754, he had apparently not taken the sacrament again until the Easter of 1761. According to later correspondence, mme Denis may have accompanied him on this occasion, but none of the other circumstances have come down to us. We know of his communion in 1761 only because he was afraid it had offended his *chers anges*: 'Il faut que j'aye commis quelque grande iniquité dont je ne me suis pas accusé en faisant mes pâques' (29 March; Best.D9706). No other evidence of the act or the reaction to it has turned up. The scarcity of evidence, in fact, suggests that the act caused no great sensation at a time when unusual events at Ferney were drawing much comment from Paris and elsewhere. Although one cannot prove it, Voltaire may have been telling the truth later on when he insisted that he had been taking communion regularly at Easter every year. Nor do the scandals of 1768 and 1769 disprove it, for they may have grown out of the provocative manner in which he did his 'duty'.

Good Friday was on 1 April in 1768. The coincidence did not escape d'Alembert, who wrote Voltaire, 'le saint *jour d'aujourdui* a été le sujet d'un grand *poisson d'avril* pour le genre humain'. Though meditating an April Fool's trick of his own, the patriarch wrote the following date line on a letter to d'Argental: '1ᵉʳ avril et ce n'est pas un poisson d'avril' (Best.D14904). D'Argental having asked why he kept an ex-Jesuit in his house, Voltaire answered, 'Je voudrais en avoir deux, et si on me fâche je me ferai communier deux fois par jour. Je ne veux pas être martyr à mon âge.' Taking communion, he thus implied, would disarm his enemies. In a letter to Choiseul on the same day, he denied responsibility for all the irreligious tracts being attributed to him and declared, 'je fais régulièrement mes pâques'. Ostensibly, therefore, he intended the claim of taking communion to dissociate him from publications offensive to the pious, whether he had written them or not.

Wagnière tells us essentially how his master celebrated Easter that year, but other sources supply a few additional details. Having invited David, the prior of the Carmelites in Gex, to dinner during the week, Voltaire confided in him, 'J'ai envie, pour le bon exemple, de faire mes pâques dimanche' (L.W. i.71). Although the friar, upon his request, absolved him of his sins for this purpose, Wagnière disappoints our curiosity about his confession, for he does not even mention it.[87] On Sunday, Voltaire told his secretary, 'A présent que je suis seul et sans embarras, je veux en qualité de seigneur du lieu aller communier à l'église: voulez-vous y venir avec moi? J'ai envie aussi de prêcher un peu ces coquins qui volent continuellement' (L.W. i.71). He was alone at Ferney because mme Denis had left after a quarrel with him over the alleged theft of some manuscript material by La Harpe.[88] A Protestant, Wagnière was unlikely to have had the opportunity to accompany him to mass before. He admits his curiosity to see the notorious enemy of the eucharist take communion. Alarmed, on the other hand, by the freethinker's intention to preach in church, the faith-

[87] he did confess, as the Church requires, for Dupan wrote to Freudenreich on 10 April: 'Il s'est confessé au prieur des Carmes de Gex pendant une minute, il en a reçu l'absolution' (Best.D14932, Commentary).
[88] for a recent account of this affair see A. Jovicevich, 'Voltaire and La Harpe – l'affaire des manuscrits: a reappraisal', *Studies on Voltaire* 176 (1979), pp.77-95.

ful secretary did his utmost to dissuade him, though in vain. Dupan and Grimm agree that Voltaire had his game wardens in uniform follow him into the church, a detail omitted by Wagnière.[89] The sources do not agree on the extent of the procession, but a procession there certainly was, since Wagnière indicates that he and Voltaire followed someone carrying 'un superbe pain bénit qu'il était dans l'usage de rendre chaque année, au jour de pâques' (L.W. i.71). This testimony implies that the patriarch had contributed the communion loaf to his parish in person every year at Easter. It seems probable, therefore, that he also took communion on all of the same occasions.

After he communed in 1768, he did stand before the congregation and begin to preach a sermon, which Wagnière and Grimm both describe as *pathétique*. Applied to Voltaire, this term can only mean an appeal to tearful sentimentality in the manner of his acting and his drama, in other words, *la sensibilité voltairienne*. Ironically, he was reintroducing into the Church his theatre of emotional edification, which he had derived in part from his knowledge of Christianity itself. In his forthcoming letter campaign, he would frequently repeat that he had spoken out against theft, but had preached no sermon. This is a semantic smoke screen. He likewise reiterated that he had exhorted his parishioners to pray for the queen's health, a point denied by none of the contemporary commentators, who seem rather to have riveted their attention on the fact of Voltaire preaching in church. Maria Leczinska was indeed ill and according to contemporaneous hearsay, Régnault notes, Beaumont seized the opportunity to complain of Voltaire's pamphlets. After receiving last rites, she solemnly asked the king to punish Voltaire, who obviously learned of the danger from his correspondents. She died several months later, despite the prayers of the Ferney parish. Realising in any case that he had offended his curate, Voltaire cut his sermon short and sought to placate Gros with flattery. Afterwards, according to Dupan, 'Il s'en est fait donner une déclaration,' signed no doubt by the curate.

The news travelled so fast that, scarcely a week later (10 April), mme Du Deffand sent him a letter full of astonishment and curiosity. Did he really confess and take communion as she had been told? If so, why did he do it? Did he intend to continue? 'Quel trouble vous allez

[89] for Dupan, see Best.D14932, Commentary. For Grimm, see *Correspondance littéraire, philosophique et critique* (Paris 1877-1882), viii.63, 65-67.

mettre dans toutes les têtes?' (Best.D14933). Manifestly, the news delighted the lady dying of boredom in Paris.

The reaction was very different in Annecy, where the bishop of Geneva resided. Mgr Biord's letter to Voltaire on 11 April (Best. D14944) showed him that he was as vulnerable to irony as his enemies. On the grounds of charity, Biord rejects the current opinion 'que c'est une nouvelle scène que vous avez voulu donner au public en vous jouant encore de ce que la religion a de plus sacré'. In reality, neither the dramatic significance of Voltaire's imposture nor his satirical intention, nor the logic behind his choice of targets escaped the bishop. Biord concedes that, since the deist has confessed and communed in good faith, he no longer leads the army of unbelievers against the Church. Despite all the impious works ascribed to him, despite 'tant de profanations dans le sanctuaire' (an acknowledgement of many previous communions), 'vous avez voulu rendre un hommage public à la religion qui vous a vu naître dans son sein'! He nonetheless invites the renegade to prove the sincerity of his reconversion by continually demonstrating his devotion to Catholicism. Having cunningly refrained from accusing him of an 'acte d'hypocrisie', he regrets 'un acte aussi éclatant' devoid of convincing circumstances. Rather than 'vous ingérer de prêcher le peuple dans l'église', he should have manifested, 'comme un Théodose, par vos soupirs, vos gémissements et vos larmes [. . .] la sincérité de votre repentir'. Indeed, it would have taken penitence of imperial proportions to heal the wound he had inflicted on the pride of the Church. Only after such a dramatic self-humiliation, says Biord, should he approach 'cette table sainte où la foi ne permet aux âmes même les plus pures de se présenter qu'avec une religieuse frayeur'. Clearly the bishop felt that the presence of Christ's body in the eucharist should strike awe in the hearts of communicants. He devotes a further paragraph to Voltaire's age, his infirmity, the proximity of death and the pressing need to prepare for an eternity which had extinguished the memory of so many famous men.

Voltaire had received his letter already by the next day, for he wrote to Jacob Tronchin, 'J'accepte le Te Deum de vôtre pauvre diable d'évêque' (Best.D14946). He knew how much sympathy to expect from a Tronchin for the Catholic bishop of Geneva in exile! Naming Biord's letter after the great Catholic hymn of thanksgiving is a sarcasm for Jacob's amusement. The patriarch alleges that Biord himself is the son of a mason, an apparently honest error which would become a dishonest refrain in his letters. He even suggests that the bishop was among the local Catholics whose fanaticism had necessitated his communion: 'Oui, par Dieu, je communie, et je communierai tant qu'il y aura une communion dans le monde, et je hurlerai avec les loups pour n'être point dévoré par eux.' The relegation of his communion to howling with the wolves likewise serves as a refrain in the correspondence from this period. It implies that the dangers of living among Catholic fanatics had forced him to participate in their most essential sacrament. This is so flagrant an exaggeration that one must wonder why he could not imagine a better excuse, especially in a letter to someone as familiar with the local situation as a Tronchin. Perhaps he wanted his correspondent to see through his excuse.

On 14 April, La Harpe declared 'Tout Paris' agog with 'la scène édifiante qui s'est passée dans l'église de Ferney' (Best.D14948, Commentary). Voltaire's reply to Biord the next day (Best.D14950) sets limits to his willingness to compromise with Catholicism. In the first place, he insists on interpreting the bishop's letter as the Te Deum he had mentioned to Tronchin and ignores his reprimands until a postscriptum at the end. This manoeuvre amounts to a denial of the bishop's authority over the lord of Ferney. In the second place, he enumerates all the duties this title allegedly imposes on him and includes Easter communion among them as if it were no more important than the others: 'Comment pouvez-vous me savoir gré de remplir des devoirs dont un seigneur doit donner l'exemple dans ses terres, dont aucun chrétien ne doit se dispenser, et que j'ai souvent remplis?' By shrugging off a compliment Biord had never made, he establishes the regularity, the responsibility and the exemplarity of his communion, but his syntax does not necessarily imply that he considers himself a Christian. He insinuates, in fact, that he is meeting a feudal, rather than a Christian, obligation incumbent upon the lord of the manor, who must encourage his vassals in their religious docility. For he spurned only those medieval institutions that did not serve his purposes! In the third place, he discreetly reminds the bishop of Geneva that Protestants occupy his seat and much of his see: 'il serait bien extraordinaire qu'un seigneur de paroisse ne fît pas dans une église qu'il a bâtie,[90] ce que font tous les

---

[90] 'je bâtis une église', he had written to Thieriot on 8 August 1760 (Best.D9124). 'Annoncez cette nouvelle consolante aux enfans d'Israel, que tous les saints s'en réjouissent. Les méchants diront sans doute que je bâtis cette église dans ma paroisse pour faire jetter à bas celle qui me cachait un beau paÿsage [. . .] Mais je laisse dire les impies, et je

prétendus réformés dans leurs temples à leur manière.' But patriotism and not piety requires the lord of the manor to support the Catholic eucharist in its competition with the Calvinist. In the fourth place, he includes in his letter an entire paragraph preaching much about God and nothing about Christ. Biord could scarcely ignore that this passage was equivalent to a deist profession of faith. In the postscriptum mentioned above, Voltaire refers, in the last place, to one of Biord's rebukes:

Vous êtes trop instruit pour ignorer qu'en France un seigneur de paroisse doit en rendant le pain bénit instruire ses vassaux d'un vol commis dans ce temps là [. . .] de même qu'il doit avertir si le feu prend à quelque maison du village [. . .] ce sont des affaires de police qui sont de son ressort.

He thus assumes the role of a country squire sure of his prerogative and confident in his ability to defeat an ecclesiastical challenge to it. Sounding the fire alarm, censuring theft and taking Easter communion are all administrative matters within his jurisdiction. His relegation of this remark to the status of an afterthought and the tone of finality he imparted to it invited the bishop to mind his own business. By crediting Biord with knowledge of what happens in France, he politely reminded him that he owed his title to the king of Savoy. Voltaire had just signed the letter with his title, 'gentilhomme ordinaire de la chambre du roi très chrétien'. Greater caution in trying to reach across the border might in fact have spared Biord future embarrassment. This was not Voltaire's intention, nevertheless. The foregoing analysis reveals a series of devices designed to prick the bishop's pride. Again and again, he plays the feudal lord and jostles the bishop in areas of jurisdictional overlap. He obviously designed the letter to provoke him without giving him any legitimate excuse for retaliation. Recognising in him an able opponent, he resorted to a tactic well above the grasp of ordinary intelligence.

In answering mme Du Deffand (18 April; Best.D14964), on the other hand, he relied on his usual tactics, for he was not only addressing the letter to her, but also to the friend who would read it to her and, inevitably, share it with others. To amplify the publicity over his communion, he teased them all by expressing surprise that anything so

---

fais mon salut.' Legal obstacles raised by local clergymen and Biord delayed the completion of the project until 1761. This chapel still stands and the inscription over the entrance, 'Deo erexit Voltaire', is still intact.

routine should excite their curiosity: 'Il faut qu'on soit bien oisif dans Paris et dans le voisinage pour avoir fait une nouvelle d'un devoir que j'ai rempli tous les ans quand ma mauvaise santé me l'a permis.' *Devoir* appears three times in this two-page letter, for Voltaire wanted to make sure that every Parisian who discussed his communion would repeat the word and associate it with the deed. In the same letter, he hopes that the deed will expose the slander of attributing certain irreligious pamphlets to him, among them the *Dîner du comte de Boulainvilliers* and the *Relation du chevalier de La Barre* which he had of course written. Perhaps the queen, in whose (temporary) return to health he rejoices, would not believe these allegations. In this way, he typically addresses the marquise's friend président Hénault, the queen's favourite. If he could persuade the queen to approve his communion, the pious faction would follow suit and the civic interpretation of the eucharist would enjoy considerable prestige. Mme Du Deffand, who was no dupe, realised that he was using her. 'Cette lettre est faite pour être montrée', she snapped in a conversation with Walpole, 'et par conséquent n'est pas digne de l'être' (Best.D14964, Commentary). But the poor lady was blind.

'Cela fait un bruit affreux,' Wagnière wrote to Damilaville on 19 April (Best.D14966). In a letter to mme Denis on the same day, Voltaire reiterated his surprise over the excitement in Paris. He had only done what all the inhabitants of Ferney did 'et ce que j'y avais déjà fait lorsque mon âge était moins avancé' (Best.D14967). He had only joined his fellow citizens in a routine observance, one which he had already begun to practise earlier in life. As in all of these remarks, he avoided connotations referring to religion. Taking the sacrament, he said was indispensable and, besides, he had to put a stop to slander. Another reason: 'il faut à la fin un bouclier à l'abri duquel on puisse finir avec tranquillité ses tristes jours'. Again, his dread of burial in the common pit! On 20 April, he confided in the comte de La Touraille, 'Je ne conçois pas comment la chose la plus simple, la plus ordinaire, et que je fais tous les ans a pu causer la moindre surprise. Je suis persuadé que vous faittes autant dans vos terres quand vous y êtes' (Best.D14971). How did La Touraille like rubbing shoulders with the count of Ferney and Tournay? He had inherited his titled estate, but Voltaire had merely bought his. Welcome or not, however, our upstart bourgeois took advantage of the opportunity to qualify his communion as a routine aristocratic example: 'Il n'y a personne qui ne doive cet exemple à sa paroisse.' No one, in other words, among those who had parishes to call their own! Since the count of Ferney accomplished this duty every year, there was no reason for the uproar in Paris. To this simple logic, he added the usual propaganda about prayers for the queen and joy over her recovery.

On 22 April (Best.D14973), he furnished d'Argental with a long list of reasons 'pour avoir changé ma table ouverte contre la sainte table', but not all of them need occupy us here. The first presents a variation on his most frequent theme: 'c'est un devoir que j'ai rempli avec mad^e Denis une fois ou deux si je m'en souviens bien'. This language reflects the need for accuracy in writing a close friend and friend of his niece. Should we therefore infer that he had been to mass only once or twice since Colmar or rather that mme Denis had not accompanied him more often than that? Since, according to Wagnière, he habitually gave and no doubt brought his parish a magnificent communion loaf every Easter, it seems reasonable to suppose that the local mass did not appeal to her. Her taste for sumptuous urban elegance tends to confirm this conjecture. The second reason Voltaire gave d'Argental amounts to howling with the wolves, but it yields additional evidence of his attitude: 'il ne m'en coûte qu'une cérémonie prescrite par les lois'. Required by law? Only in the sense that the French government disadvantaged and occasionally mistreated non-Catholics and that the Church expected all of its members to commune at least once a year at Easter. Although the loophole available to deists like Voltaire was spacious, he ignored it here to pursue the concept of a state religion. Most of the remaining items on his list are howling wolves, among whom he explicitly includes Biord. Although number eight, on the other hand, is not really a reason for taking Easter communion, it hints at one: 'On ne peut me reprocher d'hypocrisie, puisque je n'ai aucune prétention.' This remark needs underlining. Since Voltaire made no supernatural claim for his communion, it did not contradict writings in which he had ridiculed the real presence, transubstantiation, grace, etc. Eating a hostia to edify his vassals, he thought, was no hypocrisy, because he did not believe as they did that it had become the body of Christ. Nor did he feel in any way responsible for what he considered a superstition. On the contrary, he was merely assuring public order by demonstrating his respect for their cult. Number nine is even less a reason for his communion, since it asks d'Argental to burn his reasons. Did he really expect d'Argental to do it?

Biord answered him on April 25 (Best.D14980):

Je n'ais pû qu'être surpris qu'en affectant de ne pas entendre ce qui étoit fort intelligible dans ma Lettre, vous ayés supposé, que je vous savois bon gré d'une communion de politique dont Les protestans même n'ont pas été moins scandalisés, que les catholiques.

His irritation escaped him here. One suspects that Voltaire's insinuation of pretentions in excess of power had provoked him more than the deliberate misinterpretation of his letter as one of congratulation. The bishop's attempt to convert weakness into strength by citing Protestant disapproval of his communion, a well-founded argument, does not conceal the pain of the wound upon which Voltaire had thrown salt. Fortunately for Biord, Voltaire did not know what the bishop had attempted two years before, during the French mediation of a power struggle between the upper and the lower classes in Geneva. He had tried in vain to negotiate the right to reside in that city and the freedom of Catholics to practise their religion there. He was evidently not a bishop to forget all the blows Voltaire had rained on the Church. 'Une communion faite suivant Les vrais principes de La morale chrétienne', he scolds the culprit, 'exigeoit de votre part des réparations éclatantes.' Without such reparations, no priest should give him absolution or allow him to approach the sacrament. This observation not only suggests Biord's annoyance with subordinates who had committed such an indiscretion, but also his determination to see that it would not happen again. Perhaps he did not realise that, in this way, he was issuing a challenge to an implacable enemy. He easily refutes the right claimed by the lord of Ferney to address his vassals during mass[91] and condemns the retinue of armed guards (game wardens!) which he brought into church with him. Voltaire could hardly dispute these judgements in good faith. On the other hand, his age and apparent infirmity tempted Biord just as they had tempted Menoux fourteen years before. Thus the bishop reminds him of 'cette éternité à La quelle vous touchés de si près' and ends the letter with assurances of concern with his prospects for salvation. Aroused by the potential glory of converting a notorious enemy of the Church, such tactics stimulate our applause for

[91] 'La conduite d'un seigneur de paroisse [. . .] qui s' [. . .] ingère [dans l'Eglise] à donner des avis au peuple pendant la célébration de la s^{te} Messe [. . .] est [. . .] proscrite par les sages ordonnances des Rois très chrétiens qui ont toûjours distingué pour Le tems et le lieu ce qui est du Ministère des pasteurs de L'Eglise, de L'exercice de la police extérieure.'

Voltaire's resounding last laughs. Yet these letters from Biord raise him above the ranks of the deist's usual enemies, for they are lacking neither in intelligence nor in dignity. As he moves from irritation to reprobation and from reprobation to admonition, the reader detects a note of sincere regret that God-given talent should be in opposition to the Church.

Apparently Voltaire had not received this letter by 27 April when he wrote others to mme Denis and d'Alembert, each containing a full paragraph on his publicity stunt (Best.D14984, D14983). Treating his fellow *philosophe* to an ironical display of piety, he welcomes the rumours about his confession and communion as penitence for his sins. Again, he brags of doing his duty and giving his parish a communion loaf: 'il y avait une très bonne brioche pour le curé'. He says that he has also given the vestry of his chapel the sacerdotal costumes used in the Ferney production of his tragedy *Sémiramis*, a gift dramatising the responsibility for public edification which he assigns to both the theatre and the Church. As a final touch, he tells his freethinking correspondent, 'Je prétends, quand je mourrai, vous charger de ma canonisation.' Perhaps this joke obliquely cautions d'Alembert not to show the letter to the wrong people. Voltaire clearly expected his niece, on the other hand, to show the letter he wrote her to everyone who might be curious to see it. Once again, he reminds her that he had accomplished his Easter duty with her when she was at Ferney. 'Je ne pouvais m'en dispenser', he continues, 'lorsque je suis seul à Ferney chargé de la manutantion de la terre et de l'édification publique.' He could not have been more explicit. After several themes, which we have already seen, he declares, 'Je ne dois sans doute compte à personne [...] des fonctions nécessaires que j'ai remplies; mais comme vous [les] avez déjà remplies avec moi [...] je suis sûr que vous parlerez de cette affaire d'une manière convenable.' Even more than in his letter to mme Du Deffand, he was addressing himself to his correspondent's friends and acquaintances. Mme Denis was merely serving as a publicity agent, since she had already learned the basic information here from his previous letter to her. A new ingredient did enrich his propaganda, nevertheless. He now found himself accountable to no one for having fulfilled the function of edifying his vassals by his Easter exploit. He had merely hinted at this aristocratic independence in earlier correspondence.

In his second reply to Biord on 29 April, he wondered 'quels faux raports ont pu m'attirer tant d'aigreur de vôtre part' (Best.D14987).

Unable to imagine, or so he says, who might have done such a thing, he sent the bishop a copy of a notarised act drawn up in 1765 to deny the accusations of Ancian, curate of Moëns. According to this document (Best.D.app.300), Gros, Adam, David, a local curate named Fournier and several laymen testify that Voltaire 'a non seulement rempli les devoirs de la Religion Catolique', but also rebuilt the local church, maintained a schoolmaster, cleared fields for the benefit of peasants, bought ploughs, built houses and provided land for those who needed them, doubled the population of Ferney and refused aid to no one in need. Consequently, an embarrassing number of clergymen had legally certified his assiduity in performing a list of functions which assimilate religious observance to social and economic services in the public interest. Whatever the means of persuasion (which one can imagine!), common sense had convinced these poor devils that there was no harm in recognising what they knew to be true. Would they have signed such a document, if Voltaire had not effectively met the annual Easter obligation of the Church with some regularity? That would have exposed them to discipline by the bishop. Having detected Biord's chagrin over the indiscretion of clergymen at Ferney, Voltaire twists the knife in the wound: 'Vous verrez combien il est faux que les devoirs dont il est question n'aient été remplis que cette année.' Veiling deistic irony with pious sentiment, he answers the bishop's challenge in his final paragraph: 'Je tâche autant que je le puis de remplir toutes ces obligations.'

On a proximate date, he sent the same document[92] to the *Gazette d'Avignon* and denied several rumours he had heard, especially the one that his ex-Jesuit chaplain 'm'a [. . .] *confessé et traîné au pied des autels'*. He took advantage of the opportunity to publish his pet remarks about the communion loaf, the non-sermon against theft and the prayers for the queen. It was time for the general public to know that, by word and deed, Voltaire treated Easter communion as a routine civic function.

Grimm reported the incident and the reaction to it in the *Correspondance littéraire* of 1 May. Although we have already noted the details from this account that convincingly supplement Wagnière's testimony, it also evaluates the publicity Voltaire had achieved: 'Le bruit que cette nouvelle a faite à Paris et à Versailles pendant plusieurs jours est incroyable.' The king and the queen approved, says Grimm,

---

[92] *ca.* 30 April, enclosed with Best.D14989 to François de Morénas.

ut 'les dévots [. . .] les philosophes, et les gens du monde en ont été
ẟgalement scandalisés' (viii.63). Voltaire's friends and enemies alike
condemn his hypocrisy. His communion offends the devout even more
than a pamphlet might have, while socialites and neutral observers find
that it degrades him. Grimm himself, who probably reflects the opinion
of Diderot and his circle, has a more tolerant attitude: 'Cette action [. . .]
ne mérite pas d'être jugée à la rigueur, puisqu'elle ne fait de mal à personne' (viii.66). This opinion follows the general tendency of the
philosophes to predicate all moral judgements on advantages or dis-
advantages to secular society. Grimm had penetrated Voltaire's thought
in judging his act as one that harmed nobody, but he was less successful
in his attempt to motivate the act: while Voltaire certainly hoped to
persuade Louis to let him come home, he had been exaggerating his
fear of inconvenient attributions ever since the discovery that this tactic
tended to advertise the works in question.[93] Grimm does not seem to
have understood that he was deliberately exploiting the great curiosity
about everything he did. Yet the journalist acknowledged, 'L'homme
universel qui réside à Ferney [. . .] ne [peut] rien faire qui ne soit un
objet d'attention' (viii.63) for all powerful, respectable, intelligent and
cultivated Europeans. The patriarch was in fact trying to impress upon
the good sense of this influential public that, while Christianity could
not be liquidated, it could be reduced to a cult wholly dedicated to civic
edification.

The first of May brought letters from Voltaire to d'Alembert and the
marquis de Villevielle on the necessity of conforming to the unreasonable conventions of neighbours. Having recommended howling with
the wolves, he confides in the marquis: 'il y a des choses si méprisables
qu'on peut quelquefois s'abaisser jusqu'à elles sans se compromettre'
(Best.D14992). If ever the marquis finds himself in bare-bottomed
company, he should drop his breeches instead of bowing. In communion, therefore, the patriarch sees an uncivilised but harmless ceremony edifying barbarians. When surrounded by them, he tells d'Alembert, one must imitate their contortions and speak their language. 'Ce
que j'ai fait cette année, je l'ai déjà fait plusieurs fois, et, s'il plaît à Dieu,
je le ferai encore' (Best.D14991). Biord was not going to stop him.
Some people, he added, are afraid to handle spiders, but others swallow
them.

[93] see my *Voltaire and his Portable dictionary* (Frankfurt am Main 1972), p.52.

It was time for a final reply from the angry bishop. On 2 May, he protested that zeal, not *aigreur*, had dictated the tone of his last letter. He was writing this one, he said, only to exonerate the clergymen suspected by Voltaire, for public outcry had provided him with all the information he needed. The true Christian, he preaches, 'ne se flatte pas d' [. . .] avoir rempli Les devoirs [de sa religion] pour avoir fait une fois ou deux chaque année dans L'église [. . .] ni même pour avoir fait dans une longue suite d'années une ou deux communions dont le public a été plus scandalisé qu'édifié' (Best.D14995). This passage demonstrates that Biord grasped the patriarch's intentions even less firmly than Grimm. Preoccupied with the exclusion of an impostor from the ranks of true Christians, he hardly suspected the attempt to secularise the Church, despite all the innuendo in Voltaire's letters. Had he read them more carefully and discovered this design, he might have dealt with the impostor more effectively. He hastens to terminate his letter with assurances that it will be the last unless his correspondent mends his ways. Between these lines, however, Voltaire probably read the threat of more forceful measures.

In a letter to his niece on 3 May, he alludes to the dangers of living in Biord's diocese and compares himself to a herdsman minding cattle: 'il faut que je sois à leur pâturage quand ils broutent leur herbe' (Best. D14996). Mme Denis might have reminded him that, even so, there was no need to graze with them. Another letter to her on the next day contains a more successful, though less novel simile. If she should see Choiseul, she must tell him, 'j'ai déjeûné plus d'une fois avec vous [. . .] c'est une chose absolument nécessaire dans un pays où tout le monde déjeûne [. . .] les médecins ordonnent qu'on mange' (Best.D14999). Just as taking the eucharist for an ordinary meal demystifies it, treating bishops like doctors deprives them of their prestige. For the benefit of the natural light, Voltaire casts both the rite and the priest in a utilitarian role.

Allusions to his Easter communion diminish at this point in his correspondence. But a letter on 10 May to Biord from Fournier, the curate of Pregny, indicates that the bishop had asked the signers of Voltaire's notarised act for explanations. Fournier denies that he had signed a certificate stating, '*Mr. de Voltaire a rempli les devoirs de la Religion catholique dans sa Paroisse*' (Best.D15009). Yet an extant notarised copy of the act presents the same language, except that it says, 'dans la paroisse de Fernex' (Best.D.app.300), and it attests Fournier's signature. The priest claims that the certificate he had signed reads, 'Mr. de Voltaire fait profession *extérieure* de la Religion *Catolique*.' This is an unlikely claim, because such testimony was hardly worth the cost of hiring a notary. It seems more likely that Fournier was trying to lie his way out of trouble with the bishop, on the assumption that the quarrel between Biord and Voltaire would prevent Biord from consulting the original document. He even tries to divert the bishop's suspicions of him to Gros by disapproving Voltaire's continued attendance at mass. Unfortunately, he does not tell us whether the patriarch was taking communion. He nonetheless treats 'des confessions et communions qu'il a [déjà] faites' as a matter of fact. Curiously, he has a clearer perception of Voltaire's intentions than his bishop, for he notes that, according to the *Dictionnaire antiphilosophique*,[94] deists observe all cults indifferently, 'comme d'une cérémonie de bienséance'.

A letter from d'Alembert on 13 May applauds Voltaire's prank, encourages him to repeat it and informs him that 'des *Thrones*, des *dominations* et des *Puissances*' approve, an allusion to his correspondent Frederick (Best.D15016). Actually, both d'Alembert and Frederick had a very different opinion, as we shall see. After boring mme Denis, on 25 May, with standard propaganda, Voltaire rebaptised the great event as 'la chose très décente que j'ai faite' and described the bishops of Geneva and Saint-Claude as 'dogues mitrés'.[95] He acted as his own secretary and referred to himself in the third person on 30 May in answering Gay de Noblac, the self-announced author of a work on his 'rétractation' (Best.D15046). Insulted, he protests, 'Qui n'a jamais rien écrit contre ce qu'il doit respecter n'a point de rétractation à faire.' He naturally refrains from identifying exactly what it is that he respects. He likewise completes a routine explanation of his Easter performance by citing the presence of Protestants in the diocese. On 31 May, d'Alembert had the rare opportunity to send him a letter by other means than the post, thus avoiding inspection by the police. He profited from the opportunity to express a franker opinion of the Easter prank. 'Vous savez mieux que moi', he admits, 'les raisons qui vous ont déterminé' (Best.D15049). Since the devout, however, do not believe in the sacrament any more than Voltaire, they will resent his flaunting of their hypocrisy all the more bitterly. 'J'ai donc bien peur [...] que vous

---

[94] by Louis-Mayeul Chaudon, Benedictine of Cluny (Avignon 1767).
[95] Best.D15034. Voltaire was trying to obtain the liberation of serfs bound by feudal law to the monastery of Saint Claude. Full liberation was achieved only by the Revolution.

n'ayez rien gagné à cette comédie, peutêtre dangereuse pour vous.' Voltaire may have appreciated this warning, but rather because of his disciple's sincerity than his psychology of the devout. After all the hints he had given d'Alembert, on the other hand, the latter's failure to understand was surely a disappointment. This was not the only time that one of the most intelligent Frenchmen in the eighteenth century lacked imagination.[96]

Biord had meanwhile sent his correspondence with Voltaire to Saint-Florentin, the French minister, whom he asked to show it to Louis. Saint-Florentin replied on 14 June that the king applauded the 'sages conseils' and 'solides exhortations' Biord had given Voltaire. Furthermore, 'Sa M^te luy fera mander de ne plus faire dans l'église d'Eclat aussi déplacé que celuy dont vous luy avés avec raison fait reproches' (Best.D15071). The minister confirms that the lord of a private parish does not have the right to address the congregation. On this point, therefore, the bishop was vindicated. Yet the letter from Saint-Florentin says nothing about Voltaire's communion. This omission lends support to Grimm's assertion that Louis approved it[97] and amounts to a rebuke of Biord. On this more substantive issue, therefore, the bishop had suffered a setback. Saint-Florentin duly informed Voltaire of his majesty's displeasure over his intervention in church, yet without mentioning his communion (Best.D15083). Biord's appeal to Louis, which Voltaire at once guessed, naturally angered an exile anxious for a royal pardon. Five days after the date of Saint-Florentin's letter (18 June) and therefore necessarily by a return of post, he wrote to the minister to deny the charge. Along with the certificate we have already discussed (Best.D.app.300), he enclosed another signed by Gros and Adam, a document which has not been recovered. This time he reduces his intervention in church to 'avertissant à voix demi basse le curé de prier pour la santé de la Reine' (23 June; Best.D15093), a lie worse than Fournier's.

By the next day, he had learned some compromising information about Biord's past which he forwarded to his niece for dissemination: 'Le masson [...] fut repris de justice à Paris dans le temps qu'il y était

---

[96] Voltaire wrote to Beaumont *ca.* 10 June, but the text of his letter is not extant. A Jesuit hostile to Voltaire, Beaumont's biographer Régnault says that it was 'une lettre hypocrite sur son retour à la religion' (ii.166). The archbishop did not reply.

[97] Louis may also have wished to avoid any possibility of reviving the controversy over refusal of sacraments, even though Jansenists and not freethinkers had been involved.

porte Dieu' (Best.D15094). A *porte-Dieu*, who literally carries the viaticum, is a priest charged with administering last rites. Further details in a letter to d'Argental (27 July) imply that Biord had been involved in the refusal of last rites: 'cet animal là a encore sur sa friperie un décret de prise de corps du parlement de Paris, qu'il s'attira quand il était porte dieu à la s^te chapelle basse.'[98] Knowledge of his enemy's participation in the concerted denial of rites, to which Voltaire believed all dying citizens should have unconditional access, may well have strengthened his resolve to commune again during the Easter of 1769.

But he particularly resented the accusation, which Biord had communicated to the king, that he had preached a sermon in church, thus usurping the function of his curate. His satires in the form of a sermon, such as the *Sermon des cinquante*, had probably abetted this rumour, which he was determined to extinguish (Best.D15096):

Le prédicateur demande à ses anges [s'] il est convenable que mad^e Denis aille gronder m^r Le Comte de s^t Florentin respectueusement et tendrement, et lui dire qu'avant d'écrire des pouilles au nom du Roi, il n'est pas mal auparavant de s'informer si le fait est vrai.

On 29 June, he sent Richelieu a full defence of his position and hinted that he would appreciate his discussing the matter with the king. In order to amuse the blasé marshal, he infuses humour into the anecdote: 'le Roi m'a fait écrire par m^r de s^t Florentin qu'il était très mécontent que j'eusse monté en chaire dans ma paroisse, et que j'eusse prêché le jour de Pâques. Qui fut étonné? Ce fut le révérend père Voltaire' (Best.D15106). No less surprised than he, his curate, he says, immediately attested that he had merely recommended prayers for the queen's health and informed the parishioners of a theft committed during mass. After his almoner (Adam) and a notary had certified this statement, he had sent it to Saint-Florentin. The document, as we have seen, is not extant.

One must register a final comment on the communion of 1768 in a letter from Voltaire to mme Du Deffand on 13 July: 'Ne vous acquittez pas d'un usage prescrit, vous êtes un monstre d'athéisme. Acquittez

---

[98] Best.D15157. He was rather the curate of the Basse-Sainte-Chapelle from 1748 on – he was thirty years old then – according to Léon Buffet, who neither substantiates nor refutes Voltaire's allegations that he was a *porte-Dieu* and that 'il eut des démêlés avec la justice pour avoir refusé des sacrements à des malades. C'est fort possible, en un temps où le pouvoir civil intervenait jusque dans les choses religieuses' (*Monseigneur J. P. Biord*, in *Mémoires et documents publiés par l'Académie salésienne*, lvi (Annecy 1938), p.29).

vous en, vous êtes un monstre d'hypocrisie' (Best.D15139). Altho[u]
he intended this comment as a complaint against the injustice of [his]
enemies, it discloses the basic premise of his destructive strategy. Si[nce]
eucharistic dogma excluded the evidence of experience, a proponen[t]
of experience need only commune in order to sabotage the sacrament
and trap defenders of the faith in a dilemma. None of the clauses against
unworthy communicants could stop him from demonstrating that the
eucharist, of which all Catholics partook, brought no grace and from
declaring that it did not contain the transubstantiated body of Christ.
For years, Voltaire's satirical commentary on the dogma had been
stressing these very points, and so he was no more a hypocrite than an
atheist. Cries of hypocrisy merely betrayed the lack of a more appropriate epithet or, in other words, a more effective defence of the eucharist
against such an adversary.

The constructive intentions behind the communion of 1768 were
even more important to Voltaire. Since an act cannot speak for itself,
one may interpret it as one wishes. Once it is done, it can therefore lend
itself to several plausible interpretations, more than one of which may be
useful to the man responsible for it. Voltaire, as usual, varied his explanations according to the correspondent to whom he was writing.
To his friends, he confided his fear of burial in the common pit and the
affinity between his conceptions of the theatre and the church. He told
them he was performing a superstitious, but harmless ceremony to
appease his enemies and assure the allegiance of his vassals. He informed
others that he was only meeting his responsibility as the lord of Ferney,
who must set a good example and encourage his parishioners in their
practice of Catholicism, especially in an area infested with Protestants.
He admitted to no one that he was trying to appease the king in hopes of
seeing an end to his exile, but this was assuredly one of his motives too.
In nearly all of his letters, on the other hand, he insisted that he had
merely done his duty, a duty which everyone was doing and which he
had done before. Obviously, we cannot rely on his own testimony to
determine how regularly he had communed after 1761, the only docu-
mented incidence since Colmar, for his count varies from once with
mme Denis to every Easter. No one, however, and not even the bishop
denied that he had taken the annual communion required by the Church.
On the contrary, the assertions of Biord, Fournier and, above all,
Wagnière tend to confirm the notarised act of 1765. While some doubt
may remain on this point, one can scarcely dispute that he wanted his

claim to an annual observance taken seriously. Constantly, he emphasised custom, routine and generality, the very categories to which common experience consigned the eucharist in his day. Experience accommodated none of the supernatural pretentions of the Church, which he deliberately ignored throughout the controversy. In his letters to Biord, he limited his ironical piety to deism and he exploded rumours of his conversion and retraction. He never ran the risk of expounding his theory of public edification by a civic cult, but he did lavish allusions to this idea on enemies and friends alike. To no avail, however. For neither Biord, nor Grimm, nor d'Alembert could comprehend his message. Significantly, the humble Fournier came closer to understanding it than all the others. Despite Voltaire's personal demonstration of what he regarded as an unreligious rite, this concept was remote from the intellectual habits of his time.

Would Voltaire try to commune again at Easter in 1769? This question does not seem to have interested his contemporaries as much as one might expect, for there is little evidence of speculation. Meister, who replaced Grimm as the editor of the *Correspondance littéraire*, did wonder about his intentions. On 25 November 1768 the minister Moultou, on visit at Ferney, answered an inquiry from him: '[La] dévotion [de Voltaire] paraît fort rallentie, & il prétexte souvent quelque incommodité pour ne point aller à la messe. Au reste, cette farce a si mal pris la première fois, qu'il pourrait se dispenser de récidiver' (Best. D15335). The minister's bad humour,[99] which probably represents the general attitude in Geneva, distorts the evidence he reveals. Voltaire's zeal had subsided because Easter was over and he had better things to do in the off-season.

Having recognised in him a man as stubborn as himself, Biord took his precautions well in advance of Easter.[100] In a letter to Castin, his official in Gex, he gave thorough instructions, so that the fiasco of 1768 might not be repeated. Voltaire's piety the year before, he observes, had neither compensated for his pernicious works nor extinguished his rage against the Catholic religion. The sacerdotal regulations in such

[99] 'On ne peut rien promettre d'un homme aussi inconséquent et aussi variable.' This remark betrays Moultou's impatience with Voltaire's failure to behave as he expected.

[100] to the letter discussed in this paragraph (Best.D15547), Besterman assigns the date of 29 March, three days after Easter. The content of the letter, Biord's experience of Easter 1768, and his character, all tend to invalidate so late a date.

cases are explicit: 'la réparation doit être proportionnée au scandale, et comme ni la confession ni la communion ne peuvent par elles-mêmes effacer des impressions de scandale la réparation doit essentiellement précéder la confession'. Reparation must precede the administration of the sacraments, a wise precaution in dealing with so crafty a deist! As soon as Voltaire asks to confess, therefore, he must be told to renew his profession of faith from the year before, repudiate all impious works attributed to him, condemn the errors and blasphemies in them and retract everything evil or reprehensible in those he continues to recognise as his own. He must likewise sign a statement satisfying these conditions in front of witnesses and a notary, and all must sign the act. Only after these precautions, should he be allowed to confess and, if he wishes to take communion too, 'vous l'engagerez à faire en présence des témoins assistants une réparation des scandales qu'il a donnés par ses propos et par ses écrits'. Biord cites Montesquieu's deathbed retraction as an appropriate precedent. If followed, his instructions would force Voltaire to decide between the ruin of his free-thinking reputation and the abandonment of the sacraments so vital to his civic cult.

Realizing that Biord would try to stop him this time, the patriarch apparently opened his campaign on the Thursday before Palm Sunday (16 March).[101] Wagnière was taking dictation from him when, from his bed, Voltaire saw people walking in the garden and asked who they were. His secretary told him they were Gros and a Capuchin from Gex (Joseph) who was helping the curate confess his parishioners. 'Est-il vrai', Voltaire asked, 'que l'évêque d'Annecy a défendu de me confesser et de me donner la communion?' Wagnière confirmed his suspicion and Voltaire concluded: 'J'ai envie de me confesser et de communier malgré lui.' He would even receive these sacraments in his room for the bishop's sake: 'Cela pourra être fort plaisant, et nous verrons qui, de l'évêque ou de moi, l'emportera' (L.W. i.73). Consequently, he took Biord's efforts to keep him from celebrating his Easter ritual as a challenge and he meant to defy the bishop. He asked Wagnière to leave a crown on the table and call Joseph in. Once the friar had entered Voltaire told him, 'Voici le saint temps de pâques. Je voudrais [. . .] remplir aussi mes devoirs de Français, d'officier du roi et de seigneur de

---

[101] the date is undocumented, but Wagnière (whose chronology of this period is faulty) testifies that Voltaire turned to Gros in seeking a confessor three days after the incident related above. Extant correspondence dated Palm Sunday (19 March) refers to this decision (Best.D15528).

paroisse' (L.W. i.73). He was too ill, he explained, to go to church and he wished to confess in his bedroom. He gave the crown to Joseph, whom Wagnière describes as thunderstruck. On the pretext that people were waiting for him in church, the friar extricated himself with the crown in his pocket and promised to return in three days. Wagnière says he was trembling as he left the room.

By Palm Sunday (19 March) the three days had run out and he had not kept his word. Thus Voltaire sent someone to make the same request of Gros, who declined because the freethinker had not re-tracted his works against Christianity and the Church. This one gathers from a message Voltaire wrote to his curate on Palm Sunday denying the accusations of slanderers, a word which in his language always means those who attribute impious works to him, whether he had written them or not. This note warned Gros, 'rien ne doit s'opposer aux usages reçus. Vous êtes instruit sans doute des règlements faits par les parlements, et je ne doute pas que vous ne vous conformiez aux lois du Royaume' (Best.D15528). He was reminding the curate of the judicial precedents set by the *parlements* in the dispute over refusal of sacraments. A priest of Gros's calibre, he assumed, would not have the courage to face such a threat, especially when his bishop resided in a foreign country. Supervised nonetheless by Castin in Gex, Gros re-sisted.

An attestation drawn up over a month later tells us that Voltaire was indisposed in church that same day.[102] His behaviour before and after persuades us rather that he pretended to be ill, as he had in Frank-furt.[103] He probably wanted to impress Gros, who seems to have turned his back and ignored what he did not want to see. On Tuesday, Voltaire called his surgeon Burgoz into his bedroom and told him to take his pulse. Burgoz found it normal, but the patriarch exploded and bullied him into taking it again. This time the surgeon had the good sense to diagnose a dangerous fever, which Voltaire delightedly confirmed. The imminence of his death thus established, he ordered Burgoz, 'Allez

---

102 'C'est à son église paroissiale [que m. de Voltaire] tomba le dimanche de la semaine sainte dernière dans une maladie qui le mit en danger de mort' (Best.D.app.314, 12 May). Whether he attended church before or after sending the note to Gros is unclear.

103 Voltaire's secretary Collini tells how he found his master in the courtyard of the house where they were being detained: 'Je le vois courbé, se mettant les doigts dans la bouche et faisant des efforts pour vomir. Je m'écrie, effrayé, vous trouvez-vous donc mal? Il me regarde, des larmes sortant des yeux; il me dit à voix basse, *fingo . . . fingo . . .* (Je fais semblant)' (p.86).

le dire au curé, il doit savoir ce qu'il a à faire auprès d'un malade qui, depuis plus de trois jours, a une fièvre violente, et qui est en danger de mort.'[104] Now that he had been suffering from fever for several days, he was no longer asking for ordinary communion, but rather the viaticum. Gros relates his response to this request in letters he would later send Castin and Voltaire. He went immediately and saw the dying man in his château: 'Je luy dis qu'il n'étoit pas [assez] malade pour exiger [le viatique]' (Best.D15551); 'Je vous répondis aussi doucement que fit le prophète Natan à David; vous me comprites' (Best.D15559; 1 S. xii.7-15). After witnessing many false declarations and demonstrations of bad health, Gros was using his head. He realised that the hypochondriac, having been denied ordinary communion, was pretending to be dangerously ill in order to obtain the viaticum instead. Consequently, he reminded him that he would have to retract his 'mauvais ouvrages' before receiving the sacraments and we already know that Voltaire did not like retractions (see p.156). He was not used to taking no for an answer, however, and soon he tried again. Gros continues: 'Vous m'envoiâtes ensuite quérir, Comme Ochosiaz [Ahaziah] manda le prophète Elie', that is, according to 2 Kings i.2-17, with stubborn persistence and little reverence for God. Wagnière testifies that Voltaire dispatched Burgoz every morning with ever more alarming news of his health. The sick man also intensified and repeated his threat of appealing for judicial intervention: 'il n'a fait que m'inquiéter, et m'envoier des Billets et il me menace du parlement, et de l'infraction des ordonnances du Roy' (Best.D15551). He would not hear of retracting his evil works, Gros complains, and he insisted on speaking of the viaticum as 'une pure mode à suivre [...] une simple cérémonie d'état' (Best.D15559). But the curate rose to the occasion: 'j'ai fait, à cet assaut [...] comme st Michel à l'altercation qu'il eut avec le premier Ange rebelle Ebloui de l'éclat de ses lumières' (Best.D15559). This is the most preposterous of

---

[104] L.W. i.75. Wagnière sets Burgoz's examination of Voltaire three days after Joseph had taken the crown and he says that Voltaire sent Burgoz immediately to talk to Gros. Later Gros wrote to Castin (Best.D15551) and to Voltaire (Best.D15559) that he had gone and seen the lord of the parish in his château as soon as he heard that he was ill, 'le mardi de la semaine sainte' (21 March). But Voltaire was already in contact with Gros about a confession by 19 March, Palm Sunday, as indicated by the note he wrote him that day. Wagnière testifies that Voltaire did not turn to Gros until Joseph had failed to keep his word, that is, until three days had elapsed. Wagnière is therefore in error when he sets Burgoz's examination of Voltaire three days after Joseph took the crown. He may well have forgotten the exact sequence of events by the time he was writing, nine years later. This sequence does not seem to be of any special importance, however.

his three Biblical references. In Revelations xii.7-9, Michael and the good angels cast Satan and the bad angels down from heaven. According to 2 Corinthians xi.14, 'Satan himself goes disguised as an angel of light.' Mistaking the archangel for the apostle, Gros is casting himself in the role of God's triumphant general and Voltaire in that of Satan masquerading as an angel of light. He prayed God, he continues, to humble, dazzle and incline his heart to a contrition and docility more suitable for his Easter enterprise. The charitable function of prayer, the intervention of the archangel and the repentance of the sinner must have amused the lord of the parish.

His attacks of fever would continue to increase in number from letter to letter, as the months of seclusion in his bedroom at Colmar had. By Good Friday (24 March), he was claiming eight: 'Les ordonnances portent qu'au troisième accez de fièvre on donne les sacrements à un malade. M^r De Voltaire en a eu huit violents; il en avertit Monsieur le curé de Ferney' (Best.D15534). He was intensifying the urgency of his appeals to the point where their credibility was beginning to fade. Gros answered the latest note on the same day (Best.D15536) with a self-assurance born, no doubt, of support from Gex and Annecy. Acknowledging Voltaire's attacks of fever without alarm, he says his routine duties have kept him from coming to see the sick man. As if concerned, but only slightly, with the effect this excuse will have on the lord of Ferney, he complains of a sleepless night and a dry cough. Gros would in fact die a few months later.[105] Though in mortal danger, he tells Voltaire, he is anxious to provide him with the services in his competence. On the other hand, he has not forgotten Castin and Biord: 'afin de ne pas m'exposer aux menaces de mes Supérieurs [. . .] je vous prierai du fond de mon âme [. . .] de vouloir faire une rétractation devant no^{re} de tous les mauvais ouvrages que vous avez faits, en présence des témoins que vous jugerez à propos, c'est tout ce que l'on demande de vous'. This language reveals the influence of the superiors mentioned and reflects the instructions given by the bishop in the letter examined above.

In the middle of the night before Easter Sunday,[106] Voltaire ordered all of his servants out of bed and sent them to impress upon the curate

---

[105] before 6 December 1769, when Voltaire informed Pankoucke of his death (Best. D16025).

[106] nine days after Joseph had taken the crown, according to Wagnière.

the immediacy of the danger threatening his life.[107] One imagines a sleepy and dishevelled band straggling across the lawn in various stages of dress behind Wagnière who carried the most alarming report yet concocted by Burgoz. But Gros stood firm and by the end of Easter Sunday, Voltaire had neither confessed nor communed.

It must have been on Wednesday 29 March that he dispatched what Wagnière calls 'un homme de loi' (L.W. i.77) to threaten his curate with prosecution or worse. Gros later admitted to Wagnière that this move had badly scared him. He went and had a long conversation with Voltaire and, this time, the patriarch offered to make the concession demanded of him, as Gros informed Joseph the next day (30 March): 'Il est dans des dispositions de faire une rétractation [. . .] il me chargea de vous prier de [. . .] descendre samedi prochain [. . .] cela sera très honorable et pour vous et pour moi' (Best.D15550). Thus Joseph would confess Voltaire and Gros would administer the viaticum to him. The freethinker's trump card was again proving to be the very magnitude of his sins against the Church, sins which mightily inflated the potential glory of converting him. He knew that, as he increased the generosity of the concessions he offered, temptation would loosen Biord's control of Gros and Joseph. Sooner or later, the illusion of great opportunity in a lifetime of mediocrity would free them from the bishop's grasp. Suddenly subjected to unaccustomed pressure, they could be precipitated into accomplishing their habitual duties without an adequate guarantee. Under stress, Voltaire knew, the ordinary intelligence retreats from common sense to habit. He was laying a cruel trap, yet one no uglier than the ambition of the men he was luring into it.

By ten o'clock on Thursday morning (30 March), the dying man had recovered enough to dictate and sign a legal statement addressed to his curate. Despite his illness, he testifies, he was in church on Palm Sunday and has suffered several attacks of fever since then. Unable to confess and commune in church for the edification of his vassals and the Protestants living nearby, he asks the curate to obey the king's ordinances, the decrees of Parlement and the canons of the Church. The declaration emphasises the 'religion dans laquelle le dit malade est né, a vécu et

---

[107] after d'Alembert's resignation as co-editor of the *Encyclopédie* (1758), Voltaire wrote to him: 'Que ne vous adressez-vous en corps à m. de Malesherbes? [. . .] Je ne conçois pas comment tous ceux qui travaillent ne s'assemblent pas, et ne déclarent pas qu'ils renonceront à tout, si on ne les soutient [. . .] Faites un corps, messieurs; un corps est toujours respectable [. . .] Ameutez vous, et vous serez les maîtres' (19 January 1758; Best.D7592). The tactic seems naive in this case.

veut mourir, et dont il veut remplir tous les devoirs ainsi que ceux de sujet du roi, offrant de faire toutes les déclarations nécessaires, toutes protestations requises soit publiques soit particulières' (Best.D15548). To enhance the legal status of the text implied by the language, he had his secretaries Wagnière and Bigex sign it with him. Declaring himself Catholic from birth to death and promising to make any statements required of him, he was broadcasting a change of heart to Gros, as if he had panicked over the imaginary approach of death. He knew he did not have to persuade Gros that he was really dying, but merely that he feared death, a cunning tactic inspired by the pleas of Biord. But his text is full of hidden escape clauses and camouflaged omissions. He had always espoused the ancient maxim of conforming to the religion with which one must live and he had never interpreted this practice as a sincere commitment. He continued to talk of doing his duties as a loyal subject of the king. Who was to decide, moreover, what declarations were necessary? Nowhere, in any case, did he endorse the Catholic dogma. Although this document did not really fool Gros, he rushed it off with the letter of explanation mentioned above (Best.D15551) to Castin, whom he asked for detailed written instructions. This request demonstrates the effect of the bishop's displeasure over the indiscretions of David and Gros the year before.

Voltaire intended to make 'the necessary declaration' he had promised Gros, but he did not want anyone else to draw it up for him. On Friday afternoon (31 March), he called Adam, his secretary Bigex, the notary Raffo and several other favourite witnesses in for this purpose.[108] He did not invite Gros, because he knew the curate would demand stipulations laid down by Biord. He presented his statement as a reply to the slander of his enemies Nonotte and Guyon. The essential passage reads as follows (Best.D.app.300):

jamais [Voltaire] n'a cessé de respecter et de pratiquer la religion proffessée dans le Roiaume [...] si jamais il lui Etait échapé quelques indiscrétions préjudiciables à la Religion de L'Etat, il en demandait pardon à Dieu et à L'Etat [...] il a vécu et veut mourir dans L'observance de touttes les loix du Roiaume et dans la Religion Catolique, Etroitement unie à la loix.

On Friday (31 March), Castin was a busy correspondent. In a letter to Biord, he enclosed the report from Gros along with Voltaire's declaration of 30 March (Best.D15556). He informed the bishop that

---

[108] Wagnière appears to have been absent.

he had sent Gros a reply to this declaration and a statement to be signed by Voltaire, but 'seulement en cas de nécessité pressante', in other words, only if he were really dying. Otherwise, Gros should wait for the bishop's orders. Castin's fear of taking any initiative in this case, a fear that must have arisen from the bishop's anger over the communion of 1768, would result in the communion of 1769. As irony would have it, Biord would have himself especially to blame. Castin finishes the letter with assurances that, since a Capuchin will confess Voltaire tomorrow, he is sending it through Geneva and by express, so that it will arrive in time for a reply. In his letter to Gros, he says that the bishop's answer may come by tomorrow, an optimistic prediction: 'J'envois le tout à Monseigneur pour procéder ici avec plus de sûreté.' He describes the enclosures mentioned in his letter to Biord as 'un projet de lettre' and 'un projet de Déclaration', thus implying that the curate could rewrite them as he saw fit, but they were to be used 'seulement en cas de nécessité pressante'. The potential convert must not be allowed to die before he joins the Church! Although the letter will announce the declaration, 'la déclaration n'est point à lâcher qu'il n'ait promis de la signer ou même qu'il ne l'ait signé'. Here was a loophole. Castin's haste, his inability to give Gros more definite orders, his reliance on the bishop and his fear of bungling the conversion of the century betray his inexperience in such matters.

Before Joseph left for Ferney, Castin read him the drafts of a letter to Voltaire and a declaration to be signed by him. On Joseph's advice, he deleted the clause '*tandis que vous êtes peut-être menacé de plus haut vous-même*'. The friar no doubt suspected that such a statement might provoke Voltaire and spoil his inclination to convert. Joseph brought Castin's letter and declaration projects with him to Ferney the next day (1 April) and consulted Gros. Castin would later report to Biord that they used neither of these drafts. Gros may well have found the declaration project too demanding for Voltaire's willingness to compromise. In his reply to Voltaire on 1 April (Best.D15559), he did use Castin's letter draft, for he actually restored the deleted clause, '*tandis que vous êtes peutêtre menacé de plus haut* vous-même'.[109] After the review, described above (see p.163), of his recent relations with the freethinker, he exposes the discrepancies in the latter's declaration. It is vague, he objects, and

<hr />

109 Besterman assigns the date *ca.* 31 March 1769, to Best.D15559, but Gros's use of the deleted clause in Castin's letter, which Joseph brought him on 1 April, shows that the curate could not have written it before then.

neither repudiates nor condemns the horrible writings attributed to him. Fearing 'quelque surprise', he has sent to *monseigneur* to find out exactly what he should demand of Voltaire. Until the bishop answers, Gros requires retraction and repudiation according to attestation before witnesses and a notary. On this condition, he will render all the services of his ministry. Perhaps Joseph brought this letter to Voltaire himself.

Neither Castin nor Gros seems to have noticed that April Fool's Day fell on the Saturday Voltaire had asked to be confessed by Joseph. In their haste to convert a notorious enemy of Christianity, the friar, the priest and the official apparently never suspected that they were merely celebrating the feast of fools. But Voltaire, who as usual knew exactly what he was doing, particularly wanted to make a fool of the bishop. He had certainly not forgotten the letter d'Alembert had written him on 1 April 1768, describing Jesus's institution of the eucharist as 'un grand *poisson d'avril* pour le genre humain' (Best.D14909). What could be more appropriate, in view of eucharistic theology, than a commemoration of the original joke on humanity by another joke on All Fool's Day at the expense of Jesus's 'apostle' Jean-Pierre Biord? Whatever actually happened on 1 April 1769, Voltaire considered it an April Fool's prank.

Despite conflicting documents, we have a witness who stood in the patriarch's shadow day and night, an honest but unimaginative man, loyal to his master, yet inclined to detachment, and above all a Protestant.[110] Any attempt to order the chaos of this *folle journée*, this *journée des dupes*, must begin with Wagnière's testimony. When Joseph arrived, the secretary ushered him into Voltaire's bedroom, retired to an adjoining cabinet and left the door partially open. Perhaps he had permission to do just exactly that! He could see that the friar was frightened. Apparently, Voltaire had finally chosen him as his confessor because he thought he could do with him nearly as he pleased.[111]

[110] this is not to say that his testimony is flawless (see n.104). In explaining the shortcomings of early biographies of Voltaire, Besterman notes that some 'are the products of generally well-meaning men with unreliable memories (like the secretaries Longchamp, Collini and even Wagnière)' (*Voltaire* (New York 1969), pp.13-14). Besterman nonetheless finds great merit in Wagnière: 'a loyal, honest and efficient secretary [...] Wagnière's solicitude for his master's reputation and interests continued after his death, often in the face of the selfish opposition of mme Denis' (p.389).

[111] Wagnière describes Joseph as 'jeune et vigoureux'. 'Pour se créditer de côté et d'autre, [il] se vantait [...] d'avoir confessé M. de Voltaire.' When his superiors discovered that he was keeping a concubine (see n.84), they transferred him to a monastery in the remote Val d'Aoste. 'Il y arriva dans un très piteux état, car, dans un accès de

Voltaire asked Joseph to help him recite the Confiteor and the Credo. But Joseph hardly knew what he was saying, as the freethinker had probably expected. One can imagine the old versifier improvising contradictory homonyms to replace the words he did not want to say.[112] The voice of Joseph who, by force of habit, was probably saying the correct words, no doubt covered Voltaire's. Wagnière in fact states that the friar did not know what Voltaire was saying. Whatever one may think of this subterfuge, it seems unlikely that the freethinker would have stooped to a verbatim recitation of the Apostle's Creed in front of such witnesses after all he had written against the trinity, not even on April Fool's Day.

Before Joseph could confront him with an orthodox profession of faith, he abruptly professed his own faith as if his civic deism conformed to Christianity. His illness prevented him from going to mass as often as he should, he confessed, but 'J'adore Dieu dans ma chambre.' He did as much good as possible and 'j'en prends Dieu à témoin [. . .] ainsi je vous prie de me donner l'absolution' (L.W.i.80). But the Capuchin somehow found the nerve to prevaricate. Voltaire had written evil books against the good Lord, the Holy Virgin and even priests. 'Je vous serai donc obligé de signer seulement ce petit papier, qui n'est qu'une simple profession de foi' (L.W. i.80). The slip of paper, which he took from his sleeve, may well have been the note (Best.D15550) Gros had sent him asking him to come and confess Voltaire. The copyist of the only extant manuscript appended a profession of faith which formulates the trinity, implies the two natures and claims that Christ founded the Church, all of which were abhorrent to Voltaire. The copyist assumes that Voltaire signed this profession, which reappears in a notarised document, dated 15 April, making the same false claim (see p.175). Perhaps Gros or even Castin himself dictated it to Joseph as he wrote it down on Gros's letter before going to confess Voltaire. It is probably the declaration mention by Castin in his letters to Gros and Biord on 31 March (Best.D15556, D15557). Rather than accept the paper,

désespoir, il avait pris en chemin le parti de se faire la même opération qu'Origène; à force de soins, il n'en perdit pas la vie, mais ce qui la donne' (L.W. i.199-200). The secretary seems to have borrowed this joke from his master.

[112] while acting in the plays he produced, according to Wagnière, he often forgot his lines for lack of emotional self-control. Yet he spontaneously improvised new ones to replace those he could not remember. Although no one was able to record these improvisations and he could not recall them afterwards, the witnesses found them impressive. See L.W. i.50.

Voltaire argued, 'Ne venons-nous pas de réciter le Symbole des Apôtres qui contient tout? Nous devons [. . .] nous y tenir, sans quoi on pourrait avec raison vous accuser, vous et moi, d'innovation' (L.W. i.80). Good sense could scarcely deny that the Apostle's Creed defined essential Catholic orthodoxy or that innovation of any kind violated that orthodoxy. But good sense could scarcely hope to prove that the Creed adequately summarised the dogma, as Voltaire well understood, and he thought a friar sent to confess his humble parishioners unlikely to try.

At this point, Wagnière reports a contest in which Joseph kept advancing his paper and the necessity for signing it, while Voltaire insisted on the sufficiency of the Creed. After they had argued back and fourth 'pendant un demi-quart d'heure' (L.W. i.81), Voltaire began to preach slander and tolerance in the pathetic style of Easter 1768, much to the distress of the mendicant who, 'les larmes aux yeux' (L.W. i.81), continued mechanically to advance his little piece of paper. Seeing his victim ready for the kill, baron Voltaire suddenly barked, 'Donnez-moi l'absolution tout à l'heure' (L.W. i.81). Intimidated, the friar reverted to the habitual words and gesture of the absolution, while the paper went back up his sleeve unsigned and unread. Voltaire immediately summoned Gros, Adam, the notary Raffo and the other customary signers of notarised acts at Ferney. On 24 May, he would write to d'Alembert, 'Je reçois dans mon lit le saint viatique que m'apporte mon curé devant tous les coqs de ma paroisse' (Best.D15660). Having received the eucharist, he declaimed, 'Aiant mon Dieu dans ma bouche, je déclare que je pardonne sincèrement à ceux qui ont Ecrit au Roy, des Calomnies contre moi, et qui n'ont pas réussi dans leur mauvais dessein' (Best.D.app.300). Raffo duly wrote this down and everyone signed, except Wagnière. Thus Voltaire 'forgave' Biord for his 'treachery' according to the very document that attested his defiance of the bishop's orders to deny him the eucharist unless he made proper reparations.

But did Voltaire really refuse to make acceptable reparations? In his 1 April letter (Best.D15559), Gros demanded that he retract his impious and scandalous works 'selon la déclaration que je pourrois vous proposer', a declaration to be signed, witnessed and notarised. This language implies that he had neither enclosed nor in fact composed such a declaration. On 7 April, Castin told Biord that Joseph had given him Voltaire's retraction the evening before. He also said that neither Gros nor Joseph had made any use of his own 'projet de profession et de rétractation' (Best.D15575). After Joseph's return from Ferney on the previous Saturday, Castin explains, the friar 'me rendit compte [. . .] de la rétractation [. . .] qu'il fit dresser après [la] communion [de Voltaire] sans sçavoir me dire en détail ce qu'elle contenait'. The official advised him then to secure this retraction as soon as possible, for Joseph's honour as a director of conscience depended on it. He had asked the notary for it, Joseph replied, but the notary had put him off on the pretext that it had not yet been certified. The notary had nonetheless promised to let him have it later. Alarmed and impatient, Castin had tried three or four times, though in vain, to learn the contents of the retraction from the friar. What follows in Castin's letter is obscure, but he does not seem to have been satisfied with the document he finally obtained: 'tout n'est pour comble de malheur, si bien concerté et décidé, qu'on ne voit guère le moïen de rien obtenir de mieux, comme [. . .] Joseph m'a paru se Le promettre.' The 'donneurs de certificats', by which Castin means the signers of the 1768 act attesting Voltaire's 'Exactitude à remplir ses devoirs', had apparently repented. Perhaps they might be induced to 'réduire à sa juste valeur' another kind of *exactitude*, the extension of Voltaire's fief, which Churchmen naturally resented! According to the official, Biord now had 'la preuve de ses blasphêmes contre le Christ pour en former un Mémoire à la Cour', almost certainly an allusion to an enclosure. And this enclosure must be the notarised recording of Voltaire's statement upon receiving the viaticum: 'Aiant mon Dieu dans ma bouche [. . .] je pardonne sincère-ment à ceux qui ont Ecrit au Roy, des Calomnies contre moi.' The assumption that such a statement would move Louis to punish Voltaire confirms the official's innocence.

Castin's language also implies that he enclosed the retraction Joseph had attributed to Voltaire in his letter. Though undated and apparently unnotarised, such a retraction may be consulted at the Institut et musée Voltaire in Geneva (Th.B. PVA, no.35 *bis*) where it appears on the same sheet of eighteenth-century paper as a copy in the same unidentified eighteenth-century handwriting of Best.D15559 from Gros to Voltaire (Th.B. PVA. no.35). Since the letter refers to a retraction in the conditional tense, Gros had probably not written this retraction before he sent the letter, as we have seen. Is 35 *bis* therefore the retraction in question? Redundant, awkward and verbose, the style resembles

that of Gros's letters sufficiently to suggest his authorship.[113] Compared
with the elegant and precise Th.B. PVA. no.30 (Best.D.app.310, i),
almost certainly the original model retraction furnished by Biord, the
text reveals a better understanding of what Voltaire might have been
willing to sign and the desire to reconcile the curate's lord with his
bishop. After all, Gros's security depended on the relations between
them. The document emphasises the sincerity of Voltaire's Catholic
faith and his rejection of 'les [. . .] systèmes [. . .] du matérialisme, de
l'athéisme [. . .] du déisme [. . .] de la religion [. . .] des vertus purement

---

[113] Besterman intended to reproduce no.35 *bis* in Best.D.app.310, iii, but the published
text has been conflated with ThB. PVA. no.33, also reproduced in Best.D.app.310, iv.
The notarised certification of Voltaire's viaticum, which does not appear in no.35 *bis*,
has also been appended to iii. A typographical error perhaps. After reproducing most of
35 *bis*, iii shifts to 33 in the middle of a sentence. The transitional passage reads as follows:
'[Voltaire] voudrait [. . .] ne vouloir désormais employer son temps et ses talents abbé,
ayant fait contre lui des libelles [. . .] dans lesquels ils accusent [. . .] Voltaire d'avoir
manqué de respect pour la religion.' *Talents* is the last word reproduced from 35 *bis* and
abbé, the first word from 33. Here is the complete text of 35 *bis*:

'L'an 1769 et le . . . du mois de . . . par devant moi no^re et les Témoins cy après nommés
est comparu François Marie de Voltaire, Gentilhomme ordinaire de la Chambre du Roi,
seigneur de Fernex, Tournay &c^a âgé d'environ soixante et quinze ans, détenu par
indisposition dans son château, et néanmoins jouissant de tout son sens, et de toute la
vigueur de son Esprit, lequel désirant faire ses pâques avec fruit, et avec toute l'édification
qu'il doit à sa Maison et au public nous a déclaré et protesté qu'il veut vivre et mourir dans
la profession de la foi catholique, apostolique et Romaine, et dans les sentiments de
soumission et d'attachement à l'Eglise Romaine, que dieu a donné au monde pour Mère,
pour maitresse et souveraine dans l'ordre de la foi, de la croïance, et du culte qu'on doit
à Dieu. Conséquemment qu'il adhère et se soumet à tous ses dogmes, à sa morale, et à sa
Discipline, qu'en qualité d'autheur et d'Ecrivain, chargé des plus mauvaises imputations,
il désavoue, et déteste comme les dernières extravagances de l'esprit, et comme le comble
de la perversité du cœur humain les vieux systèmes, renouvellés en ces jours, du matérialisme, de l'Athéisme, ou du Déisme. Qu'il proteste contre la suffisance de la Religion de
l'équité et des vertus purement naturelles pour le salut, ajoutant que rien n'est plus
contraire à l'esprit de J. C., de l'Eglise, et du Christianisme que l'indifférence du culte,
et que les systèmes du Tolérantisme qu'il désavoue, et déteste tous les ouvrages qui y
conspirent, qu'il gémit devant Dieu des outrages qu'il en a reçus, des maux que l'église en a
souferts, et des scandales que le public en a vus, qu'il demande très humblement pardon
à tous ceux qu'il a offensés par ses discours ou ses traits de plume, notamment dans le
livre des honnêtetés littéraires, qu'il voudroit au prix de sa vie guérir toutes les plaies
qu'il peut avoir faites au cœur du prochain, et effacer entièrement toutes les fâcheuses
impressions qui peuvent rester dans les Esprits, de ses conversations, de ses Délyres
poétiques, et de ses autres Ecrits Et ne vouloir désormais emploïer son temps et ses
talents qu'à sa sanctification, qu'à l'édification de l'Eglise et qu'à la gloire de Dieu.
'Voulant qu'à ses frais extrait de la présente soit expédié à M. le curé de Ferney, le
fasse imprimer, et tiré autant d'exemplaires qu'il qu'il [*sic*] jugera à propos, le priant de
les envoier partout où il le croira nécessaire pour l'honneur de la [ou *sa*] croyance de ses
plus sincères dispositions et pour la satisfaction de la chrétienté fait et passé etc.'

naturelles [de] l'indifférence du culte [. . .] du tolérantisme'.[114] However contradictory, a list of all accusations made against Voltaire was bound to include the appropriate ones! If the deist saw this list, he could take comfort in the first two items and the next to the last. Perhaps the only passage totally unacceptable to him in this retraction is one repudiating his 'délyres poétiques' and impious works like the *Honnêtetés littéraires*. All in all, it would be difficult to assign this text to someone other than Gros.

Castin's disappointment and his plea for Biord's indulgence are understandable: 'je compte bien que votre grandeur ne trouvera ici qu'une tragi-comédie' (7 April; Best.D15575). Although the bishop included Voltaire's declarations of 31 March and 1 April in his *Lettres de mgr l'év. ... de G... à monsieur de V...* (1769), he omitted the retraction concocted by Gros. Obviously he did not trust it. Joseph's inability or refusal to disclose the contents before 6 April must have raised his suspicions. The style, the content, the lack of a date, notarisation and, above all, Voltaire's signature, justified Castin's forebodings. Biord could scarcely have failed to perceive that publication would damage the Church, not Voltaire.

If Gros had produced the retraction when he came to administer the viaticum, Wagnière would not have failed to mention it. Asking Voltaire to sign would inevitably have resulted in the kind of resistance that had thwarted Joseph. It seems more likely that Gros lost his nerve at the last minute and gave Voltaire the sacrament without even taking the retraction out of his pocket.

Afterwards, as soon as Voltaire found himself alone with his secretary, he jumped out of bed and declared, 'J'ai eu un peu de peine avec ce drôle de capucin, mais cela ne laisse pas que d'amuser et de faire du bien. Allons faire un tour de jardin' (L.W. i.82). He had predicted that his contest with Biord would be amusing. He had won. He had again embarrassed his enemy, profaned a sacred mystery and practised a civic rite despite concerted efforts to stop him. In his *Commentaire historique*, a peculiarly appropriate title in this instance, he remarks, 'Les plaisants de Paris croiront que c'est un poisson d'avril' (M.i.115). As usual, he allowed several days for rumours to herald the event in advance of his

I wish to thank m. Charles Wirz, Director of the Institut et musée Voltaire, for his assistance in solving this problem.

[114] he borrowed this language from Biord's model retraction (Best.D.app.310, i), as we shall see presently.

letters explaining it. He does not mention it in two long letters, dated 3 April, to mme Denis, whom he was trying to dissuade from returning to Ferney (Best.D15565, D15568). Only in letters to Dupont and Saint-Lambert on the fourth and to Saurin on the fifth did he open his publicity campaign (Best.D15569, D15570, D15572). A selective synopsis of the three letters, which contain familiar themes, will suffice. He counts his attacks of fever as if he were keeping score, twelve in all, but ten by the time he had received the viaticum. He did his duty as an officer of the king's bedchamber, a member of the French Academy, the lord of a country parish and a citizen who must die in the religion of his king and country. He must protect his family and his body after his death, and so he has sent a copy of the notarised attestation to the Academy for deposit in the archives. The only fresh idea to emerge here is an allusion to the establishment of a national religion '*by act of parliament*' (to Saint-Lambert). He translates this phrase into French for Saurin and informs him that occupation of any office in England, including that of the king, requires the practice of this religion. He also invites Saurin to discuss the matter with d'Alembert, whose disapproval of his 1768 communion he had not forgotten.

It is regrettable that Biord's letter to Saint-Florentin (*ca.* 5 April) protesting against his profanation of the sacraments has not turned up in Besterman's exhaustive investigations of his correspondence. We can only speculate on the bishop's reaction to the April Fool's communion, but we can at least determine how Gros and Joseph manoeuvred to escape his wrath. They could not have been very serene when each discovered that the other had failed to obtain the prerequisite signature on his paper. Wagnière, in whom the dying curate would confide his troubles, confirms Gros's consternation. Knowing that the bishop would discipline them if he found out what they had done, they resorted to the contrived retraction we have just seen and the expedient of claiming that Voltaire had said the profession of faith up Joseph's sleeve.[115] In his report to Biord on 7 April, Castin says he had just asked Joseph for 'une copie de la profession de foi qu'il a substituée à mon projet, comme l'ayant trouvé trop long et trop fort'. A briefer text, Joseph must have argued, was more convenient for an oral profession and a

[115] see Best.D15550, Commentary. The copyist introduces a following statement, the confession of faith intended for Voltaire, as 'copie au net de profession de foi que M. de Voltaire a faite entre les mains de son confesseur et qu'il a réitérée avant la communion'. This claim is of course unsubstantiated.

more conciliatory one, more likely to be accepted. Perhaps he had already explained that Voltaire would have refused or even that he had refused to sign a written profession. After all, a minor concession in no way detracted from the triumph of the Church over its most notorious living enemy! Joseph did not give Castin the profession in time for his letter, but sent it directly to the bishop later on with a letter of his own. In this letter, which Besterman dates 7 April (Best.D15576), Joseph told the bishop that he was enclosing both Gros's request for him to come and confess Voltaire, and the profession itself. This statement tends to confirm the hypothesis that he had simply written the profession on the same paper as Gros's letter of 30 March. Joseph assured the bishop that everything he had done was in co-operation with the curate, a lie covering his failure to obtain Voltaire's signature on the profession. In view of Biord's attitude, he had little choice.

Voltaire would describe Biord's reaction to his viaticum and his notarised forgiveness of slander as follows: 'Voilà mon maçon d'Annecy furieux, désespéré comme un damné, menaçant mon bon curé, mon pieux confesseur et mon notaire' (to d'Alembert, 24 May; Best.D15660). Although he was angry with Biord when he wrote this sentence, he was not entirely wrong, as we shall see. Both Voltaire and Wagnière say that, on 15 April, Gros and Joseph secretly assembled Raffo, Burgoz and other 'donneurs de certificats' in the presbytery of the Ferney church. All, except the notary, attested that, before receiving the viaticum, Voltaire had made a profession of faith which they dictated to Raffo: 'Pas celle du vicaire savoyard', Voltaire comments, 'mais celle de tous les curés de Savoie [. . .] Ils envoient cet acte au maçon sans m'en rien dire, et viennent ensuite me conjurer de ne les point désavouer. Ils conviennent qu'ils ont fait un faux serment pour tirer leur épingle du jeu.' This false attestation, which appears in Best.D.app.310 under ii ascribes to Voltaire nearly the same profession of faith as the one Joseph seems to have written at the end of Gros's letter.[116] One sentence has been added to the beginning and two to the end. The second of these, which now concludes the profession, betrays the personal concern that dictated it: 'Je déclare de plus que j'ai fait cette même confession de foi entre les mains dudit R^d Père capucin avant que de me confesser.'[117]

---

[116] except for the following changes: the phrase *réellement distinctes* is missing in Best.D.app.310, ii, and the latter substitutes *à laquelle* for *à qui*.

[117] apparently Joseph had already made these changes in the text of the profession he sent Biord, for otherwise he would have given himself away.

As Voltaire would later object, he had not even signed this document.[118] Joseph took it back to Gex with him, had it certified there on the same day and forwarded it to the bishop on the next day. In his covering letter, he explained: 'J'ay exécuté Les ordres que votre Grandeur Avoit donnés à Monsieur L'official au sujet de la confession de foi de M. De Voltaire, que vous trouverez ci-incluse' (Best.D15595).

Voltaire reacted to this pious fraud and the insubordination of his employees with surprising benevolence. According to Wagnière, he called them in, reprimanded them and let them go without further ado. Gros told Castin a different story. In an undated letter to Biord (Best. D15720), the official reports: '[Voltaire] en a querellé le curé de Fernex Et les témoins, et menacé le notaire de le perdre comme un faussaire; le curé de Fernex est fort en colére.' Castin says he now hopes that Gros will cooperate in drawing up further legal documents against Voltaire, something he refused to do in the past. In view of Wagnière's testimony, however, Voltaire's anger and Gros's resentment seem to have been exaggerated in order to make a proper impression on the official. Voltaire confirms his secretary's version of the reprimand in his correspondence and particularly in a letter to an anonymous addressee in April or May (Best.D15621). Although he dissociates himself from their 'Savoyard' style, 'ils n'en ont pas moins exprimé la substance de mes opinions'. He would only ask 'les pieux faussaires' of 15 April never to lie in favour of the truth, for everyone knows that the Catholic religion needs no such support! Several of these 'witnesses' admit to having been suborned, but they all thought they were doing the right thing and their intentions are above reproach. Besides, pious fraud has been in fashion for 1600 years! Besterman classifies this letter as ostensible, that is, intended for all willing readers. While it could not serve as legal evidence of impiety, they would know where to insert the exclamation marks. It informed them that he had not subscribed to the profession of faith assigned to him. It implied approval of his employees' piety, which he felt it his duty to encourage by his example. It further insinuated that the real culprits were not the poor devils at Ferney, but rather the bishop in Annecy who had induced them to lie.

After twelve attacks of fever, he told mme de Fontaine, he had sent for the viaticum, and now he was well (Best.D15577). To the reasons d'Argental had heard too often before, he added on 9 April, 'Il faut

118 in Best.D15863, dated 1 September 1769, which he may have sent to Moultou.

être poli et ne point refuser un diné où l'on est prié, parce que la chère est mauvaise' (Best.D15578). Having repeated others, he confided in Richelieu (15 April), 'je compte plus sur vôtre protection que sur vos plaisanteries' (Best.D15589). On the same day, the *Correspondance littéraire* reported that the pious activity in Ferney was causing a scandal in Paris. But mme Du Deffand found the scandal more exciting than Grimm. She wrote to Voltaire, that same day, 'Hâtez-vous, hâtez-vous, Monsieur, de me rendre raison de la nouvelle [. . .] qui a fait tomber tous les autres sujets de conversations' (Best.D15591). Among the many pressing questions that followed, one finds an excellent guess: 'sontce les billets de Confessions qui vous ont fait naître cette idée?' She likewise wanted to know why he had not told his friends in Paris the role he wanted them to play. He must have savoured this letter.

His letters to La Harpe and mme Denis on 17 April (Best.D15598, D15596) repeat the usual propaganda, except for a discreet wish revealed to the latter: 'J'ai donné même un éxemple que tout bon citoien suivra peut être.' He hoped that his spectacular demonstration of the civic cult would introduce it to the main stream of commonsense ex-perience, a futile wish. Common sense naturally continued to interpret communion as an expression of orthodox Catholicism. In his act, it only saw a dishonourable surrender to the enemy he had long been fighting tooth and nail. The scandal in fact waned more quickly this time, for on 23 April, mme Denis wrote, 'J'ai fait usage de votre lettre dans toutes les occasions [. . .] On parle des choses quatre jours et puis on en parle plus' (Best.D15603).

He tried to revive interest by his answer to mme Du Deffand on 24 April, but he only succeeded in extending a worn metaphor. Viaticum is a medicine prescribed by his doctor (Biord) and administered by his apothecary (Gros). Since he does not have two hundred thousand men at his orders (like Frederick), 'J'ai [. . .] pris le parti de rire de la médecine avec le plus profond respect, et de déjeuner comme les autres avec des attestations d'apoticaires' (Best.D15605). On the latter score, he regrets that he cannot disclose 'des friponneries de la faculté [de médé-cine]' for fear of inculpating some poor devils who perjured themselves by trying to help him. In any case, he was only dining in accordance with the custom of his country. Would he eat a Turkish meal if he were a Turk? 'Oui, Messieurs.'

Having obtained no satisfaction from the French court, Biord decided to complain directly to Voltaire on 5 May (Best.D15631). An elegant blend of veiled threat and charitable exhortation, his letter might have made a more profound impression on the addressee if he had not already tried and failed to have him punished. According to Biord, Voltaire himself had described the Easter communion of 1768 as '*une grimace*'. Since this word does not appear in his correspondence, he must have said it in front of someone who repeated it to the bishop's informant. Citing several recent works ascribed to Voltaire,[119] Biord wonders how he could have 'participé dignement et avec fruit au plus saint et au plus auguste de nos sacrements'. He could not have, of course, which is precisely the point he was trying to make. The bishop accredits the 15 April attestation and quotes the entire profession of faith, as if to shame him into a more convenient attitude. In fact, he devotes most of his letter to contradictions in his conduct which he felt exposed his hypocrisy. He scolds him for having refused to commune in church, 'sous prétexte d'une maladie dont la durée était fixée à la quinzaine de pâques'. Rather than protest against slanderers, the communicant should regret having scandalised true Christians by his writings. His equivocal declaration of 31 March, in any case, does not allay public suspicion. Where the bishop saw hypocrisy, however, the patriarch saw subterfuge all the more legitimate because clerical chicanery was obstructing the citizen's right to the sacraments. Speaking of hypocrisy, moreover, Biord ignores the retraction fabricated by Gros, an omission implying repudiation. Nor does he mention the refusal of sacraments, in which he had once been involved. To disprove his responsibility for the *Lettres de mgr. l'év. de G. . .* , which had since appeared, he alleges alterations in the text that Besterman could not find. The last paragraph in his letter contains his habitual warning against continued impiety and alarm over the imminent death of an unrepentant enemy of the Church. Evidently, he was preaching because he could not punish, and Voltaire must have realised it over a month after his April Fool's communion.

Finding his angels disgruntled over his exploit, Voltaire assured them on 8 May, 'On ne peut donner une plus grande marque de mépris pour ces facéties que de les jouer soi même' (Best.D15635). One should not fear to participate in such jokes like 'qui vous savez' (Louis living in sin with mme Du Barry), but follow the example of 'laquelle vous

[119] *Cinquième homélie prononcée à Londres* (1769), *Discours aux confédérés catholiques* (1768), *Discours de l'empereur Julien* (1769). Voltaire's authorship of the last work is uncertain.

savez' (the king's new mistress who 'affiche [...] la dévotion'). On 17 May, he answered Biord under the name of de Mauleon, an alleged nephew of his and officer in the royal army. 'De Mauleon' refuses to believe the bishop could have written his letter of 5 May and assumes the impostor who did to be the same as the one who had dared to publish Saint-Florentin's letter: 'Il est de l'honneur de Monsieur l'évêque de Genève de découvrir & de dénoncer l'imposteur' (Best.D15653). De Mauleon likewise denies that a member of the French Academy could have used so vulgar a word as *grimace*. Although this letter did little for Voltaire's reputation, he would not have written it if he had believed the bishop capable of retaliation. A truculent remark in a letter to the angels on 23 May confirms this feeling of security: 'je [...] traduirai [l'imposteur d'Annecy] hautement au parlement de Dijon s'il a l'audace de faire un pas contre les lois de l'état.'[120] He devotes most of this letter to apology for his pious activity in 1768 and 1769 in hopes of convincing the sceptical d'Argentals. A letter to d'Alembert the next day (Best.D15660) presents invective against Biord and an account of his attempts to punish Voltaire. The bishop 'jure comme un diable qu'il me fera brûler', a wild assumption no doubt.

Voltaire may well have sent a copy of the *Lettres de mgr. l'év. de G...* to Saint-Florentin, for the minister wrote to Biord on 27 May to express his irritation over the appearance of the bishop's correspondence with him and with Voltaire in print. 'Si vous n'y avés aucune part', he remarks, 'je ne puis comprendre quel peut en être l'auteur' (Best. D15665). He assures Biord that Voltaire was seriously ill during Easter and regrets that the bishop should have incited public suspicion of a dying man's intentions. His defence of Voltaire implies that the patriarch had managed to involve him in his quarrel with the bishop and that Louis had approved his second annual communion. Towards 30 May, Biord asked Voltaire about the insulting letter from his 'nephew' and demanded an unequivocal answer, which he did not receive (Best D15672). In a letter to d'Alembert on 4 June, Voltaire regretted that he did not have 12,000 men to expel him from Annecy, just as the Genevans had expelled his predecessor from their city (Best.D15676). In a scornful reply to the bishop (mid-June), de Mauleon censures his unauthorised publication of correspondence and his lack of respect for a minister of

---

[120] Best.D15659. Later he would discover that Biord himself had tried and failed to persuade the same *parlement* to proceed against him for his impious works.

the French crown. He answers his reminders of the patriarch's approaching death by evoking 'le lit de mort où [Voltaire] souffre et où vous serez comme lui' (Best.D15688). As for the profession of faith attributed to his uncle, 'Quel sacristain ivre a pu composer un pareil galimatias?' Nor does he, in turn, shrink from a veiled threat: 'Les faussaires qui l'ont rédigée et l'ont fait signer longtemps après par des gens qui n'y étaient pas, seraient repris de justice, si on les traduisait devant nos tribunaux.' Of all the false witnesses listed in the 15 April attestation, he continues, only Joseph had been present two weeks before, when Voltaire allegedly made this profession. He insinuates that these false witnesses might be induced to testify against the real perjurers, the official and the bishop. Recalling Biord's involvement with the refusal of sacraments, he threatens to inform the Dijon parlement should he engage in such activities again. This letter serves no other purpose than defiance of an enemy.

The 1769 campaign had failed even more quickly than the 1768 campaign. By 19 June, Voltaire was resorting to predictions of success in a distant future for lack of any actual encouragement. In a letter to the d'Argentals, he declares that fanaticism may gloat over his communion now, but it will one day serve to manifest 'la turpitude de ce monstre infernal' (Best.D15693). It would be dangerous to speak his mind openly at present, for 'Le public juge de tout à tort et à travers.' This prophecy would no more be fulfilled than those of the Old Testament which he had so often disproved. The project had won support from virtually none of his admirers. One might have expected Frederick to relish the idea of a patriotic cult for the discipline of the vulgar, yet he does not conceal his disappointment from d'Alembert on 2 July: 'Après d'aussi belles choses [contre le christianisme], je suis un peu fâché que ce même Voltaire fasse si platement ses pâques, & donne une farce aussi triviale au public' (Best.D15725). Voltaire, as Frederick sees it, is merely joining the vulgar and by no means converting their trivial farce into something that might have appealed to his royal interests. A second failure was enough, moreover, to persuade Voltaire that he could more profitably expend his energy on writing and publishing. On 23 April 1773 he assured mme Necker that the letter he had received from her was more precious to him than all the sacraments of his church: 'Je ne les ai point reçus cette fois cy. On s'était trop moqué à Paris de cette petite facétie, et [...] mon Evêque [...] avait trop crié contre ma dévotion' (Best.D18333). As the latter consideration indicates, he had finally realised that, despite his claims to the contrary, his annual communion was jeopardising his chances for a decent burial after death. Now that he had dashed the bishop's hopes of converting him, Biord's preoccupation with his forthcoming death might revert to thoughts of revenge. Exasperating him further would only determine him perhaps to desecrate the body of the old man who had twice made a fool of him. Voltaire received last rites once again in 1777 when smallpox threatened his life[121] and refused them in 1778 as he lay dying in Paris.[122] On both of these occasions, he seems to have been uniquely concerned with preserving his body from desecration after death, a wish eventually fulfilled.

Defiance of Biord eclipses all other motives for the April Fool's communion of 1769. But repetition might have strengthened Voltaire's demonstration of the civic rite, if his vendetta had not drawn the attention of the public away from it. He had extorted the sacraments from the Church, forced a priest and a friar to perjure themselves twice, frustrated the authority of the bishop and his official, embarrassed the bishop and even flaunted the bishop's inability to retaliate. After outwitting Biord at every turn, however, he had nothing more to show for it than a Pyrrhic victory. The power to crush any further attempts to profane the sacraments remained intact, the bishop's determination to use it had increased and the sympathy of Catholics, Protestants and freethinkers alike, which might have hindered it, had all but disappeared. He had proved to common sense that he was cleverer than Biord, but certainly not that communion had only a patriotic significance or that everyone had the right or duty to celebrate it. In all probability, however, he could not have proved this point even if he had concentrated all his efforts on it, for the Christian significance of the eucharist was too deeply rooted in the experience of his public.

Voltaire did not suspend his writing and publishing activity during

---

[121] 'A courageous (or foolhardy) priest, who had no fear of contracting the pox, asked to see Voltaire. The latter accepted the visit, received the last rites [. . .] and resigned himself to death [. . .] By December first Voltaire was recovered sufficiently to be transported to Paris' (A. Owen Aldridge, *Voltaire and the century of light* (Princeton 1975), p.46).

[122] Wagnière relates the bedside visit of abbé Gautier: 'Il proposa ensuite au malade de lui donner la communion. Celui-ci répondit: "M. l'abbé, faites attention que je crache continuellement du sang; il faut bien se donner garde de mêler celui du bon Dieu avec le mien." Le confesseur ne répliqua point' (*Relation du voyage de m. de Voltaire à Paris en 1778 et de sa mort*, L.W., i.132-33).

these Easter seasons. Nor did he spare the eucharist in the publications of 1768 and 1769 while he was profaning it in practice.

The *Relation du banissement des jésuites de la Chine*, which he first mentioned in a letter to Chardon on 16 March 1768 (Best.D14841), contains a sharp attack on the sacrament. Since we have already discussed most of the themes woven into this story in connection with earlier works, a synopsis and commentary indicating how Voltaire has applied them here will be sufficient. In explaining his religion to the emperor of China, the Jesuit Rigolet anticipates his majesty's pleasure upon eating Christ after his conversion to Christianity, which Rigolet appears to take for granted. 'Vous mangez votre dieu?' asks the astonished emperor. 'Je le fais et je le mange,' replies the Jesuit. The pretention of creating the creator, which the author unfairly attributes to all priests, is already preposterous, but the further pretention of eating the divinity just created exceeds absurdity. Rigolet nonetheless brags that he has made four dozen gods this morning, a multiplication of the divinity (Berengar), and he offers to show them to his majesty. The emperor naturally accepts this offer: 'Je vais [...] ordonner à mes cuisiniers de se tenir prêts pour les faire cuire; tu leur diras à quelle sauce il les faut mettre' (*Dial.*, p.227). He supposes a dish of gods to be delicious; never will he have eaten so sumptuous a meal. Rigolet soon returns with a sort of tobacco tin and the emperor hastens to see 'ton dieu qui est dans ta boîte'. Voltaire is ridiculing the material confinement of a spiritual substance, just as he had in the Leningrad Notebook forty-two years before (see p.102). Rigolet shows the emperor 'une douzaine de petits morceaux de pâte ronds et plats comme du papier'. They do not look very filling, his majesty objects, for 'Un dieu [...] devrait être un peu plus dodu' (*Dial.*, p.229). Far from detecting anything divine, the senses perceive nothing more than an absurdly inadequate meal.

What does Rigolet expect him to do with these little pieces of glue? His majesty need only order some red wine and 'vous verrez beau jeu' (*Dial.*, p.229). Why red wine and not white, which is more appropriate for lunch?[123] The Jesuit explained,[124] 'Il allait changer le vin en sang,

[123] the emperor of China is a connoisseur of wine! In the *Histoire de l'empire de Russie*, Voltaire had underlined the inconvenience of exporting the eucharist to countries that produce no wine (see p.125). Such contradictions did not bother him when he was composing *rogatons*, which thrived rather on heedless fantasy.

[124] Voltaire alternates narrative in the past with dialogue in the present, hence the mixed tenses.

et [. . .] il était bien plus aisé de faire du sang avec du vin rouge qu'avec du vin paillet' (*Dial.*, p.229). The reassurance he finds in the resemblance of colour reveals the ease with which he indulges in self-delusion. The emperor, who agrees with him, sends for the wine like any European prince! Rigolet states that Christ was a priest in the order of Melchizedek when he gave the disciples his body to eat. A priest himself, he will change these pieces of bread into gods: 'chaque miette de ce pain sera un dieu en corps et en âme; vous croirez [. . .] manger du pain, et vous mangerez Dieu' (*Dial.*, p.230). Thus Voltaire continues to exploit Berengar's caricature of concomitance and transubstantiation. But Rigolet unwittingly exhibits additional absurdities in the latter doctrine: 'Quoique le sang de ce dieu soit dans le corps que j'aurai créé avec des paroles, je changerai votre vin rouge dans le sang de ce dieu même [. . .] je le boirai' (*Dial.*, pp.230-31). Rigolet is substituting himself for the Holy Spirit by creating the creator with words. He therefore succumbs, as Voltaire believed most priests do, to the temptation of magic. He does not deviate from dogma, on the other hand, when he observes that transubstantiation produces the blood of Christ twice, once in the eucharistic body and again in the eucharistic blood itself. Voltaire is insinuating that the inventors of miracles cover initial fraud by further fraud which they found on it.

At this point, Rigolet consecrates and consumes two dozen communion wafers and a bottle of wine. Impressed, the emperor wonders what will happen to his god 'quand tu auras besoin d'un pot de chambre' (*Dial.*, p.231). The reappearance of Stercoranism was inevitable in such a story, but no Jesuit is at a loss for words, no Jesuit at least in Voltaire's works. What happens to God in the digestive tract concerns God alone and by no means Rigolet, or so he says. Some theologians believe God to be defecated and others, to be transpired, but Rigolet suspends his judgement. Needless to say, no theologian ever believed anything of the sort, as Voltaire well knew, yet he strongly suspected them of preoccupation with such minutiae. No theologian himself, Rigolet acknowledges that he looks forward to a good dinner after this (bad) lunch and a little money for his trouble, a swipe at private mass. The emperor wonders if the other Catholic orders in China eat God too. Yes, concedes the Jesuit, but they are only condemning themselves. Voltaire thus implies that the traditional clause excluding heretics serves as a convenient partisan weapon. Rigolet takes advantage of the opportunity to invite his majesty to expel the other orders. The next day, the emperor does just that and the Jesuits along with their rivals.

Rigolet is a far cry from the defenders of civic rites Voltaire had admired in the *Siècle*. Instead of justifying Jesuit missionaries in China, the *Relation* demotes them to the presumptuous ranks of the rival orders. Rigolet's self-defeating candour and zeal caricature Jesuit discipline and intelligence, which Voltaire no longer respected. His rash confidence in his ability to convert the emperor mocks Jesuit enterprise several years after their explulsion from France, an event in the back of Voltaire's mind. He unwittingly acts as the jester of his majesty, who elegantly personifies the natural light. Yet the emperor holds reason in reserve behind a screen of bemused irony, which Rigolet mistakes for sympathy with Christianity. After explanation of the eucharist and demonstration of communion, his good sense triumphs over nonsense.

Since Voltaire's *Epître aux Romains* appeared towards the end of May in 1768, he could not have put his Easter prank entirely out of mind while writing it. In the opening paragraph, he imagines doctors trying to resolve the dispute over whether Paul was from Giscala or Tarsus by supposing him to have been born in both places at the same time. As a precedent, he cites 'certains corps qui sont créés tous les matins avec des mots latins, et qui se trouvent en cent mille lieux au même instant' (M.xxvii.83). Transubstantiation and concomitance. Comparing them to the hypothesis of Paul's dual and simultaneous birth suggests the temptations of supernatural solutions for religious problems of any kind. Reminding the public of the absurdity in eucharistic dogma so soon after his Easter communion prevented them from taking it seriously, but the gesture was bound to anger a bishop like Biord.

One finds the earliest allusion to his *Conseils raisonnables à m. Bergier pour la défense du christianisme* in the *Correspondance littéraire* of 1 June 1768. This is an answer to Bergier's *Certitude des preuves du christianisme* (1767) which, though especially devoted to a refutation of the *Examen critique des apologistes de la religion chrétienne* (1766), also attacks Voltaire. This polemical ricochet does not interest us here, but Article 11 in the *Conseils* presents several historical facts about the Council of Constance that Voltaire's Christian contemporaries refused to acknowledge. He observes that John Hus was a victim of judicial murder and, as a foreigner, of an infraction against international law. The Council liquidated them because it found them heretical and not because they were fomenting rebellion in Bohemia. This liquidation caused the rebellion and not the other way around, but the Church had no jurisdiction in such matters anyway. The Council treated John XXIII, a profoundly corrupt pope, with relative leniency. It burned Hus and Jerome at the stake for resisting such corruption and for defending laymen's rights to the cup of the eucharist. Voltaire never learned the role of remanence in the condemnation of Hus. In Article VI, however, he reinforced his defence of the lay cup: '[Les] *Evangiles* n'ont point dit [...] que les laïques ne dussent pas faire la pâque avec du vin' (M.xxvii.39). Perhaps he would have gladly enriched the satirical pomp of his own Easter communion with this additional ceremony. The truth about the Council of Constance and the refusal of the Church to recognise this truth tended to persuade his public not to trust the Church.

While the brunt of this attack fell on the Church rather than the eucharist, he aims a passage in the *Profession de foi des théistes*, circulating in Paris by the end of May, directly at the sacrament. One paragraph contains a scornful description of what allegedly happens when the eucharist is celebrated and another examines the consequences from a theist point of view. In the first paragraph, the theist adds an arm to Voltaire's arsenal: 'Se mettre à la place de Dieu qui a créé l'homme, créer Dieu à son tour, faire ce Dieu avec de la farine et quelques paroles' (M.xxvii.60). Here Voltaire bypasses the dogma itself to assault what he suspects most priests and laymen actually believe. Paschase attributed the presence of Christ's body in the eucharist to God's creative power, but Guitmund discarded this argument and, after him, theologians merely claimed that the power to create implies the power to assure the real presence. Most other Christians, however, did not have the acumen to discriminate between creation and transubstantiation as sharply as they did. While even these would not have admitted reversing the roles of creator and creature in the eucharist, many of them may well have believed something approximately equivalent to that. For commonsense analysis of the relationship between transubstantiation and creation tends to yield such a result on its own. Perhaps Voltaire merely isolated this tendency in order to condemn it from his theist viewpoint. To the magic of making God with words, he adds the idolatry of making him with flour, an idea already implicit in the dialogue between Rigolet and the emperor. The rest of his description consists of familiar objections: a thousandfold God who nonetheless remains unique; the destruction of the flour from which he was made (without destroying him); the conversion of wine into blood which already exists in the body just created; the destruction of this wine, eating God and drinking his blood. All of these concepts violate the theist's good sense.

We know little about this imaginary spokesman except that, according to Voltaire, he wrote the original version of the *Profession* in German. Initials in the subtitle suggest, moreover, that he is addressing himself to the *roi de Prusse*. In his concluding paragraph, he protests against 'un pareil excès de bêtise et d'aliénation d'esprit' (M.xxvii.61), the eucharist in other words, which he would even refuse to believe of the Hottentots or the Kaffirs. His allusion to these African peoples, then considered ultimately primitive, implies that the natural light cannot tolerate the eucharist. It should be possible only in a fabulous land, the theist argues, and yet it is celebrated every day in the most civilised countries of Europe. Princes allow it and wise men say nothing. 'Que faisons-nous à l'aspect de ces sacrilèges?' he asks. 'Nous prions l'Etre éternel pour ceux qui les commettent' (M.xxvii.61). The elderly Voltaire is admitting a limited providence to which one might appeal in such cases.[125]

He must have published major Kaiserling's alleged *Discours* to the Polish confederates a month later, for the *Mémoires secrets* reported it on 24 July. This work contains another list of eucharistic doctrines differing from sect to sect. The Turks do not eat God; the Greeks eat him without being sure that they do it in the Roman manner; the Swedes, the Danes and the Prussians also eat him, but in a way different from the Greeks who 'croient manger du pain et boire un coup de vin en mangeant Dieu' (M.xxvii.76). Impanation. In several Prussian churches along the Polish border, 'on ne mange point Dieu, mais [. . .] on fait seulement un léger repas de pain et de vin en mémoire de lui' (M.xxvii.76). These are reform churches on the model of those founded by Zwingli, Calvin and Knox. In view of his Easter communion, Voltaire would seem to agree with them. Kaiserling, in any event, assures his Polish listeners that none of these variations deserves to spill any blood.

He wrote and published all of these pamphlets between March and July of a year in which he himself communed on Easter Sunday, 3 April. None of them could have reassured the bishop of Geneva or any other devout Catholic on his acceptance of eucharistic dogma or his respect for the authority of the Church in such matters. He certainly attacked

---

[125] the quoted sentence continues as follows: 'si pourtant nos prières peuvent quelque chose auprès de son immensité, et entrent dans le plan de sa providence'.

the eucharist at this time because his Easter communion and the quarrel with Biord were on his mind. He may well have done so deliberately, in fact, so as to block any attempt to interpret his participation in the sacrament as a conversion. He no doubt intended his polemics against the eucharist to complement his effort to transform the Christian rite into a civic one by his example.

He actually anticipated the communion he expected to celebrate at Easter in 1769 by adding a *Cinquième Homélie prêchée à Londres . . . le jour de pâques* to the other four he had already published in 1767. Since the earliest report of this publication occurred in the *Correspondance littéraire* of 15 March, he had provided for the distribution of the pamphlet to his public in advance of Easter Sunday, 26 March. Presumably the same English Protestant devotes this sermon to communion, which he defines as a celebration of fellowship commemorating the Last Supper: 'Nous nous acquittons d'une cérémonie que nous croyons nécessaire [. . .] parce qu'elle nous rend plus chers les uns aux autres' (M.xxvii.559). Upon reading these unaccustomed words, one can scarcely avoid wondering what Voltaire is premeditating. Another passage confirms, at any rate, that he is not promoting brotherhood gratuitously: 'A quoi nous servirait cette communauté de nourriture si nous n'avons une communauté de charité, de bienfaisance, de tolérance, de toutes les vertus sociales' (M.xxvii.557). The juxtaposition of the Christian *charité* and the philosophic *bienfaisance*, which are otherwise synonyms, illustrates the concept of tolerance following them. The final term in the enumeration assimilates all three to social virtues contributing to the moral health of a community. This wording implies the abandonment of eucharistic dogma and Church discipline as well as the limitation of communion to the promotion of social welfare, the function to which the *philosophes* wanted to confine religion in general. Voltaire is pioneering the ideological conversion of the Christian sacrament to a civic rite.

He likewise amplifies the theory that nearly all men are essentially theist brothers, whether they recognise this fact or not. His English spokesman exhorts his listeners not to look upon the members of other sects as enemies, but rather as 'frères dont nous n'entendons pas le langage' (M.xxvii.560). This quotation concludes another Voltairian list of doctrinal variations: Quakers, Baptists and Menonites who take no communion; Presbyterians who eat Christ spiritually; Lutherans and Anglicans who eat his body together with the bread and drink his

blood together with the wine of their eucharist, and papists 'qui prétendent manger le corps et boire le sang, en ne touchant ni au pain ni
au vin' (M.xxvii.560). Thus the language of transubstantiation is the
most incomprehensible of all. The preacher's advocacy of tolerance
does not preclude disapproval of Catholic intolerance. In England, he
observes, 'Nous participons tous au même pain et au même vin', while
in Ireland, the pope, a foreigner, imposes a communion which 'n'est
que la rejection des autres hommes' (M.xxvii.561). The Catholic Church
has prostituted communion not only by misusing it to exclude dissidents,
but also by adulterating its significance. While *sacrament* used to mean
oath in Latin, it now means *mystery*: 'Pourquoi faut-il qu'il y ait des
choses cachées dans la religion? Tout ne doit-il pas être public? Tout
ne doit-il pas être commun à tous les hommes que le même Dieu a fait
naître?' (M.xxvii.559). Here Voltaire applies his belief in the clarity of
religious truth to communion. His assault on Pascal's apology for
Christian obscurity in the twenty-fifth *Lettre philosophique* had strengthened a conviction he owed to the distant influence of Descartes. For
the equation of truth to clarity, which seems out of place in his English
preacher, definitely belongs to Cartesian good sense. The idea of the
natural light emanating from God underlies the principle that everyone
should be able to understand the cult in which he participates. 'Tout
ne doit-il pas être commun à tous les hommes que le même Dieu a fait
naître?' This thought combines theism with religious democracy in a
peculiarly Voltairian blend.

His preacher refuses to discuss the disputes between proponents of
real and spiritual manducation, Innocent III's speculations on what
happens to the eucharistic body when the communicant has diar-
rhoea,[126] Toledo's claim that a priest can transubstantiate a baker's
stock of bread and an innkeeper's supply of wine,[127] the necessity for
deliberate intention on the part of a celebrant before transubstantiation
can take place, or certain examples of theological hairsplitting which
he duly notes.[128] Debating these questions will not improve morality,

[126] 'Quod si forte sucessus vel fluxus aut vomitus post solam eucharistiae perceptionem
evenerit ex accidentibus et humoribus generatur, cum inter humores alsque cujus libet
cibi materia vel effluant in secessum vel emittantur ad vomitum' (*De sacro altaris mysterio
libri sex*, Migne, ccxvii.867).

[127] Francisco Toledo, *Summa conscientiae, seu instructio sacerdotum* (Rome 1618).
Voltaire refers to book II, chapter 25.

[128] 'Plusieurs docteurs disent que dans l'eucharistie il y a quantité sans *quantum* et
accident sans substance; ils déclarent qu'on peut être camus sans avoir de nez, et boiteux
sans avoir de jambes, *simitas sine naso, claudicatio sine crure*' (M.xxvii.558).

that is, will not make society function more smoothly. On the contrary, Bloody Mary burned over eight hundred Englishmen for rejecting transubstantiation. Such violations of good sense may seem laughable, but they sometimes result in enormous crimes.

Nor does Voltaire spare the authenticity of communion itself. 'Plusieurs savants s'inquiètent', warns the preacher, 'que l'*Evangile de saint Jean* ne dise pas un mot de l'institution de l'Eucharistie' (M.xxvii. 562). Shifting the viewpoint to these shadowy scholars allows Voltaire to venture into an area his spokesman would ordinarily avoid. Exegetes have in fact always puzzled over the absence of any explicit reference in the fourth gospel to so important an event (see p.17). This omission has an even greater impact on the unspecialised intelligence, which lacks the experience from which one may draw possible explanations. Communion would be more vulnerable to civic conversion, Voltaire thought, if he could weaken its historical foundations in the minds of his public. This was certainly one of his intentions in the *Cinquième homélie*, which Biord cites as proof of his hypocrisy in taking the viaticum (see p.178). The bishop may well have understood that Voltaire intended the pamphlet to qualify the communion he expected to take at Easter. This communion would have symbolised his fellowship with other men and his faith in civic virtue. It would not have been an endorsement of the exclusive privilege or supernatural pretentions he associated with the Catholic sacrament.

He may well have foreseen the necessity for a retreat from Easter communion to the viaticum and even the tactics he would use in this contingency. Several pages towards the end of the *Histoire du parlement*, begun in January and published in late May, relate the dispute over refusal of last rites. Although he had already treated this subject in the *Précis*, he did not really repeat himself in the *Histoire*. According to Wagnière, the ministry (probably Choiseul) had secretly asked him to compose the work (L.W. i.229), a manoeuvre no doubt intended to embarrass Parlement. Despite the possibility of this motive, Voltaire avoids polemic more scrupulously than in his other historical works. He no longer affirms, moreover, that Beaumont started the dispute to distract Parlement from taxation of the Church. The archbishop of Paris, he explains, 'se laissa persuader qu'il extirperait le jansénisme' (M.xvi.79). Beaumont ordered the curates in his diocese to refuse the viaticum[129] to dying Jansenists who, in rejecting Unigenitus, had appealed to the higher authority of a council or who had confessed to priests who had done so.

An older man, Voltaire now had greater sympathy for the victims of this tyranny: 'Dans les lois de tous les peuples, le refus des derniers devoirs aux morts est une inhumanité punissable' (M.xvi.79). This sentence secularises the sacrament and transforms it into the legal right that he demanded and finally obtained on April Fool's Day. Might he not also have asked, who has the prerogative to decide whether a man is dying if not that man himself? Although what followed proves that he was not himself in danger as he pretended, a man's desire, he obviously felt, should enable him to obtain immediate and unquestioned access to last rites. Since the Catholic sacraments enjoyed traditional respectability in his country, priests must not be allowed to use them for doctrinal or political coercion. The refusal of last rites, he argues, not only infringed on the rights of dying men, but also degraded the sacraments themselves: 'L'archevêque [...] ne s'apercevait pas qu'en voulant forcer ses diocésains à respecter la bulle, il les accoutumait à ne pas respecter les sacrements' (M.xvi.79-80). Elsewhere in the same text, he finds that Catholicism itself was losing the respect of the public and he is almost certainly right. He likewise condemns confession certificates, which Beaumont was using against dying Jansenists: 'Cette innovation était regardée par tous les esprits sérieux comme un attentat contre la société civile' (M.xvi.80). This is of course an exaggeration intended to convince common sense, for confession certificates were in fact disrupting society. Besides, any such innovation, in Voltaire's opinion, contradicted the Church's constant profession of fidelity to its traditions.

He illustrates these critical remarks by several incidents, two of which involve Boitin (actually Bouëttin), the curate of the strategic Saint-Etienne-du-Mont in Paris. In the following summaries, critical rectifications drawn from *La Bulle Unigenitus* (1936) by Jacques Parguez appear in parentheses.[130] In the first incident, Boitin refused to administer last rites to Coffin, a famous Jansenist professor (because the latter had no confession certificate) and Coffin died without them. The curate then tried to prevent his burial in sacred ground (false),

129 which, as Voltaire explains, originally meant '*provision de voyage*' (M.xvi.79). Such remarks are rare in this text.

130 see Parguez, pp.121-22, 126-27.

but Coffin's nephew, a counselor at the Châtelet, forced him to yield (also false: while Bouëttin did not dare to interfere with the burial, the counselor organised a campaign to denounce his refusal of last rites). Six (eighteen) months later, the nephew himself lay dying and Boitin 'lui signifia qu'il ne serait ni communié, ni oint, ni enterré, s'il ne produisait un billet [de confession]' (M.xvi.80). Parlement censured, fined and briefly imprisoned the curate. In the second incident, the unrepentant Boitin refused last rites to a Jansenist priest named Le Maire (Lemaire; because he had no confession certificate). This time Parlement tried to force Beaumont to let Le Maire have last rites, but 'le prélat le laissa mourir' (M.xvi.82). (After a second appeal from Parlement, Louis, who otherwise supported the archibishop, sent a Capuchin to give Lemaire his last rites, but the friar did not reach him in time.) The details of the general conflict that followed need not occupy us here. Hardly a week went by, says Voltaire, 'où il n'y eût un arrêt du parlement pour communier [. . .] et un arrêt du conseil [royal] pour ne communier pas' (M.xvi.84). The denial of communion to (the aged paralytic) sister Perpétue, a name Voltaire must have relished, resulted in a protracted legal battle: 'Ce qui aigrit le plus les esprits, ce fut l'enlèvement de sœur Perpétue' (M.xvi.84). In this case as well as the others, the crown sided with the Church against Parlement. The author entitles the next chapter 'Suite de ces folies' and, in the one after that, he records a statement by Damiens, addressing himself to the (absent) king whom he had nicked with a penknife: 'Vous n'avez pas la bonté pour votre peuple d'ordonner qu'on lui accorde les sacrements à l'article de la mort [. . .] L'archevêque de Paris est la cause de tout le trouble' (M.xvi.95). It is not difficult to understand why Voltaire valued this testimony. While blaming each other for Damiens's act, the constitutional (pro-Unigenitus) and appellant (anti-Ungenitus) parties managed to blame the *philosophes* too. A royalist himself, Voltaire had no great pity for 'ce misérable' (M.xvi.98), who was drawn and quartered.

In accordance with his usual philosophy of history, he derives important effects from trivial causes in his study of the dispute over refusal of last rites. His constant thesis consists in the absurdity of the issue behind all the turmoil and he even avoids explicit justification of Parlement's resistance to the Church and the crown, an attitude dictated no doubt by Choiseul's patronage, the exile's wish to go home and Parlement's persecution of him. Since the facts nonetheless spoke for themselves, his April Fool's viaticum might have opened the eyes of his public, if the latter had been able to understand his reinterpretation of the sacrament. His renewed investigation of the dispute may well have suggested to him the role of the dying man in need of last rites, the role he played that spring. His threats of complaining to the Dijon parlement for refusal of sacraments had no more immediate source.

Although his history of Parlement has its value, detachment did not really suit him as a writer. When he returned to the eucharist that autumn, therefore, he was in the mood for satire. In his *Dieu et les hommes* (1769), the Englishman Dr Obern assures us: 'Loin d'abolir le culte public, nous voulons le rendre plus pur et moins indigne de l'Etre suprême' (M.xxxviii.241). With this purpose in mind, Obern imagines what Jesus did not say about original sin, the trinity and the two natures. He likewise excludes the following statement from Jesus's sayings: 'Je vous ordonne de mettre, par des paroles, dans un petit morceau de pain mon corps tout entier, mes cheveux, mes ongles, ma barbe, mon urine, mon sang, et de mettre en même temps mon sang à part, dans un gobelet de vin; de façon qu'on boive le vin, qu'on mange le pain, et que cependant ils soient anéantis' (M.xxviii.225). The mere thought of consuming these bodily substances, which Voltaire has chosen deliberately, repels the reader. This thought impresses upon common sense the preposterous and disgusting material consequences of a doctrine cloaked, according to Voltaire, in spiritual respectability. Although we have already seen most of the other elements in the passage, he has renewed them by arranging them in a sort of recipe. In this unsaid statement, Jesus is giving instructions for the preparation of a meal – for Voltaire continues to consider the eucharist a meal – almost as if he were talking to his cook in the kitchen. Yet Voltaire mixes exotic ingredients into this domestic soup: a magic formula, enclosure of a large object within a smaller one, the inedible liquids and solids already mentioned, the simultaneous existence of the same blood in two different places and the disappearance of food and drink, even though eating and drinking them tend to prove their existence. The contrast between the matter-of-fact form and the fantasy of the contents ridicules the manner in which Voltaire thought dogma has been formulated. Theologians, in his opinion, have combined abstractions just as cooks mix ingredients, yet without the discipline of any final test, such as the taste of the soup.

In 1769, therefore, one finds a greater variety in the relationships between writings concerned with the eucharist and his spring communion than in 1768. The *Cinquième homélie* qualifies the Easter com-

munion he failed to obtain. New information available to him for the
Histoire du parlement seems to have inspired his attempt to substitute
the viaticum for communion. A passage in *Dieu et les hommes*, on the
other hand, announces a return to unprogrammed satire of the eucharist
after the abandonment of his efforts to convert the sacrament to a civic
rite by coordinated publicity stunts and campaigns. This technique
had failed because he had overestimated the capacity of common sense.
His satirical propaganda had usually succeeded because he had long
since learned to gauge his reader's mentality accurately.

One expects the fecundity of an ageing writer to slip before his pro-
ductivity actually begins to decline. This symptom does not seem to
have plagued Voltaire in his last writings on the eucharist. Two pamphlets published in 1770, when he reached his seventy-sixth birthday,
do present examples of repetition unenriched by variation, but they
set no trend.

A passage in the *Entretiens chinois* tends to echo the unforgettable
conversation between Rigolet and the emperor. A mandarin, who
lacks his Majesty's finesse, is making the usual complaint to a Jesuit
(*Dial.*, p.245):

Vous nous dites que nous serons damnés si nous ne mangeons de votre pain;
et puis, quand quelques-uns de nous ont eu la polititesse d'en manger, vous
leur dites que ce n'est pas du pain, que ce sont des membres d'un corps
humain et du sang, et qu'ils seront damnés s'ils croient avoir mangé du pain.

Never had Voltaire spelled out the logic of his objections to the Catholic
eucharist more clearly, and yet this sentence tells us practically nothing
that we do not already know. In the past, he had usually found a more
curious approach to the presumption of foreigners threatening hospit-
able natives with damnation if they do not abandon the natural light for
distasteful and unfounded doctrine.

A passage in the *Discours du conseiller Anne Dubourg*, which sets a
similar protest in a historical situation, attacks a scholastic formulation
of transubstantiation. Sentenced to death for his resistance to the
persecution of Protestants, the sixteenth-century counselor in Parlement
accuses his judges of several arbitrary and repressive acts, among them
the following (M.xxviii.471):

Pour joindre le ridicule à l'atrocité [...] vous ordonnez que Paul de Foix
déclare devant les chambres assemblées [du Parlement] *que la forme est*

inséparable de la matière dans l'eucharistie: qu'a de commun ce galimatias péripatétique avec la religion chrétienne [. . .] avec le bon sens?

Paul de Foix was a fellow counselor implicated in the same affair on a lesser charge. Thomas Aquinas had derived the peripatetic nonsense in question from Aristotle's distinction between form and matter. In connection with transubstantiation, he defined the accidental bread and wine as form and the substantial body and blood as matter. The separation of form and matter in de Foix's case implies that the dual process of transubstantiation cannot bring them together. The statement imposed on him therefore amounts to an endorsement of this dogma,[131] but Voltaire is substituting good sense for religious freedom as the motive of Dubourg's martyrdom.

Several articles in the 1771 edition of his *Questions sur l'Encyclopédie* directly or indirectly concern the eucharist. 'Fanatisme II' is a fable about a Basque bishop with a diocese partly in France and partly in Spain, and the squire of a French parish in his see, which was formerly inhabited by Moors. The squire incurred the bishop's suspicion by asserting that Moroccans are not necessarily hostile to the Supreme Being. The bishop asked the king of France to transfer the squire to Brittany or Normandy, where he could no longer mislead Basques by his bad jokes, but the king refused. The fable omits the Easter communion of 1768, but not the April Fool's viaticum of 1769. Learning that the squire was dangerously ill, the bishop

défendit au porte-dieu du canton de le communier, à moins [qu'il] ne donnât un billet de confession par lequel il devait apparaître que le mourant [. . .] condamnait [. . .] l'hérésie de Mahomet, et tout autre hérésie [. . .] comme le calvinisme et le jansénisme, et qu'il pensait en tout comme lui évêque biscayen.[132]

Confession certificates were very much in fashion then, explains Voltaire, thus rolling the time of his story back to a more 'fabulous' past. He thus assimilates the profession of faith Biord tried to wrest from him with the confession certificates of the bishop's earlier career. The squire, he continues, sent for his drunken imbecile of a curate and 'le menaça de le faire pendre par le parlement de Bordeaux, s'il ne lui donnait pas

[131] according to Eugène and Emile Haag, de Foix had to declare before Parlement 'qu'au sacrement de l'autel la forme est inséparable de la matière, et que le sacrement ne peut s'administrer autrement que ne le fait l'Eglise romaine'. He was cleared and later became archbishop of Toulouse ('De Foix, Paul', *La France protestante* (Geneva 1966)).
[132] M.xix.83.

tout à l'heure le viatique, dont lui mourant se sentait un extrême besoin' (M.xix.83). Intimidated, the curate gave him the viaticum. The squire then declared before witnesses that he was not a Mohammedan but a Christian and that the bishop had slandered him. But Voltaire does not characterise this Christianity as strictly civic in nature. Having signed his statement, the squire 's'en porta mieux, et le repos de la bonne conscience le guérit bientôt' (M.xix.83). At this point, the story seems even more fabulous than before! In retaining the fiction of his brush with death, however, Voltaire may have had an ironical intention. He was not the first, as he well knew, to exaggerate the healing power of a clear conscience. The fable ends with an account of the fraudulent retraction ascribed to him two weeks after his viaticum. Although this fable proves that the ageing Voltaire could still tell a pretty good story, he blurs its true moral, the utility of communion as a means of patriotic edification. Both the squire in the fable and the lord of Ferney in 1769 used the sacrament to declare their independence of foreign domination.

To 'Confession', already published in the *Dictionnaire*, he added a subsection in 1771 entitled 'Des Billets de confession'. This time he took the trouble to explore the origin of the device. When one confesses venial sins in Italy, he relates, 'on vous donne [...] un reçu imprimé moyennant quoi vous communiez'.[133] The contrast between this relatively harmless precedent and Beaumont's atrocious innovation has a calculated impact on good sense which he fully exploits. He in fact hooks the archbishop – for everything is possible in writing! – on the horns of a dilemma: 'Si l'on peut être sauvé sans ce viatique, vos billets sont inutiles. Si les sacrements sont absolument nécessaires, vous damnez tous ceux que vous en privez; vous faites brûler pendant toute l'éternité six à sept mille âmes [...] cela est violent' (M.xviii.231). By six or seven thousand people, or nine-tenths of Paris as he claims in the context, he apparently meant the number of potential victims if Beaumont had applied his policy rigorously. Neither did this happen nor could it have, since the archbishop's power was limited. Prosecuting the potential effect rather than the actual deed nonetheless enables Voltaire to impugn Beaumont's humanity and intelligence. The archbishop's responsibility for the souls of his diocese should have weighed more heavily in his decision to deny so many of them the alleged means of access to salvation. In reasoning with Beaumont, therefore, Voltaire

---

[133] M.xviii.230; apparently an allusion to the policy of Borromeo, bishop of Milan, in the sixteenth century. See p.91.

remains within the bounds of Catholicism and attacks the abuse of the sacraments rather than their significance. He is appealing, for once, to a Catholic common sense.

He takes it upon himself to 'legislate' for the Church in section VI of 'Droit canonique', which he entitles 'Inspection des magistrats sur l'administration des sacrements'. The title alone was enough to infuriate clerical enemies like Biord, yet the article fulfils the promise of the title, and especially when Voltaire prohibits withholding the eucharist on any ground whatsoever: 'Aucun pasteur pécheur ne peut avoir le droit de refuser [...] l'eucharistie à un autre pécheur. Jésus-Christ, impeccable, ne refusa pas la communion à Judas' (M.xviii.442). Last rites, he adds, are subject to the same law. Here he finally reveals the principle behind his determination in the spring of 1768 and 1769. What right does one sinner have to deny remission of sins to another? Again he is pleading within the framework of Catholic common sense. His first question obliges proponents of confession certificates to plead a lesser degree of sin in clergymen, an embarrassing plea for clergymen themselves. His second question nonetheless blocks even this escape, for how can one who speaks in Christ's name repudiate his example? He had long since learned that the most devastating weapon against Christianity was the very conduct of its founder. Nothing does greater violence to reason than the contrast between the two, hence, in Voltaire's opinion, the desperate necessity for faith.

In 'Conscience VI' or 'Liberté de conscience', he pretends to have translated a German dialogue, in which the almoner of a Catholic prince threatens an Anabaptist with exile. The almoner describes the three sects allowed in the Holy Roman Empire as 'celle qui mange Jésus-Christ sur la foi seule, dans un morceau de pain en buvant un coup; celle qui mange Jésus-Christ Dieu avec du pain; et celle qui mange Jésus-Christ Dieu en corps et en âme, sans pain ni vin' (M.xviii. 238 n.3). Since the Anabaptist does not eat God in any way, says the almoner, he is not worthy to live under the prince's rule. The three kinds of communion correspond to 1. the Calvinists, 2. the Lutherans and the Anglicans, and 3. the Roman Catholics. The sly omission of *Dieu* after *Jésus-Christ* in the first instance refers to the Socinianism of Voltaire's Genevan neighbours. The Anabaptist's reasonable opinion, which enjoys the prestige of finality in the enumeration, contrasts with the absurdity of the other three and suggests the futility of distinguishing between them so methodically.

One finds a more explicit and comprehensive attack on the sacrament itself in 'Eucharistie'. Voltaire deplores the division of Europe into two hostile camps – how familiar this sounds! – over a word which, according to his etymology, means *douce charité*.[134] Although he is speaking of *eucharist*, the next paragraph designates transubstantiation as the source of the trouble. Twenty nations abhor this dogma in which they see the utter limit of human folly. They cite the famous passage in *De natura deorum* in which Cicero says, 'Les hommes ayant épuisé toutes les épouvantables démences dont ils sont capables, ne se sont point encore avisés de manger le dieu qu'ils adorent.'[135] Thus the twenty Protestant countries take comfort in the thought that devouring one's god revolted Cicero as much as it revolts them. They suspect that this notion has evolved from the tendency of the vulgar to construe in a concrete sense what they cannot understand in a figurative sense. They insist that Jesus could not have held his body in his hands in order to feed it to his disciples; that a body cannot be in a hundred thousand places, and in bread and a cup at the same time; that bread eliminated as excrement and wine as urine cannot be identical to the creator of the universe. These examples not only violate common sense, but arouse disgust. How indeed could they have come down to us from reasonable men?

To the Catholic dogma, Voltaire opposes the doctrine of the Stoics, who 'entendent par ces mots: "Je porte Dieu dans moi," la partie de l'âme divine, universelle, qui anime toutes les intelligences' (M.xix.38). The all-pervading universal soul in Stoicism is in fact the most ancient ancestor of the natural light, which Voltaire endorses in this passage. He has not forgotten the awe of belief in the real presence of God within the communicant's body: 'L'imagination est subjugée, l'âme est saisie et attendrie. On respire à peine, on est détaché de tout lien terrestre, on est uni avec Dieu, il est dans notre chair et dans notre sang. Qui osera, qui pourra commettre après cela une seule faute?' (M.xix.38). No mystery, he comments, could have inspired virtue more powerfully than this one.

134 'Eucharist [. . .] the term which derives from the "thanksgiving" of Jesus at the Last Supper means the "proper conduct of one who is the object of a gift"' ('Eucharist', *Sacramentum mundi* (London 1968-1970)).

135 M.xix.37. 'When we speak of corn as Ceres and wine as Liber, we employ a familiar figure of speech, but do you suppose that anybody can be so insane as to believe that the food he eats is a god?' (*De natura deorum*, translated by H. Rackham (London 1933), iii.16).

ønetheless produces a roll of pious criminals undeterred by the
ence of God within them. Louis XI poisoned his brother. The
op of Pisa a celebrant, and the Pazzi, communicants,
d the Medici in the cathedral of that city.[136] Upon leaving the
ɒeɑ oɪ ɦis bastard daughter, Alexander VI administered the eucharist
to his bastard son Cesare Borgia and together they hanged, poisoned or
stabbed the owners of all property coveted by them. Jules II defiles
himself with the carnage of battle, while 'Léon X tient Dieu dans son
estomac, ses maîtresses dans ses bras, et l'argent extorqué par les indulgences dans ses coffres' (M.xix.39). Trolle, archbishop of Upsala,
watched his henchmen massacre the Swedish senate[137] and Van Galen,
bishop of Munster, made war on his neighbours and distinguished
himself by his rapacity. Voltaire terminates the list with a deliberate
anticlimax, Father N., an average priest apparently,[138] who corrupts his
penitents and steals from them. 'Que conclure de ces contradictions?
que tous ces gens-là [...] n'ont jamais imaginé avoir Dieu dans leur
estomac' (M.xix.39). Since the real presence had no effect on the morality
of men expected to set an example for others, they could not have taken
it seriously. The dogma therefore fails the only test by which common
sense can judge it, the evaluation of its empirical results.

Despite the age of the author, 'Eucharistie' is one of his most convincing essays on the subject. Nor do the other articles treating the
sacrament in the *Questions* of 1771 deserve neglect. Voltaire in fact
introduces a new tactic, arguing within the confines of the faith in
pursuit of a Catholic common sense. Thus the decline which one might
expect after the mediocre passages in the *Discours* and the *Entretiens* of

[136] in *Les Médicis* (Lausanne 1968), Albert Jourcin gives the following details: Easter
Sunday, 26 April 1478. At the moment of elevation during high mass, Bernardo Bandini
stabbed Julio Franceschino and kept on stabbing him, nineteen times in all, and even
stabbed himself in the leg in his frenzy. The priests Antonio and Stefano attacked Lorenzo
de Medici. Antonio grabbed him by the shoulder and, when he turned around, stabbed
him in the throat. As Lorenzo tried to defend himself, the brothers Cavalcanti helped the
murderers to flee. Bandini then killed Francesco Nori who tried to block their escape
(see pp.162-65).

[137] a conflict between Church and state opposed Trolle, archbishop of Upsala, to
Sten Sture, the regent of Sweden, which then belonged to the Danish crown. Kristian II
of Denmark defeated the regent, who died in battle, and entered Stockholm with his ally
Trolle. Trolle accused the entire Swedish senate, which had supported the regent, of
'heresy' (resistance to papal authority) and persuaded Kristian to have them beheaded.
Mass executions took place on 8 and 9 November 1520. See Michael Roberts, *The Early
Vasas: a history of Sweden, 1523-1611* (Cambridge 1968), pp.11-19.

[138] his identity is unknown.

1770 did not materialise in 1771. Henceforth, however, he would practically abandon the subject.

Voltaire's interest in the eucharist began in earnest at a time in life when one faces an immediate, rather than a distant possibility of death. Yet he did not react to this threat as others do and as ambitious clergymen hoped. Instead of anticipating death in one way or another, the playwright-actor explored and exploited the grey zone of infirmity. With more complaints than symptoms, he accustomed himself to the comfort and convenience of his bed where, for indefinite periods of time, he could work and receive visitors. Like Argante,[139] he used his bedroom as a stage and played the sick man to the audience beyond it. Once his public had learned the conventions of this strange dramaturgy, he could count on almost every degree and manner of approaching death for a particular response. Although he played this role over and over again, it bored practically no one, not only because he knew his part and played it well, but also because no one, himself included, had the faintest idea when, at his age, he might be playing it for the last time.

Perhaps he was lying in bed wondering about his most recent complaint when he remembered what he must have discovered as a child: 'Un dieu réellement présent [...] dans l'estomac [...] remplissait [un communiant] d'une terreur religieuse' (*Essai*, i.488). Man could not, according to him, have conceived of a more compelling mystery, and yet it had deterred none of the notorious criminals he listed in 'Eucharistie'. Susceptibility to such emotion made him all the more wary of it, for he knew that the few could use it to dominate the many. His tragedies as well as his impromptu sermons, in church in 1768 and in his bedroom in 1769 (despite his special motive), were nothing less than attempts to inspire religious terror for the purpose of moral edification. Convinced that the Church had always used the eucharist to consolidate its authority, he wanted to break this authority by destroying faith in the dogma and by converting the sacrament into a civic rite. Both of these objectives seem to have evolved from the Colmar experience.

Since he had been attacking other dogmas long before he turned to the eucharist, he capitalised on this experience in seeking to destroy faith in the dogma. The historical research necessary for the *Essai* gave him the opportunity to study the development of the dogma. Though

---

[139] in Molière's *Malade imaginaire* (1673).

faulty, his knowledge of this background enabled him to exploit the weaknesses already exposed by the controversies of the past. His own analysis soon produced others, which he supplemented by the results of his research into the refusal of last rites. The proliferation of *rogatons* in the sixties resulted in the usual repetition of satirical devices, themes and materials, but he usually managed to enliven them with clever variation. This is also true of his alphabetical essays and especially those in the *Questions* of 1771.

A review of critical and satirical themes confirms the appeal to common sense indicated by the analysis of his texts on the eucharist. The institution narratives in the New Testament, he finds, do not justify the sacrament and Jesus, in any case, was celebrating a Jewish custom. The opposition of sincere and competent theologians to the real presence and transubstantiation beginning in the early Middle Ages reveals that these dogmas do not enjoy universal and permanent consent.

Putting God in a piece of bread or a cup of wine, confining a spiritual being to a tiny portion of matter and reducing the Almighty to a perishable triviality are absurd propositions. To eat anyone else alive is worse than cannibalism and even worse than that should someone eat his own body. Some of the components of a body are less edible than others, such as hair, fingernails and worse. This body is said to contain Christ's soul and his divinity. How can one eat a soul? How can one eat God? Is this not worse than idolatry? If one can eat God, what is to prevent the unworthy, the indifferent and even animals from eating him too? Why quarrel over how to eat God without any evidence that he can be eaten? How can one eat the Son without eating the Holy Spirit and the Father too? The rejection of the real presence by infidels, despite the efforts of missionaries, confirms the absurdity of the dogma. This polemic is massive and destructive, but not comprehensive, for Voltaire does not exploit the vulnerable distinction between the bodies in heaven and on the altar.

The substantial conversion of bread and wine into the body and blood of Christ occurred to Christian theologians late in the history of a Church claiming continuous inspiration by the divinity. The dogma of transubstantiation resulted from a decision to embrace mystery and reject reason, which the creator shares with all men and which, according to Malebranche and Voltaire, flows directly from him. How can a creature create the creator? How can bread have become body when the senses continue to perceive bread? How can wine have become blood when they continue to perceive wine? A magic formula and vague similarities will convince only fools and fanatics that a change has taken place. Yet the gratuitous manipulation of abstractions in order to demonstrate this change has not only provoked disputes, but also split Europe into hostile camps.

One can neither multiply God nor distribute him in crumbs of bread and drops of wine, each of which contains Christ in body and soul by dint of concomitance. For Voltaire believed that the Council of Trent had legislated the idolatry of every drop and crumb. Though scant, the eucharistic meal, which affects the body as any other food or drink, undergoes the same digestion and elimination. If communicants eat God, they defecate God. Voltaire thought Stercoranism no more blasphemous than the real presence, transubstantiation and concomitance which, in his opinion, necessarily imply it. Despite his gaiety, this blasphemy offended him, for Besterman has not succeeded in impugning the sincerity of his deism.[140] Among his many professions of belief in God above the suspicion of attempting to edify the people, those in his correspondence with Biord adequately prove the point.

No less than the falsity of the eucharist, the advantage it afforded the clergy excited his suspicion. It enabled them, he found, to insinuate that they had supernatural powers without imposing any moral discipline on them. He accused them of yielding to the temptations of power, wealth and prestige. Priests convicted of having acquired wealth by dishonest means convinced him that they could hardly believe they held the divinity in their hands at mass. How then could they intend to consecrate, the minimum requirement for transubtantiation? Voltaire echoed Luther's charge of cupidity against private mass and, unfairly, accused celebrants of moral and even hygienic corruption.

Although his attitude towards the dispute over refusal of sacraments changed according to circumstances, the fundamental elements remained constant. He insisted on treating the dispute as a civil disturbance perpetrated by irresponsible clergymen on the pretext and at the expense of religion, which he considered necessary to society. How can one sinner deny forgiveness of sins to another? Every citizen has a right to the sacraments and especially those traditionally preceding

---

[140] he includes a chapter on 'Voltaire's god' in his *Voltaire*. In his opinion, 'Voltaire was at most an agnostic; and were any toughminded philosopher to maintain that this type of agnosticism is indistinguishable from atheism, I would not be prepared to argue with him' (p.223).

death, for decency depended on them. Since the Church can justify itself only by the services it renders society, it has no right to refuse the sacraments to anyone, whatever the excuse, and particularly to dying citizens who ask for them. While confession certificates did not seem vicious to Voltaire, but ridiculous, he nonetheless attacked the intrusion of legalistic coercion in private matters of no concern to the Church. He likewise objected to the tardy suppression of the lay cup, which he attributed to clerical pursuit of privilege and prestige. He felt that the state should police the administration of the sacraments to ensure that the Church is meeting its obligations to society.

He might have emphasised the political chicanery and treachery conditioning the evolution of Eucharistic dogma more than he did. He nonetheless ridiculed Christian missionaries trying to propagate the eucharist in countries where bread and wine were unknown, a reminder that the sacrament contains elements incompatible with the universalism to which they pretended. On the other hand, he envisaged a few reforms intended to make communion more useful to society. He implicitly approved the spiritual communion practised by the Quakers, proposed to celebrate the theist brotherhood in which all men participated by means of the sacrament and explicitly endorsed the civic interpretation of the Chinese rites promoted by the Jesuits. These constructive ideas facilitate understanding of his own participation in the eucharist.

Among the reasons he gave for taking the sacrament, the one he repeated most often and amplified most shrilly inspires the least confidence. He could scarcely have believed that the pious and complacent would credit an act blatantly contradicting his frequently published opinion. Like his denials of responsibility for subversive pamphlets, this claim served especially as publicity and even more in 1768-1769 than in 1754. He probably did intend to placate Louis xv, who seems to have approved of these communions, but rather as acts of submission to authority than as expressions of religious sincerity. If this hypothesis is true, the king's attitude bore some resemblance to Voltaire's conception of the civic cult. The writer's ceremonial submission, however, did not tempt Louis to let him return from exile. Volture hinted at his profoundest motive several times without daring to explain it very clearly. There can be little doubt that he hoped to transform the eucharist into a rite dedicated to civic and patriotic virtue. How many times in 1768 did he describe his Easter communion as a duty, an obligation, a necessary function or a ceremony (to be) required by law? Frequently, according to the extant documentation. The gentleman of the king's bedchamber and lord of Ferney insisted that he had participated in the cult of his king, his country, his parish. Every lord sets this example for his parish (1768); every good citizen follows this example (1769). One must respect and practice the state religion, the religion established 'by act of parliament'. The celebration of the theist fellowship by communion, Voltaire thought, would encourage cultivation of all the social virtues, such as tolerance and beneficence. His civic rite would also exalt love of country and stiffen the national resolve against foreign infiltration, interference and intrusion. This aspect of his theory reinforced his determination to commune in spite of Biord, a foreign bishop, and embarrass him by subverting his local authority. A patriotic rite would encourage independence from the pope in conjunction with the resistance to his authority already prevalent in France under the banner of Gallicanism. The desire to assure himself a respectable death and burial also motivated Voltaire's communions. Rather than appease clerical authorities, however, he sought to establish his right to the sacraments by taking them and thus accustom these authorities to a routine hypocrisy from which he knew other impious communicants were benefiting. Such a routine, he seems naively to have assumed, might spare him the shame of the common pit after his death. His communions therefore served three interrelating purposes, a decent burial, a return from exile, and the conversion of the eucharist into a civic rite. Neither unique nor permanent, the third motive was nonetheless the most original of the three.

But his public could comprehend only the first two, because the third lay beyond their experience. Since the first two depended on the tactics designed to achieve the impossible third, all three failed, for Voltaire eventually obtained a decent burial by other means.[141] Common sense could not follow him in his attempt to transform the eucharist into a civic rite, but it responded as usual to his satire of the eucharist. While freethinkers, neutral observers, and the devout all misunderstood and disapproved his publicity stunts and campaigns, each segment of public opinion played the role he assigned it in the reading of his works.

[141] before his death was known, his friends and family had his body driven from Paris to the Abbey of Sellières in Champagne where he was buried. Father Mignot, his grand nephew, was the abbot of Sellières. According to Wagnière, Beaumont had written to his suffragan Biord three times asking him to warn Gros not to bury Voltaire in hallowed ground. See *Relation*, L.W., i.162-64.

The freethinkers applauded, the neutral observers enjoyed them, and the devout reacted with customary outrage. Lethal as usual in the destructive mode, the appeal to common sense proved ineffective in the pursuit of a constructive project.

Works cited

Adam, Antoine, *Du mysticisme à la révolte*. Paris 1968

Aelfric, the Grammarian, *The Sermones catholici or homelies of Aelfric*, trans. Benjamin Thorpe. London 1846

Aldridge, Owen, review of Ira Wade, *The Intellectual development of Voltaire*, *Comparative literature* 23 (1971), p.189.

—, *Voltaire and the century of light*. Princeton 1975

Ambrose, *Select works and letters*, trans. Henri de Romestin, *Select library of Nicene and post-Nicene Fathers*, 2nd series, vol.x. Grand Rapids 1955

—, *Theological and dogmatic works*, trans. Roy Deferrari, *The Fathers of the Church*, vol.xliv. Washington 1963

Anchor Bible. New York 1964

Arnason, H. H., *The Sculptures of Houdon*. London 1975

Assisi, sister Francis, *The Eucharist, the end of all the sacraments according to st Thomas and his contemporaries*. Sinsinawa, Wisc. 1972

Augustine, *The City of God*, trans. Marcus Dods, *Select library of Nicene and post-Nicene Fathers*, 1st series, vol.ii. Grand Rapids 1956

—, *Expositions on the Book of Psalms*, trans. A. Cleveland, *Select library of Nicene and post-Nicene Fathers*, 1st series, vol.viii. Grand Rapids 1956

—, *Homelies on the Gospel according to st John*, trans. John Gibb and James Innes, *Select library of Nicene and post-Nicene Fathers*, 1st series, vol.vii. Grand Rapids 1956

—, *Letters 83-130*, trans. Wilfrid Parsons, *The Fathers of the Church*, vol.viii. New York 1953

—, *Sermons on the liturgical seasons*, trans. Mary Muldowney, *The Fathers of the Church*, vol.xxxviii. New York 1959

—, *Tractatus sive sermones inediti ex Codice Gulferbytana*. Zürich 1918

—, *The Writings against the Manichaeans and against the Donatists*, trans. Richard Stothert, *Select library of Nicene and post-Nicene Fathers*, 1st series, vol.iv. Grand Rapids 1956

Bayle, Pierre, *Recueil de quelques pièces curieuses concernant la philosophie de monsieur Descartes*. Amsterdam 1684

Becker, Carl, *The Heavenly city of the eighteenth-century philosophers*. New York 1960

Berengar, *Berengarii Turonensis de sacra coena*, ed. Friedrich Vischer. Berlin 1834

Besterman, Theodore, *Voltaire*. New York 1969

Bossuet, Jacques, *Correspondance*. Paris 1909-1925

—, *Discours sur l'histoire universelle*. Paris 1966

Brémond, Henri, *Histoire littéraire du sentiment religieux en France depuis la fin des guerres de religion*. Paris 1968

Brown, Harcourt, 'The composition of the *Letters concerning the English Nation*', *The Age of the Enlightenment*, ed. W. H. Barber et al. Edinburgh, London 1967 [pp.15-34]

Buffet, Léon, *Monseigneur J. P. Biord*, in *Mémoires et documents publiés par l'Académie salésienne*, lvi. Annecy 1938

Caussy, Fernand, 'Les pâques de m. de Voltaire', *Le Figaro littéraire*, 13 avril 1912

Chaunu, Pierre, *La Mort à Paris (XVIe, XVIIe, XVIIIe siècles)*. Paris 1978

Cicero, *De natura deorum*. London 1933

Collini, Côme-Alexandre, *Mon Séjour auprès de Voltaire*. Paris 1807; rpt. Paris 1970

Concilii Tridentini Autorum. Acta Concilii Iterum Tridentum congregati a Massarello conscripta (1551-1552). Freiburg, Brisgau 1961

Cyprian, *Letters 1-81*, trans. Rose Donna, *The Fathers of the Church*, vol.li. Washington 1958

Delumeau, Jean, *Le Catholicisme entre Luther et Voltaire*. Paris 1971

Denziger, Heinrich, *The Sources of Catholic dogma*, trans. Roy Deferrari. St Louis, London 1957

Descartes, René, *Œuvres philosophiques*. Paris 1967-1973

Dictionnaire de théologie catholique. Paris 1930-1950

The Didache, The Epistle of Barnabas, etc., trans. James Kleist. Westminster, Maryland 1961

Diderot, Denis, *Encyclopédie ou dictionnaire raisonné des sciences, des arts et des métiers*. Paris 1751-1766

—, *Le Neveu de Rameau*, ed. Jean Fabre. Paris 1950

Encyclopedia of religion and ethics. Edinburgh 1933

Fahey, John, *The Eucharistic teaching of Ratramn of Corbie*. Mundelein, Illinois 1951

Fénelon, François de Salignac, *Œuvres complètes*. Paris 1850

Fontius, Martin, *Voltaires literarische Hilfsmittel in Berlin*. Berlin 1964

Gazier, Augustin, *Histoire générale du mouvement janséniste*. Paris 1923

Geiselmann, Josef, *Die Eucharistielehre der Vorscholastik*. Paderborn 1926

Gielly, Louis, *Voltaire; Documents iconographiques*. Geneva 1948

Godard, Philippe, *La Querelle des refus de sacrement, 1730-1765*. Paris 1937

The Great sermons of the great preachers. London 1858

Grimm, Melchior, *Correspondance littéraire, philosophique et critique*. Paris 1877-1882

Guitmund of Aversa, *De corporis et sanguinis Christi veritate in eucharistia*, ed. H. Hurter. London 1879

Guy, Basil, *The French image of China before and after Voltaire*, Studies on Voltaire 21. Genève 1963

Haag, Eugène et Emile, *La France protestante*. Genève 1966

Hefele, Charles-Joseph and Henri Leclercq, *Histoire des Conciles*. Paris 1910-1916

Hilgenfeld, Hartmut, *Mittelalterlich-traditionelle Elemente in Luthers Abendmahlsschriften*. Zürich 1971

Irenaeus, *Irenaeus against heresies*, trans. Alexander Roberts and James Donaldson. Buffalo 1887

Jaubert, Annie, *La Date de la Cène*. Paris 1957

Jedin, Hubert, *Geschichte des Konzils von Trent*. Freiburg 1970

Jerusalem Bible. New York 1966

Johanny, Raymond, *L'Eucharistie centre de l'histoire du salut*. Paris 1968

Jourcin, Albert, *Les Médicis*. Lausanne 1968

Justin Martyr, *Writings of Justin Martyr*, trans. Thomas Falls, *The Fathers of the Church*. New York 1948.

Kelly, John, *Early Christian doctrines*. London 1958

Kieffer, Eugène, 'De la vie et de la "mort" de M. de Voltaire à Colmar', *Annuaire de la Société historique et littéraire de Colmar* 3 (1953), pp.85-115

Kilmartin, Edward, *The Eucharist in the primitive Church*. Englewood Cliffs 1965

Larousse du XXe siècle. Paris 1931

Leroy, Alfred, *Quentin de La Tour et la société française du XVIIIe siècle.* Paris 1953

Levesque, E., 'Introduction à un fragment de Bossuet, *Examen d'une nouvelle explication du mystère de l'Eucharistie'*, *Revue Bossuet* (1900), pp.129-58

Longchamp, Sébastien and Jean-Louis Wagnière, *Mémoires sur Voltaire et sur ses ouvrages.* Paris 1826

Lubac, Henri de, *Corpus mysticum: l'eucharistie et l'Eglise au moyen-âge.* Paris 1949

Luther, Martin, *D. Martin Luthers Werke.* Weimar 1901

—, *Luther's Works*, ed. Abel Ross Wentz. Philadelphia 1959

MacDonald, A. J., *Lanfranc: a study of his life, work and writing*, 2nd ed. London 1944

Malebranche, Nicolas de, *Œuvres complètes.* Bruxelles 1977

Das Marburger Religiongespräch 1529: Versuch einer Rekonstruktion, ed. Walther Köhler, *Schriften des Vereins für Reformationsgeschichte*, Jahrgang 48 n.148. Leipzig 1929

Meslier, Jean, *Œuvres complètes*, ed. Roland Desné, Jean Deprun, Albert Soboul. Paris 1970-1972

Montaigne, Michel de, *Essais.* Paris 1953

Monty, Jeanne, *Etude sur le style polémique de Voltaire:* Le Dictionnaire philosophique, Studies on Voltaire 44 (Genève 1966)

New Catholic encyclopedia. Toronto 1967

Nixon, Edna, *Voltaire and the Calas case.* New York 1961

Noyes, Alfred, *Voltaire.* New York 1936

Oxford dictionary of English etymology. Oxford 1966

Pappas, John, 'La Rupture entre Voltaire et les jésuites', *Lettres romanes* 13 (1959), pp.351-70

Parguez, Jacques, *La Bulle Unigenitus et le jansénisme politique.* Paris 1936

Pascal, Blaise, *Pensées*, ed. Louis Lafuma. Paris 1962

Pascal, Georges, *Largillière.* Paris 1928

Patrologiae latinae cursus completus, ed. J. Migne. Paris 1878-1890

Plato, *The Timaeus and the Critias or Atlanticus*, trans. Thomas Taylor. Washington 1944

Petau, Denis, *De la pénitence publique et de la préparation à la communion.* Paris 1644.

Pichon, Jean, *L'Esprit de Jésus-Christ et de l'Eglise sur la fréquente communion.* Paris 1745

Pomeau, René, *La Religion de Voltaire.* Paris 1956

Ratramn, *The Book of Ratramn . . . on the body and blood of the Lord*, trans. H. W. and W. C. C. Oxford 1838

—, *De corpore et sanguine domini*, ed. J. N. Bakhuizen van den Brink. Amsterdam 1974

Régnault, Emile, *Christophe de Beaumont.* Paris 1882

Rendtorff, Rolf, *Studien zur Geschichte des Opfers im alten Israel.* Neukirchen-Vluyn 1967

Roberts, Michael, *The Early Vasas: a history of Sweden, 1523-1611.* Cambridge 1968

Robson, John, *Wyclif and the Oxford schools.* Cambridge 1961

Rousseau, Jean-Jacques, *Œuvres complètes.* Paris 1959-1969

Rowbotham, Arnold, 'Voltaire, sinophile', *Publications of the Modern Language Association* 47 (1932), pp.1050-65

—, *Missionary and mandarin.* Berkeley 1942

Rowley, Harold, *From Moses to Qumram: studies in the Old Testament.* London 1963

Sacramentum mundi. New York, London 1968-1970

Sales François de, *Introduction à la vie dévote.* Paris 1628

Sarpi, Pietro, *Istoria del concilio tridentino.* Bari 1935

Snoeks, Rémi, *L'Argument de tradition dans la controverse eucharistique entre catholiques et réformés français au XVIIIe siècle*. Louvain 1951

Solano, Jesus (ed.), *Textos eucaristicos primitivos*. Madrid 1952-1954

Stacey, John, *John Wyclif and the Reform*. London 1964

Thomas of Aquinas, *Summa contra gentiles*, trans. English Dominican Fathers, vol.iv. London 1929

—, *Summa theologiae*, trans. David Bourke, James Cunningham, William Barden, Thomas Gilby. vols lvi-lix. New York 1965-1975

Trapnell, William, 'Survey and analysis of Voltaire's collective editions', *Studies on Voltaire* 67 (1970), pp.105-99

—, *Voltaire and his portable dictionary*. Frankfurt am Main 1972

Turmel, Joseph, *Histoire des dogmes*, vol.v. Paris 1936

Van Kley, Dale, *The Jansenists and the expulsion of the Jesuits from France, 1757-1765*. New Haven 1975

Vernet, Jacob (ed.), *Recueil de pièces fugitives sur l'eucharistie*. Genève 1730

Voltaire, *Candide*, ed. René Pomeau. Paris 1959

—, *Complete Works of Voltaire*, ed. Theodore Besterman *et al.* Banbury 1968-

—, *Dialogues et anecdotes philosophiques*, ed. Raymond Naves. Paris 1961

—, *Dictionnaire philosophique*, ed. Raymond Naves. Paris 1961

—, *Essai sur les mœurs*, ed. René Pomeau. Paris 1963

—, *Voltaire: Facéties*, ed. Jean Macary. Paris 1973

—, *Letters concerning the English nation*, London 1926; rpt. New York 1974

—, *Lettres philosophiques*, ed. Gustave Lanson. Paris 1924

—, *Œuvres complètes*, ed. Louis Moland. Paris, 1877-1882.

—, *Taureau blanc*, ed. René Pomeau. Paris 1956

Vovelle, Michel, *Piété baroque et déchristianisation en Provence aux XVIIe et XVIIIe siècles*. Paris 1973

Wade, Ira, *The Intellectual development of Voltaire*. Princeton 1969

Werner, Martin, *The Formation of Christian dogma*. New York 1957

Wiclif, John, *On the eucharist*, in *Advocates of reform*, trans. Matthew Spinka. London 1953

Wright, Lawrence, *Clean and decent*. London, 1960

Index

Index

Pompadour, Jeanne de, 109
Porrentruy, 110, 112
Port-Royal, 73, 84, 94
Portatif. See *Dictionnaire philosophique*
power: behind figure, 31, 36, 38, 40, 57; words, 32, 34, 64; reliance on God's, 42-43, 45-46; intrinsic, of words, 47-48, 52
Précis du siècle de Louis XV, 127-29, 189
Profession de foi des théistes, 185
Psalms, 71

Quakers, 103-104, 187, 202
Queen of France. See Maria Leczinska
Quesnel, Pasquier, 87
Questions sur l'Encyclopédie, 194-98, 200
Questions sur les miracles, 133-37

Raban Moor, 34
Raffo, 166, 170, 175
Ratramn, 34-39, 40, 54-55, 98, 117-19, 131
realism: sacramental, 31-32, 39; scholastic, 54-56, 58, 60
reason: opposed to transubstantiation, 56, 65, 74, 77, 82; to faith, 37-38, 39-40, 42, 75, 80, 98-99; by Voltaire, 10, 100; his confidence in, 43, 53, 101-203
receptionism, 32, 38, 59
redemption: through Christ's self-sacrifice, 14, 22, 24-25, 37, 72, 100; through eucharist, 16-17, 18; access by communion, 20, 26-27, 63
Reformation, 25, 56, 67, 122, 142
refusal of last rites, 89-97, 99, 27-129, 189-92, 200; Voltaire's objections to, 126-27, 129, 137, 196, 201; Biord's participation in, 158, 178; opposition by *parlements*, 162. *See also* viaticum
Régnault, Emile, 91, 126, 145, 157
Relation du banissement des jésuites de la Chine, 182-84
Relation du chevalier de La Barre, 149
Remarques pour servir de supplément à l'Essai sur les mœurs, 129
remanence, 57, 60, 185
remonstrance, 93, 96
Renaudot, Eusèbe, 75
resurrected body of Christ: saves, 18, 24; spiritual treatments, 21, 38, 79; in

heaven, 27-28, 32, 35-37, 43, 58; resuscitates daily, 138
retraction, 156, 160, 161, 163-80, 195
Revelations, 164
Revolution, French, 99
Richelieu, duc de, 158, 177
Rigolet, 182-84, 185, 193
rites controversy, 106-108, 115
Rivotte, 90-91
Roberts, Michael, 198
Robson, John, 54
Rome, 18, 62, 86, 88, 119
Rothelin, Charles de, 104
Rousseau, Jean-Jacques, 132-33, 134-36
Rowbotham, Arnold, 106, 107

sacrifice: Hebraic to Jewish, 13-14; to Christian, 16, 18, 20-21, 24, 62-63, 71-72; enrichment, distortion, 97-98; eucharistic, 20, 37, 53, 62-63, 70, 73; redemptive, 22, 26-27, 100; by self-sacrificing priest, 27, 71-72, 98; constantly reactualised, 34; of books, 110
Saint-Aimé, 90-91
Saint-Claude, bishop of, 156
Saint-Cyran, abbé de, 84
Saint-Etienne du Mont, 91-94, 190-91
Saint-Eustache, 105
Saint-Florentin, comte de, 157, 158, 174, 179-180
Saint-François, sister, 96-97
Saint-Jean de Beauvais, 92
Saint-Lambert, marquis de, 174
St Martin's School in Tours, 39, 43, 45
Saint-Médard, 94
Sainte-Agate, 94
Sainte-Chapelle, 158
saints, veneration of, 107
Samuel, 124
Sarpi, Paolo, 122-23
Saul, 124
Saurin, Bernard-Joseph, 174
Savoyard Vicar, 134-35, 175
Scholasticism, 23-24, 34, 47, 53, 98, 119; and transubstantiation, 48-49, 54, 76, 77, 80, 104
Secundum quendam modum, 27-28, 35, 41
self-condemnation, 21-22, 30, 38, 67, 130, 183
Sémiramis, 152
sermon, Voltaire's, 145, 153, 158

Index

Index